Collins

OCR Gateway GCSE (9–1)

Biology for Combined Science

Student Book

John Beeby
Anne Pilling
Series editor: Ed Walsh

William Collins' dream of knowledge for all began with the publication of his first book in 1819.

A self-educated mill worker, he not only enriched millions of lives, but also founded a flourishing publishing house. Today, staying true to this spirit, Collins books are packed with inspiration, innovation and practical expertise. They place you at the centre of a world of possibility and give you exactly what you need to explore it.

Collins. Freedom to teach

HarperCollins Publishers
1 London Bridge Street
London SE1 9GF

Browse the complete Collins catalogue at
www.collins.co.uk

First edition 2016

10 9 8 7 6 5 4 3 2 1

© HarperCollins Publishers 2016

ISBN 978-0-00-817499-6

Collins® is a registered trademark of HarperCollins Publishers Limited

www.collins.co.uk

A catalogue record for this book is available from the British Library

Commissioned by Lucy Rowland, Lizzie Catford and Joanna Ramsay

Edited by Hamish Baxter

Project managed by Elektra Media Ltd

Development edited by Rebecca Ramsden and Ashley Craig

Copy edited by Sophia Ktori and Anna Clark

Proofread by Judith Shaw and Laurice Suess

Typeset by Jouve India and 2Hoots Publishing Services Ltd

Cover design by We are Laura

Printed by Grafica Veneta Spa

Cover images © Shutterstock/Komsan Loonprom, Shutterstock/Everett Historical

OCR Endorsement statement

This resource is endorsed by OCR for use with specification J250 GCSE (9–1) Gateway Science Suite – Combined Science A. In order to gain OCR endorsement, this resource has undergone an independent quality check. Any references to assessment and/or assessment preparation are the publisher's interpretation of the specification requirements and are not endorsed by OCR. OCR recommends that a range of teaching and learning resources are used in preparing learners for assessment. OCR has not paid for the production of this resource, nor does OCR receive any royalties from its sale. For more information about the endorsement process, please visit the OCR website, www.ocr.org.uk.

ACKNOWLEDGEMENTS

The publishers gratefully acknowledge the permissions granted to reproduce copyright material in this book. Every effort has been made to contact the holders of copyright material, but if any have been inadvertently overlooked, the Publisher will be pleased to make the necessary arrangements at the first opportunity.

Chapter 1
Pg. 12 Claudio Divizia/Shutterstock, A. BARRINGTON BROWN, GONVILLE AND CAIUS COLLEGE/SCIENCE PHOTO LIBRARY, Valeriy Velikov/Shutterstock, fusebulb/Shutterstock; Pg. 13 royaltystockphoto. com/Shutterstock, hxdbzxy/Shutterstock, royaltystockphoto. com/Shutterstock, Digieva/Shutterstock, Knorre/Shutterstock; Pg. 14 Africa Studio/Shutterstock; Pg. 15 Jubal Harshaw/Shutterstock; Pg. 16 Jose Luis Calvo/Shutterstock, Ed Reschke/Getty; Pg. 18 nyaivanova/Shutterstock, Ed Reschke/Getty, Visuals Unlimited, Inc. /Dr. Gladden Willis/Getty; Pg. 19 D. Kucharski K. Kucharska/Shutterstock, toeytoey/Shutterstock, Lebendkulturen. de/Shutterstock; Pg. 20 DR. MARLI MILLER/ VISUALS UNLIMITED, INC. /SCIENCE PHOTO LIBRARY; Pg. 21 Scivit/Shutterstock, Santia/Shutterstock; Pg. 22 Pan Xunbin/Shutterstock, royaltystockphoto. com/Shutterstock; Pg. 23 toeytoey/Shutterstock, Dlumen/Shutterstock, DR JEREMY BURGESS/SCIENCE PHOTO LIBRARY, CNRI/SCIENCE PHOTO LIBRARY, AMMRF, UNIVERSITY OF SYDNEY/SCIENCE PHOTO LIBRARY; Pg. 24 StudyBlue inc; Pg. 25 StudyBlue inc; Pg. 26 A. BARRINGTON BROWN, GONVILLE AND CAIUS COLLEGE/SCIENCE PHOTO LIBRARY, adike/Shutterstock; Pg. 34 Ralf Herschbach/Shutterstock; Pg. 35 BMJ/ Shutterstock, Dave Massey/Shutterstock; Pg. 36 wavebreakmedia/Shutterstock, Knorre/Shutterstock; Pg. 37 Africa Studio/Shutterstock; Pg. 38 Bettmann/Getty; Pg. 48 Andreas Altenburger/Shutterstock, bjul/Shutterstock, Anton_Ivanov/Shutterstock; Pg. 98 JONATHAN PLEDGER/Shutterstock;

Chapter 2
Pg. 58 STEVE GSCHMEISSNER/SCIENCE PHOTO LIBRARY, Jubal Harshaw/Shutterstock; Pg. 59 eAlisa/Shutterstock, SUSUMU NISHINAGA/SCIENCE PHOTO LIBRARY; Pg. 69 Jose Luis Calvo/Shutterstock; Pg. 70 Leptospira/Shutterstock; Pg. 72 Lisa S. /Shutterstock; Pg. 73 royaltystockphoto/Shutterstock; Pg. 76 SCIENCE SOURCE/SCIENCE PHOTO LIBRARY, Sakarin Sawasdinaka/Shutterstock; Pg. 77 dreamerb/Shutterstock, Lebendkulturen. de/Shutterstock, Abel Tumik/Shutterstock, Monika Vosahlova/Shutterstock; Pg. 84 PROFESSORS P. M. MOTTA & S. CORRER/SCIENCE PHOTO LIBRARY; Pg. 87 Claudio Divizia/Shutterstock; Pg. 91 Jubal Harshaw/Shutterstock; Pg. 93 Stephen VanHorn/ Shutterstock; Pg. 94 D. Kucharski K. Kucharska/Shutterstock;

Chapter 3
Pg. 106 Pavel Chagochkin/Shutterstock, istanbul_image_video/Shutterstock; Pg. 107 Johanna Goodyear/Shutterstock, Image Point Fr/Shutterstock, Steven Allen/Shutterstock; Pg. 108 3Dme Creative Studio/Shutterstock; Pg. 110 bikeriderlondon/Shutterstock; Pg. 112 India Picture/Shutterstock; Pg. 115 STEVE GSCHMEISSNER/SCIENCE PHOTO LIBRARY; Pg. 119 Robert Przybysz/Shutterstock; Pg. 120 Steve Buckley/Shutterstock, UNIVERSITY OF DURHAM/SIMON FRASER/SCIENCE PHOTO LIBRARY; Pg. 121 EPSTOCK/Shutterstock; Pg. 122 NYPL/SCIENCE PHOTO LIBRARY; Pg. 124 ZEPHYR/SCIENCE PHOTO LIBRARY; Pg. 126 Pamela Moore/iStock; Pg. 131 areeya_ann/Shutterstock; Image Point Fr/Shutterstock; Roman Prishenko/Shutterstock; Image Point Fr/Shutterstock; Michael Kraus/Shutterstock; JPC-PROD/Shutterstock; Pg. 134 Keystone/Getty, originalpunkt/Shutterstock; Pg. 135 nevodka/Shutterstock; Pg. 136 ALAIN POL, ISM/SCIENCE PHOTO LIBRARY; annedde/iStock; Pg. 138 Daxiao Productions/Shutterstock; MARTIN SHIELDS/SCIENCE PHOTO LIBRARY; Pg. 141 Barbol/Shutterstock; Pg. 143 Pat_Hastings/Shutterstock; Pg. 145 Jamroen Jaiman/Shutterstock, ElecImagery/Alamy Stock Photo; Norman Pogson/ Shutterstock; Pg. 146 Izf/Shutterstock; Pg. 147 STEVE GSCHMEISSNER/SCIENCE PHOTO LIBRARY; Pg. 148 Joseph Giacomin/Getty; Pg. 152 Santibhavank P/Shutterstock; Pg. 154 Andrey_Popov/Shutterstock; Pg. 155 AnglianArt/Shutterstock; Pg. 165 Anest/Shutterstock;

Chapter 4
Pg. 168 apiguide/Shutterstock; patostudio/Shutterstock; Peshkova/Shutterstock; BMJ/Shutterstock; Pg. 169 Ludmila Lemke/Shutterstock, Ethan Daniels/Shutterstock; fotoJoost/Shutterstock; Pg. 170 topten22photo/Shutterstock; Pg. 171 Marek Velechovsky/Shutterstock; Pg. 172 Carlos Caetano/Shutterstock; Pg. 173 DrObjektiff/Shutterstock; Pg. 174 Joanna Stankiewicz-Witek/Shutterstockl; JFs Pic Factory/Shutterstock; Pg. 176 Tischenko Irina/Shutterstock; Pg. 177 Zack Frank/Shutterstock, Martin Fowler/Shutterstock, Ron Zmiri/Shutterstock; Pg. 178 Vaclav Volrab/Shutterstock; SJ Travel Photo and Video/Shutterstock; Joanne Weston/Shutterstock; Pg. 180 so51hk/Shutterstock; Pg. 182 bjul/Shutterstock, paula french/Shutterstock, Tom Roche/Shutterstock; Pg. 183 Polarpx/Shutterstock; Pichai Tunsuphon/Shutterstock; 7382489561/Shutterstock; Pg. 184 Onsuda/Shutterstock, Aquapix/Shutterstock, Leonardo Gonzalez/Shutterstock, Masahiro Suzuki/Shutterstock, Ugo Montaldo/Shutterstock;

Chapter 5
Pg. 194 itsmejust/Shutterstock, Sergey Novikov/Shutterstock, Kjersti Joergensen/Shutterstock, Esteban De Armas/Shutterstock; Pg. 195 Giovanni Cancemi/Shutterstock; Pg. 196 Levent Konuk/Shutterstock; Pg. 197 Africa Studio/Shutterstock; Pg. 198 PHILIPPE PSAILA/SCIENCE PHOTO LIBRARY; Pg. 199 alybaba/Shutterstock; Pg. 200 khemporn tongphay/Shutterstock; Pg. 204 Puwadol Jaturawutthichai/Shutterstock; Pg. 206 SCIENCE PHOTO LIBRARY; Pg. 207 Kazakov Maksim/Shutterstock, MARK THOMAS/SCIENCE PHOTO LIBRARY; Pg. 210 catwalker/Shutterstock; Pg. 212 Charlotte Purdy/Shutterstock; Pg. 213 BMJ/Shutterstock, outdoorsman/Shutterstock, photos2013/Shutterstock; Pg. 214 Tanor/Shutterstock; Pg. 218 Steve McWilliam/Shutterstock; Pg. 221 Ryan M. Bolton/Shutterstock, Claude Huot/Shutterstock, Guido Vermeulen-Perdaen/Shutterstock, Ben Queenborough/Shutterstock, NATURAL HISTORY MUSEUM, LONDON/SCIENCE PHOTO LIBRARY, Joe Ravi/Shutterstock; Pg. 222 Chantelle Bosch/Shutterstock; Pg. 223 Patricia Chumillas/Shutterstock, Ben Queenborough/Shutterstock, Stubblefield Photography/Shutterstock, MIGUEL CASTRO/SCIENCE PHOTO LIBRARY; Pg. 224 manfredxy/Shutterstock; Pg. 225 Martin Fowler/Shutterstock, Steve McWilliam/Shutterstock; Pg. 226 Olga Popova/Shutterstock; Pg. 228 PAUL TAFFOREAU/ESRF/PASCAL GOETGHELUCK/SCIENCE PHOTO LIBRARY; Pg. 229 Natursports/Shutterstock; Pg. 230 Everett Historical/Shutterstock; Pg. 232 NATURAL HISTORY MUSEUM, LONDON/SCIENCE PHOTO LIBRARY; Pg. 233 Alexandr79/Shutterstock, chris2766/Shutterstock, SCIENCE PHOTO LIBRARY; Pg. 234 SCIENCE PHOTO LIBRARY, NATIONAL LIBRARY OF MEDICINE/SCIENCE PHOTO LIBRARY; Pg. 235 Studiotouch/Shutterstock, HERMANN EISENBEISS/SCIENCE PHOTO LIBRARY;

Chapter 6
Pg. 246 Stefano Carnevali/Shutterstock, royaltystockphoto. com/Shutterstock, Critterbiz/Shutterstock; Pg. 247 esolla/Shutterstock, JPC-PROD/Shutterstock, Kazakov Maksim/Shutterstock; Pg. 250 Yellowj/Shutterstock, Yellowj/Shutterstock; Pg. 251 Gajic Dragan/Shutterstock; Pg. 252 ChiccoDodiFC/Shutterstock, Lukas Gojda/Shutterstock, Anton Gorlin/Shutterstock; Pg. 253 Konstantin Stepanenko/Shutterstock; Pg. 254 Richard Thornton/Shutterstock; Pg. 255 photoneye/Shutterstock, Lodimup/Shutterstock; Pg. 256 Gary Andrews/Shutterstock; Pg. 257 Bildagentur Zoonar GmbH/Shutterstock, Nathape/Shutterstock; Pg. 259 bikeriderlondon/Shutterstock, BOONCHUAY PROMJIAM/Shutterstock; Pg. 260 Huguette Roe/Shutterstock; Pg. 261 Anticiclo/Shutterstock; Pg. 262 Randimal/Shutterstock, Gubernat/Shutterstock; Pg. 268 Orla/Shutterstock; Pg. 264 Stephen Lavery/Shutterstock, sunsetman/Shutterstock; Pg. 265 Ilona Ignatova/Shutterstock, seaphotoart/Shutterstock; Pg. 266 Sergei Butorin/Shutterstock; Pg. 267 montree hanlue/Shutterstock; Pg. 268 Vladislav Gajic/Shutterstock; Pg. 269 Randimal/Shutterstock, Egon Zitter/Shutterstock; Pg. 270 dwphotos/Shutterstock, Nate Allred/Shutterstock; Pg. 271 Eric Isselee/Shutterstock, Sergey Fatin/Shutterstock, Henk Vrieselaar/Shutterstock; Pg. 272 Volodymyr Stakhiv/Shutterstock; Pg. 273 Bildagentur Zoonar GmbH/Shutterstock, Jorge Salcedo/Shutterstock, Gordana Sermek/Shutterstock, Texturis/Shutterstock; Pg. 274 Goldenrice. org; Pg. 275 Denton Rumsey/Shutterstock; Pg. 276 sunsetman/Shutterstock; Pg. 277 Lightspring/Shutterstock, Geoffrey Budesa/Shutterstock; Pg. 279 stocksolutions/Shutterstock, a katz/Shutterstock; Pg. 280 www. GloFish. com; Pg. 281 VOLKER STEGER/SCIENCE PHOTO LIBRARY; Pg. 283 Antonio Guillem/Shutterstock; Pg. 284 IAN GOWLAND/SCIENCE PHOTO LIBRARY; Pg. 285 Chaikom/Shutterstock, muuraa/Shutterstock; Pg. 290 NORM THOMAS/SCIENCE PHOTO LIBRARY; Pg. 291 Jina K/Shutterstock; Pg. 292 MichaelTaylor3d/Shutterstock, royaltystockphoto. com/Shutterstock, Freedom_Studio/Shutterstock; Pg. 294 Author's own, © Nigel Cattlin/Visuals Unlimited/Corbis; Pg. 296 NORM THOMAS/SCIENCE PHOTO LIBRARY, popular business/Shutterstock, kay roxby/Shutterstock; Pg. 297 Christian Musat/Shutterstock, PHOTO FUN/Shutterstock; Pg. 298 anyaivanova/Shutterstock, GEOFF KIDD/SCIENCE PHOTO LIBRARY; Pg. 299 vladimir salman/Shutterstock; Pg. 302 Roberto Piras/Shutterstock; Pg. 306 JPC-PROD/Shutterstock; Pg. 308 EM Karuna/Shutterstock, Zaharia Bogdan Rares/Shutterstock, P. FERGUSON, ISM/SCIENCE PHOTO LIBRARY; Pg. 310 borzywoj/Shutterstock; Pg. 314 Sarah Marchant/Shutterstock, Hellen Sergeyeva/Shutterstock, TwilightArtPictures/Shutterstock; Pg. 316 WitthayaP/Shutterstock; Pg. 317 Edyta Pawlowska/Shutterstock; Pg. 320 Maksym Bondarchuk/Shutterstock Australis Photography/Shutterstock, 157854569/Shutterstock; Pg. 323 Ehab Edward/Shutterstock; Pg. 324 Elena Pavlovich/Shutterstock; Pg. 325 Santibhavank P/Shutterstock; Pg. 326 Gio. tto/Shutterstock, isak55/Shutterstock; Pg. 329 PETER MENZEL/SCIENCE PHOTO LIBRARY;

Contents

How to use this book

Remember! to cover all the content of the OCR Gateway Biology Specification you should study the text and attempt the End of chapter questions.

These tell you what you will be learning about in the lesson and are linked to the OCR Gateway specification.

This introduces the topic and puts the science into an interesting context.

Each topic is divided into three sections. The level of challenge gets harder with each section.

Each section has level-appropriate questions, so you can check and apply your knowledge.

Biology – Photosynthesis (B1.4)

Increasing photosynthesis

Learning objectives:

- identify factors that affect the rate of photosynthesis
- interpret data about the rate of photosynthesis
- explain the interaction of factors in limiting the rate of photosynthesis.

KEY WORDS

limiting factor

Plants grow faster in summer than in winter. This means that they must produce more food to allow them to grow in summer. Some factors can increase the rate of photosynthesis.

Plants in different habitats

Plants are found in every ecosystem, but their size, appearance and adaptations mean that they look very different. Tropical rainforests have dense plant life. In contrast, few plant species grow in tundra (Arctic regions with permanently frozen subsoil) and desert regions.

Figure 1.42 What are the environmental conditions of these habitats?

1. How would you describe environmental conditions in tropical forest, tundra and desert ecosystems?

2. Suggest how the conditions you have described affect photosynthesis in each habitat.

Limiting factors

Some students investigated the effect of light on the rate of photosynthesis. Look at their results (Figure 1.43). The students found that:

- Between A and B, the rate of photosynthesis increases as the light intensity increases. Because the rate depends on the light intensity, light intensity is called the **limiting factor**.
- Between B and C, increasing the light intensity has no effect on the rate of photosynthesis. Another factor is now the limiting factor.

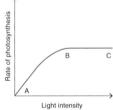

Figure 1.43 Can you explain the shape of the graph between B and C

KEY INFORMATION

Remember that enzymes denature at temperatures greater than 40°C.

44   OCR Gateway GCSE Biology for Combined Science: Student Book

---

What other factors might limit the rate of photosynthesis between B and C?

...nts need carbon dioxide to photosynthesise but there is ...y 0.04% in the atmosphere. It is often the limiting factor ...trolling the rate of photosynthesis.

...bon dioxide levels around plants rise when there is ...light. This is because the plants are respiring but not ...otosynthesising. As light levels increase the plants use the ...bon dioxide up.

HIGHER TIER ONLY

...nteracting limiting factors

...ver one day, light, temperature and carbon dioxide levels ...hange. Carbon dioxide may be the limiting factor when ...lants are crowded on a sunny day. Temperature may be the ...miting factor in cooler months. Light may be the limiting ...actor at dawn.

...lants living in continual shade can adapt. They have a ...igher ratio of leaves to roots than other plants. The leaves ...re thinner, have a larger surface area and contain more ...hlorophyll to absorb light. A shortage of chlorophyll can ...mit the rate of photosynthesis.

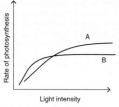
Figure 1.45 Photosynthesis in normal (A) and shade-adapted (B) leaves

...he graph shows that shade-adapted leaves (B) are more ...fficient at absorbing low intensity light than normal ...eaves (A).

4 Suggest the limiting factors for photosynthesis over one complete warm summer's day.

5 Describe and explain adaptations for photosynthesis shown by some shade-tolerant plants.

6 Suggest an advantage of a tree having needles rather than flat, broad leaves.

1.16

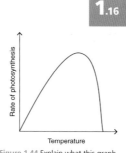
Figure 1.44 Explain what this graph shows

DID YOU KNOW?

Pine trees grow in a cone shape to expose more needles to the sun, increasing the rate of photosynthesis.

Biology

The first page of a chapter has links to ideas you have met before, which you can now build on.

This page gives a summary of the exciting new ideas you will be learning about in the chapter.

CHAPTER OPENING

The Key Concept pages focus on a core ideas. Once you have understood the key concept in a chapter, it should develop your understanding of the whole topic.

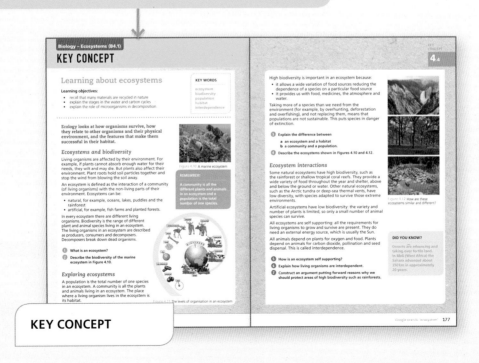

KEY CONCEPT

There are dedicated pages for practicals. They help you to analyse the practical and to answer questions about it.

The tasks – which get a bit more difficult as you go through – challenge you to apply your science skills and knowledge to the new context.

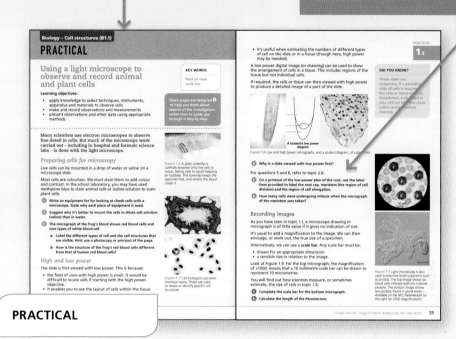

PRACTICAL

The Maths Skills pages focus on the maths requirements in the OCR Gateway specification, explaining concepts and providing opportunities to practise.

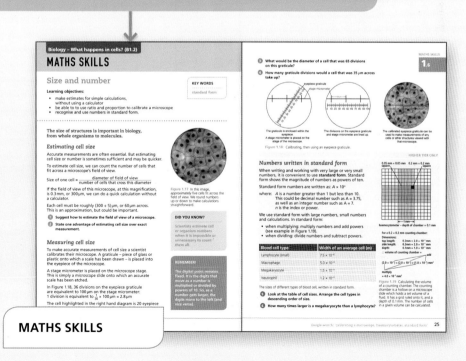

MATHS SKILLS

These lists at the end of a chapter act as a checklist of the key ideas of the chapter. In each row, the green box gives the ideas or skills that you should master first. Then you can aim to master the ideas and skills in the blue box. Once you have achieved those you can move on to those in the red box.

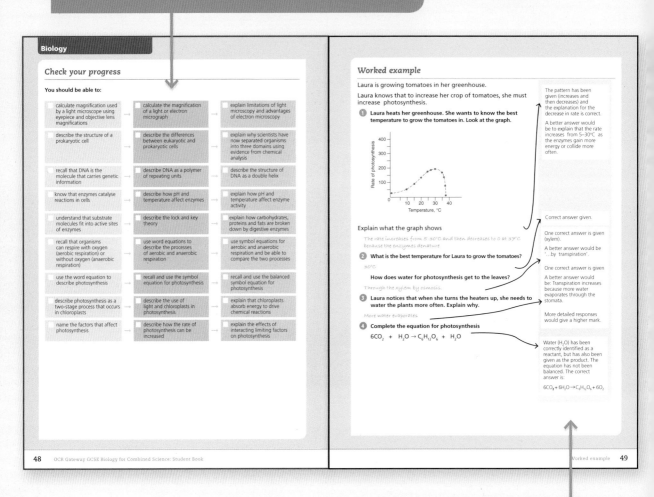

Use the comments to help you understand how to answer questions. Read each question and answer. Try to decide if, and how, the answer can be improved. Finally, read the comments and try to answer the questions yourself.

END OF CHAPTER

The End of chapter questions allow you and your teacher to check that you have understood the ideas in the chapter, can apply these to new situations, and can explain new science using the skills and knowledge you have gained. The questions start off easier and get harder. If you are taking Foundation tier, try to answer all the questions in the Getting started and Going further sections. If you are taking Higher tier, try to answer all the questions in the Going further, More challenging and Most demanding sections.

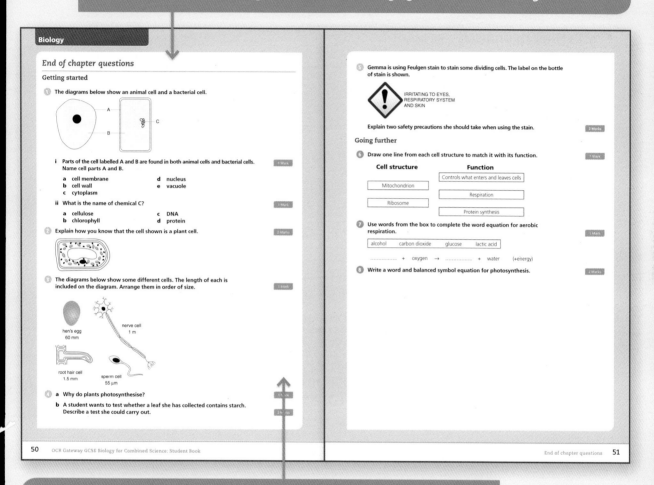

There are questions for each assessment object (AO) from the final exams. This will help you develop the thinking skills you need to answer each type of question:

AO1 – to answer these questions you should aim to **demonstrate** your knowledge and understanding of scientific ideas, techniques and procedures.

AO2 – to answer these questions you should aim to **apply** your knowledge and understanding of scientific ideas and scientific enquiry, techniques and procedures.

AO3 – to answer these questions you should aim to **analyse** information and ideas to: interpret and evaluate, make judgements and draw conclusions, develop and improve experimental procedures.

CELL LEVEL SYSTEMS

IDEAS YOU HAVE MET BEFORE:

ALL LIVING ORGANISMS ARE MADE OF CELLS

- Cells are the building blocks of life.
- Cells contain specialised structures.
- Organisms such as bacteria are unicellular.
- All plants and animals are multicellular.

THE CELL CONTAINS GENETIC INFORMATION

- Genetic information is contained within genes on our chromosomes.
- Our chromosomes and genes are found in the nucleus of our cells.

ENZYMES ARE IMPORTANT FOR THE REACTIONS THAT OCCUR IN OUR BODY

- Enzymes speed up reactions inside the body.
- Different enzymes are used to speed up different reactions.
- The digestive system uses enzymes to digest food.

ORGANISMS OBTAIN ENERGY BY THE PROCESS OF RESPIRATION

- The energy that is released drives all the processes necessary for life.
- Most organisms use oxygen for aerobic respiration.
- Some cells or organisms can survive without oxygen. They respire anaerobically.
- Energy is transferred between living organisms.

PLANT CELLS ARE ADAPTED TO CARRY OUT THEIR FUNCTIONS

- Chloroplasts absorb energy from light for photosynthesis.
- Most photosynthesis happens in the mesophyll cells in leaves.
- The amount of photosynthesis can be affected by a range of different factors.

STUDYING CELL STRUCTURE AND FUNCTION

- The structures inside cells do different jobs within the cell.
- Cells can be studied using different types of microscopes.
- The cells of animals, bacteria and plants are structurally different.

THE STRUCTURE OF DNA

- DNA is a polymer of repeating units.
- The shape of DNA is called a double helix.
- Chromosomes and genes are found in the nucleus of cells.

HOW ENZYMES WORK

- Many reactions in cells are controlled by enzymes.
- The lock-and-key theory can be used to explain enzyme function and specificity.
- There are specific enzymes in the digestive system; their action is affected by different factors.

HOW ORGANISMS OBTAIN THEIR ENERGY FROM FOOD

- Anaerobic respiration: when organisms or cells respire without oxygen.
- Many microorganisms can respire anaerobically, as can the muscles of mammals for short periods.

FACTORS WHICH AFFECT THE PHOTOSYNTHESIS REACTION

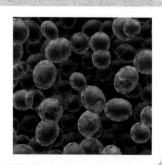

- Leaves are adapted to absorb energy from light energy for photosynthesis.
- Substances move in and out the leaf during photosynthesis.
- The products of photosynthesis are simple carbohydrates and oxygen.
- Different environmental factors interact to limit the rate of photosynthesis in different habitats at different times.

The light microscope

Learning objectives:

- observe plant and animal cells with a light microscope
- understand the limitations of light microscopy.

KEY WORDS

magnification
resolving power
micrographs

The type of microscope you have used in the school laboratory is called a light microscope. Microscopes produce a magnified image of the specimen you are looking at, making them look bigger than they are.

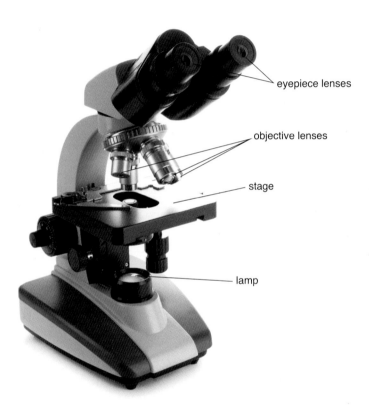

eyepiece lenses

objective lenses

stage

lamp

Figure 1.1 A light microscope

DID YOU KNOW?

British scientist Robert Hooke first used the term 'cell'. He recorded the first drawings of cells using a compound microscope in his book *Micrographia*, which was 350 years old in 2015.

You may also have heard of Hooke for his law of elasticity, Hooke's law, in physics.

Magnification

The magnified image is produced by two lenses, an eyepiece and an objective lens. There is usually a choice of objective lenses.

> **Total magnification = magnification of eyepiece × magnification of objective lens**

For instance, if the eyepiece has a **magnification** of ten, which is written ×10, and the objective lens has a magnification of ×40, the total magnification is ×400.

1 Calculate is the total magnification with an eyepiece magnification of ×15 and an objective lens magnification of ×40?

2 What magnification would the objective lens need to be to give a total magnification of ×300 with an eyepiece of ×15?

Magnification of images

The magnification described on the previous page is the magnification used to *view* an image. Microscope images, or **micrographs**, in books or scientific papers must show the magnification, to be meaningful.

$$\text{magnification of the image} = \frac{\text{size of image}}{\text{size of object}}$$

The cell in Figure 1.2 is 50 mm across on the page. In real life, it measures 40 μm.

To calculate the magnification, first convert the 50 mm into micrometres (or convert 40 μm to millimetres).

50 mm = 50 000 μm

The cell measures 40 μm

Therefore, the magnification of the image = $\frac{50\,000}{40}$ = ×1250.

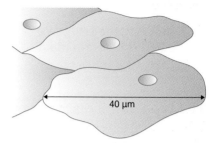

Figure 1.2 A drawing of a micrograph of a cell

3 A micrograph of a plant cell in a book is 150 mm long. The plant cell measures 120 μm long. Calculate the magnification.

4 Why is it essential to state the magnification of an image of a cell in a book but of little value on a website?

The limits of the light microscope

Very high magnifications are not possible with the light microscope. This is because of the light-gathering ability of the microscope and the short working distances of high-power lenses. The highest magnification possible is around ×1500.

Using higher magnification does not always mean that you can see greater detail in an image. This depends on the **resolving power**, or resolution. This is the ability to distinguish between two points. In other words, whether you see them as two points, or one.

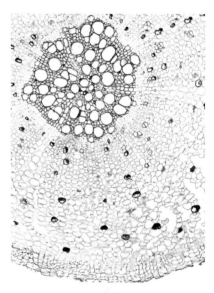

Figure 1.3 A micrograph of the cross section of a root. Magnification ×100

The resolving power of a light microscope is around 0.2 μm, or 200 nm. This means that you could not separately pick out two points closer than 200 nm apart.

5 What is the maximum resolving power of the light microscope?

6 What is the maximum magnification possible with a light microscope?

7 Make a table to show the pros and cons of using a light microscope.

COMMON MISCONCEPTIONS

Do not confuse magnification, which is how much bigger we can make something appear, with resolving power, which is the level of detail we can see.

Think about a digital photo. You can make it as big as you like, but at a certain point you will not be able to see any more detail.

Looking at cells

Learning objectives:

- describe the structure of eukaryotic cells
- explain how the main sub-cellular structures are related to their functions.

KEY WORDS

chloroplast
chlorophyll
chromosome
eukaryotic
order of magnitude

Cell biology helps us to understand how parts of the cell function and interact with each other. It also helps us to learn how we develop, and about our relationships with other organisms.

Biomedical scientists use cells to look for signs of disease and in new drug development.

Plant and animal cells

Almost all organisms are made up of cells. Cells are the fundamental units of living organisms. Plant and animal cells have a basic structure.

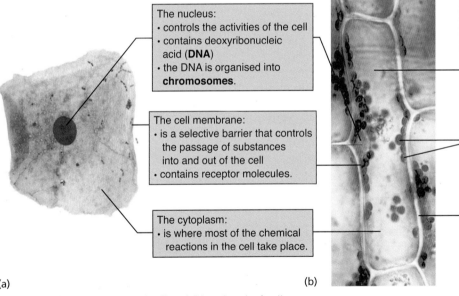

The nucleus:
- controls the activities of the cell
- contains deoxyribonucleic acid (**DNA**)
- the DNA is organised into **chromosomes**.

The cell membrane:
- is a selective barrier that controls the passage of substances into and out of the cell
- contains receptor molecules.

The cytoplasm:
- is where most of the chemical reactions in the cell take place.

The vacuole:
- surrounded by a membrane and fluid filled
- the fluid is called cell sap
- vacuoles are permanent structures in plants.

The **chloroplasts**:
- are found in plant cells above ground
- contain **chlorophyll** that absorbs the light the plant needs for photosynthesis.

The cell wall:
- is an additional layer outside the cell membrane
- made from cellulose fibres
- contains fibres that provide strength
- unlike the cell membrane, does not regulate what enters or leaves the cell.

(a)   (b)

Figure 1.4 (a) A simple animal cell and (b) a plant leaf cell

This type of cell, containing a true nucleus in the cytoplasm, is called a **eukaryotic** cell.

1. List the sub-cellular structures found in both plant and animal cells.

2. Which sub-cellular structures are found only in plant cells?

   What is the function of:

   - the nucleus
   - the cell membrane?

3. What structure gives strength to a plant cell?

Cell size

The smallest thing we can see is about 0.04 mm, so you can see some of the largest cells with the naked eye. For all cells, however, we need a microscope to see them in any detail.

Most animal and plant cells are 0.01–0.10 mm in size. The unit we use to measure most cells is the micrometre, μm. For some sub-cellular structures, or organisms such as viruses, it is best to use a smaller unit: the nanometre, nm.

1 millimetre (mm) $= \frac{1}{1000}$ m   or 10^{-3} m

1 micrometre (μm) $= \frac{1}{1000}$ mm   or 10^{-3} mm   or 10^{-6} m

1 nanometre (nm) $= \frac{1}{1000}$ μm   or 10^{-3} μm   or 10^{-9} m

4 **What size is the smallest thing our eye can see, in mm?**

5 **What is the range in size of most animal and plant cells, in μm?**

Order of magnitude

Figure 1.5 shows the size of plant and animal cells compared with some other structures.

When comparing the sizes of cells, scientists often refer to differences in **order of magnitude**. That's the difference calculated in factors of 10.

> **REMEMBER!**
>
> You'll notice that this system of units uses, and gives names to, multiples and sub-multiples of units at intervals of thousands (10^3) or thousandths (10^{-3}). A common exception is the centimetre, $\frac{1}{100}$ or 10^{-2} of a metre. But it is often convenient to use centimetres, particularly in everyday life.

| ant length 3 mm | hair diameter 100 μm | leaf cell length 70 μm | red blood cell diameter 7 μm | bacterium length 1 μm | HIV diameter 100 nm | DNA diameter 2.5 nm | carbon atom diameter 0.34 nm |

Figure 1.5 Size and scale

So, the difference in order of magnitude for the HIV and the plant cell:

The plant cell in Figure 1.4b is 100 μm = 0.1 mm = 10^{-4} m.

The human immunodeficiency virus (HIV) is 100 nm = 0.1 μm = 10^{-4} mm = 10^{-7} m.

The difference in order of magnitude is 10^3, expressed as 3.

6 **A cell membrane measures 7 nm across. Convert this to micrometres.**

7 **A white blood cell measures 1.2×10^{-5} m. An egg cell measures 1.2×10^{-4} m. Calculate the difference in order of magnitude.**

PRACTICAL

Using a light microscope to observe and record animal and plant cells

Learning objectives:

* apply knowledge to select techniques, instruments, apparatus and materials to observe cells
* make and record observations and measurements
* present observations and other data using appropriate methods.

These pages are designed ❶ to help you think about aspects of the investigation rather than to guide you through it step by step.

Many scientists use electron microscopes to observe fine detail in cells. But much of the microscope work carried out – including in hospital and forensic science labs – is done with the light microscope.

Preparing cells for microscopy

Live cells can be mounted in a drop of water or saline on a microscope slide.

Most cells are colourless. We must stain them to add colour and contrast. In the school laboratory, you may have used methylene blue to stain animal cells or iodine solution to stain plant cells.

Figure 1.6 A glass coverslip is carefully lowered onto the cells or tissue, taking care to avoid trapping air bubbles. The coverslip keeps the specimen flat, and retains the liquid under it

❶ Write an equipment list for looking at cheek cells with a microscope. State why each piece of equipment is used.

❷ Suggest why it's better to mount the cells in dilute salt solution (saline) than in water.

❸ The micrograph of the frog's blood shows red blood cells and two types of white blood cell.

   a Label the different types of cell and the cell structures that are visible. Hint: use a photocopy or printout of the page.

   b How is the structure of the frog's red blood cells different from that of human red blood cells?

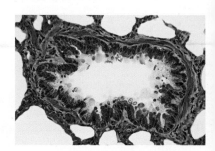

High and low power

The slide is first viewed with low power. This is because:

* the field of view with high power is small. It would be difficult to locate cells if starting with the high power objective.
* it enables you to see the layout of cells within the tissue.

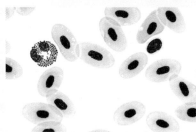

Figure 1.7 Cell biologists use other chemical stains. These are used to reveal or identify specific cell structures

- it's useful when estimating the numbers of different types of cell on the slide or in a tissue (though here, high power may be needed).

A low power digital image (or drawing) can be used to show the arrangement of cells in a tissue. This includes regions of the tissue but not individual cells.

If required, the cells or tissue can then viewed with high power to produce a detailed image of a part of the slide.

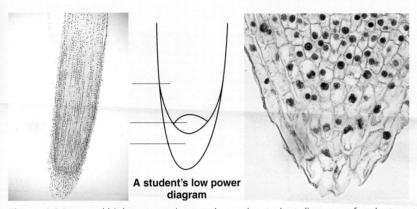

A student's low power diagram

Figure 1.8 Low and high power micrographs, and a student diagram, of a plant root

4 Why is a slide viewed with low power first?

For questions 5 and 6, refer to topic 2.6.

5 On a printout of the low power plan of the root, use the label lines provided to label the root cap, meristem (the region of cell division) and the region of cell elongation.

6 How many cells were undergoing mitosis when the micrograph of the meristem was taken?

Recording images

As you have seen in topic 1.1, a microscope drawing or micrograph is of little value if it gives no indication of size.

It's usual to add a magnification to the image. We can then envisage, or work out, the true size of a specimen.

Alternatively, we can use a **scale bar**. Any scale bar must be:

- drawn for an appropriate dimension
- a sensible size in relation to the image.

Look at Figure 1.9. For the top micrograph, the magnification of ×1000, means that a 10 *millimetre* scale bar can be drawn to represent 10 *micrometres*.

You will find out how scientists measure, or sometimes estimate, the size of cells in topic 1.6.

7 Complete the scale bar for the bottom micrograph.

8 Calculate the length of the *Paramecium*.

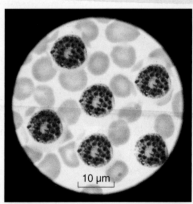

10 μm

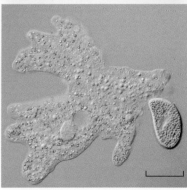

Figure 1.9 Light microscopy is also used to examine small organisms such as protists. The top image shows six blood cells infected with the malarial parasite. The bottom image shows two protists found in pond water – *Amoeba* on the left; *Paramecium* on the right (at ×200 magnification)

Primitive cells

Learning objectives:

- describe the differences between prokaryotic cells and eukaryotic cells
- explain how the main sub-cellular structures of prokaryotic and eukaryotic cells are related to their functions.

KEY WORDS

genome
plasmid
prokaryotic cells
eukaryotic cells

The oldest fossil evidence of life on Earth comes from Australia. It confirms that there were bacteria living around 3.5 billion years ago.

The bacteria probably formed thin purple and green mats on shorelines. The bacteria would have photosynthesised, but produced sulfur as waste instead of oxygen.

Prokaryotic cells

Bacteria are among the simplest of organisms. Along with bacteria-like organisms called Archaeans, they belong to a group of organisms called the prokaryota. These are single cells with a **prokaryotic cell** structure.

The cells of most types of organisms – such as all animals and plants – are **eukaryotic**. These have a cell membrane, cytoplasm containing sub-cellular structures called organelles and a nucleus containing DNA.

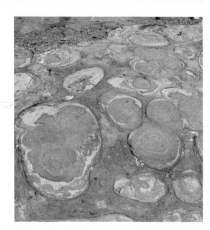

Figure 1.10 The organisms in this fossil are similar to purple bacteria that are living today

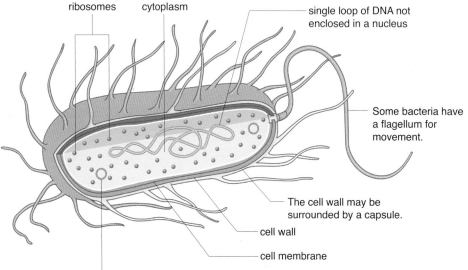

ribosomes   cytoplasm   single loop of DNA not enclosed in a nucleus

Some bacteria have a flagellum for movement.

The cell wall may be surrounded by a capsule.

cell wall

cell membrane

Small ring of DNA called a plasmid (one or more in a cell). Genes in the plasmids can give the bacterium advantages such as antibiotic resistance.

Figure 1.11 The structure of a prokaryotic cell

Prokaryotic cells are much smaller than eukaryotic cells, around 1 µm across. Their DNA is not enclosed in a nucleus. It is found as a single molecule in a loop. They may also have one or more small rings of DNA called **plasmids**.

1 List the differences between prokaryotic and eukaryotic cells.

2 Where is DNA found in prokaryotic cells?

A new classification system

Traditionally, prokaryotic organisms have been grouped together, but now many scientists suggest that they should be divided into two sub-groups – the Bacteria and Archaea.

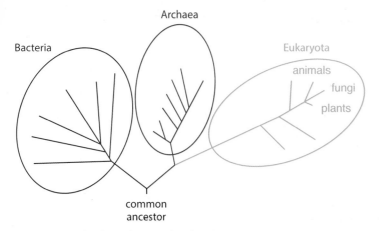

Figure 1.12 The three-domain classification system

Many people think of bacteria as causing disease, but most are free-living. They live in all habitats on the planet.

Population explosions of blue-green bacteria sometimes cause 'blooms' in rivers, lakes and the sea.

3 Which types of organism are prokaryotic?

4 Give three habitats where prokaryotic organisms live.

Looking at cells in more detail

Learning objectives:

- identify the differences in the magnification and resolving power of light and electron microscopes
- explain how electron microscopy has increased our understanding of sub-cellular structures.

KEY WORDS

scanning electron
  microscope (SEM)
transmission electron
  microscope (TEM)
resolution

The *transmission electron microscope* (TEM) uses an electron beam instead of light rays.

Some of the electrons are scattered as they pass through the specimen. Those able to pass through it are focused in TEMs using electromagnetic coils instead of lenses.

Electron microscopes

TEMs are used for looking at extremely thin sections of cells. The highest magnification that can be obtained from a transmission electron microscope is around ×1 000 000, but images can also be enlarged photographically.

The limit of resolution of the transmission electron microscope is now less than 1 nm.

The **scanning electron microscope (SEM)** works by bouncing electrons off the surface of a specimen that has had an ultra-thin coating of a heavy metal, usually gold, applied. A narrow electron beam scans the specimen. Images are formed by these scattered electrons.

SEMs are used to reveal the surface shape of structures such as small organisms and cells. Because of this, **resolution** is lower and magnifications used are often lower than for TEM.

Electrons do not have a colour spectrum like the visible light used to illuminate a light microscope. They can only be 'viewed' in black and white. Here, false colours have been added.

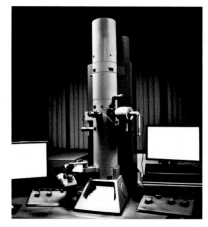

Figure 1.13 A transmission electron microscope. The electrons are displayed as an image on a fluorescent screen

1. What is the maximum resolution of an electron microscope?

2. What types of samples would a TEM and an SEM be used to view?

3. How has electron microscopy improved our understanding of cells?

Figure 1.14 A scanning electron micrograph of a cancer cell

Cell ultrastructure

The TEM reveals tiny sub-cellular structures that are not visible with the light microscope. It also shows fine detail in those structures.

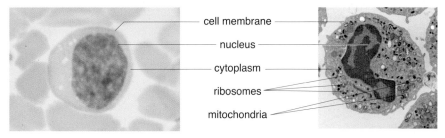

cell membrane

nucleus

cytoplasm

ribosomes

mitochondria

Figure 1.15 A white blood cell, as seen with a light microscope and a transmission electron microscope

We can see mitochondria and chloroplasts with the light microscope, but the electron microscope reveals their internal structure.

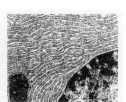

(a)

Mitochondria are where aerobic respiration takes place in the cell. Mitochondria contain the enzymes for respiration. A mitochondrion has a double membrane. The internal membrane is folded.

(b)

Chloroplasts are the structures in the plant cell where photosynthesis takes place. Like mitochondria, they also have a complex internal membrane structure.

(c)

Ribosomes are tiny structures where protein synthesis takes place. You can see them as dots in the micrograph. They can either lie free in the cytoplasm or may be attached to an internal network of channels within the cytoplasm.

Figure 1.16 Viewing (a) mitochondria, (b) chloroplasts and (c) ribosomes by transmission electron microscopy

The size of sub-cellular structures is important. Mitochondria and chloroplasts vary in size and shape. The complexity of a mitochondrion indicates how active a cell is. Chloroplast size varies from one species to another. Scientists sometimes investigate the ratio of the area of the cytoplasm to that of the nucleus in micrographs. A high ratio of cytoplasmic: nuclear volume can indicate that the cell is about to divide. A low one can be characteristic of a cancer cell.

4 **Name one structure visible to the electron microscope, but not the light microscope.**

5 **What process happens in ribosomes?**

6 **Which type of microscope would be best suited to viewing the 3D structure of a cell? Explain why.**

COMMON MISCONCEPTIONS

Don't assume that we always use electron microscopes in preference to light microscopes, or that electron microscopes are always used at high magnifications. Confocal microscopy is used in a lot of biomedical research. It can give high resolution images of live cells. And SEM is often used at low magnifications.

DID YOU KNOW?

Three scientists won the Nobel Prize in 2014 for the development of super-resolved fluorescence microscopy. It allows a much higher resolution than normal light microscopy. And, unlike electron microscopy, it has the advantage of allowing scientists to look at living cells.

MATHS SKILLS

Size and number

Learning objectives:

- make estimates for simple calculations, without using a calculator
- be able to to use ratio and proportion to calibrate a microscope
- recognise and use numbers in standard form.

The size of structures is important in biology, from whole organisms to molecules.

Estimating cell size

Accurate measurements are often essential. But estimating cell size or number is sometimes sufficient and may be quicker.

To estimate cell size, we can count the number of cells that fit across a microscope's field of view.

$$\text{Size of one cell} = \frac{\text{diameter of field of view}}{\text{number of cells that cross this diameter}}$$

If the field of view of this microscope, at this magnification, is 0.3 mm, or 300 μm, we can do a quick calculation without a calculator.

Each cell must be roughly (300 ÷ 5) μm, or 60 μm across. This is an approximation, but could be important.

1. **Suggest how to estimate the field of view of a microscope.**

2. **State one advantage of estimating cell size over exact measurement.**

Measuring cell size

To make accurate measurements of cell size a scientist calibrates their microscope. A graticule – piece of glass or plastic onto which a scale has been drawn – is placed into the eyepiece of the microscope.

A stage micrometer is placed on the microscope stage. This is simply a microscope slide onto which an accurate scale has been etched.

In Figure 1.18, 36 divisions on the eyepiece graticule are equivalent to 100 μm on the stage micrometer:
1 division is equivalent to $\frac{1}{36} \times 100\,\mu m = 2.8\,\mu m$

The cell highlighted in the right hand diagram is 20 eyepiece divisions across: the width of the cell = (20 × 2.8) μm = 56 μm

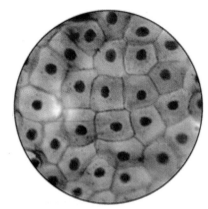

Figure 1.17 In this image, *approximately* five cells fit across the field of view. We round numbers up or down to make calculations straightforward.

DID YOU KNOW?

Scientists *estimate* cell or organism numbers when it is impossible or unnecessary to count them all.

REMEMBER!

The digital point remains fixed. It is the digits that move as a number is multiplied or divided by powers of 10. So, as a number gets larger, the digits move to the left (and vice versa).

3 What would be the diameter of a cell that was 65 divisions on this graticule?

4 How many graticule divisions would a cell that was 35 μm across take up?

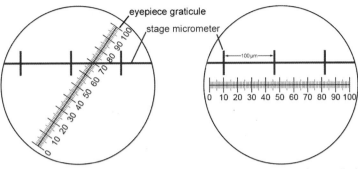
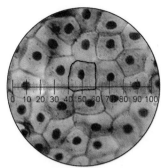

The graticule is enclosed within the eyepiece.
A stage micrometer is placed on the stage of the microscope.

The divisions on the eyepiece graticule and stage micrometer are lined up.

The calibrated eyepiece graticule can be used to make measurements of any cells or other structures viewed with that microscope.

Figure 1.18: Calibrating, then using an eyepiece graticule.

Numbers written in standard form

When writing and working with very large or very small numbers, it is convenient to use **standard form**. Standard form shows the magnitude of numbers as powers of ten.

Standard form numbers are written as: $A \times 10^n$

where: A is a number greater than 1 but less than 10. This could be decimal number such as $A = 3.75$, as well as an integer number such as $A = 7$.
n is the index or power.

We use standard form with large numbers, small numbers and calculations. In standard form:

- when multiplying: multiply numbers and add powers (see example in Figure 1.19).
- when dividing: divide numbers and subtract powers.

Blood cell type	Width of an average cell (m)
Lymphocyte (small)	7.5×10^{-6}
Macrophage	5.0×10^{-5}
Megakaryocyte	1.5×10^{-4}
Neutrophil	1.2×10^{-5}

The sizes of different types of blood cell, written in standard form.

5 Look at the table of cell sizes. Arrange the cell types in descending order of size.

6 How many times larger is a megakaryocyte than a lymphocyte?

HIGHER TIER ONLY

0.05 mm × 0.05 mm square   0.2 mm × 0.2 mm square

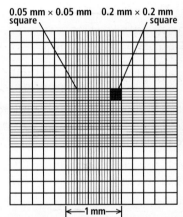

←1 mm→
haemocytometer – depth of chamber = 0.1 mm

For a 0.2 × 0.2 mm counting chamber:

Dimensions:
top length: 0.2mm = 2.0×10^{-1} mm
side length: 0.2mm = 2.0×10^{-1} mm
depth: 0.1mm = 1.0×10^{-1} mm

∴ volume of counting chamber =

add

$(2.0 \times 10^{-1}) \times (2.0 \times 10^{-1}) \times (1.0 \times 10^{-1})$ mm³

multiply
= 4.0×10^{-3} mm³

Figure 1.19 Calculating the volume of a counting chamber. The counting chamber is a hollow on a microscope slide which holds a set volume of a fluid. It has a grid ruled onto it, and a depth of 0.1 mm. The number of cells in a given volume can be calculated.

The structure of DNA

KEY WORDS

DNA
double helix
polymer

Learning objectives:

- describe the structure of DNA as two strands that form a double helix shape
- describe DNA as a polymer.

In April 1953, Francis Crick and James Watson, working in the Cavendish Laboratory in Cambridge, produced the breakthrough scientific paper in which they revealed the structure of DNA.

The discovery of the structure of DNA

On 25 February 1953, Francis Crick walked into the Eagle pub in Cambridge and announced,

'We have found the secret of life!'.

He was referring to the structure of deoxyribonucleic acid (DNA) – the molecule that carries our genes, and ultimately, determines who we are.

Figure 1.20 Watson and Crick with their model of the structure of DNA Laboratories in Cambridge are still at the forefront of current work in genomics.

The DNA double helix

A molecule of DNA has a structure like a ladder that has been twisted. The shape is called a **double helix**.

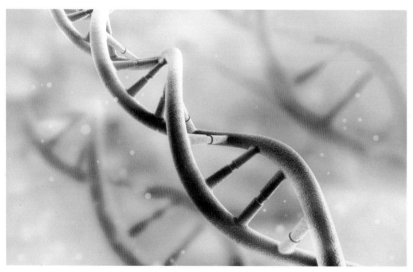

Figure 1.21 An illustration of DNA. The molecule consists of two strands and is like a ladder that has been gently twisted

1. What is the name given to the shape of the DNA molecule?
2. Describe this shape.

DNA is a polymer

The DNA molecule is a polymer made up of repeating units. These units contain the genetic code.

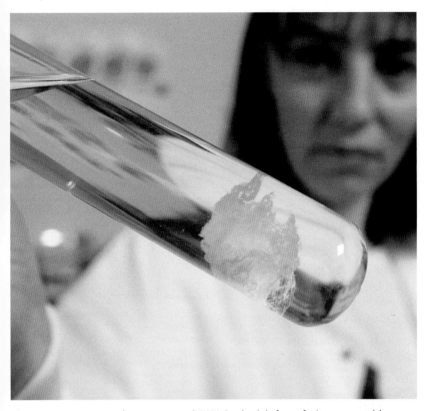

Figure 1.22 You may have extracted DNA in the lab from fruit or vegetables, such as kiwi, strawberries or peas

Working scientifically

The discovery of the structure of DNA is a good example of how scientific theories develop over time. In the late 1940s and early 1950s, several scientists had been trying to unravel the structure of DNA at the same time. But it was Crick and Watson who put the evidence together and worked out that the structure of DNA is a double helix.

It had been established in the 1940s that genes work by controlling enzyme synthesis. Following the description of the molecular structure of DNA, Francis Crick continued his work and established how the genetic code in the DNA molecule controls protein synthesis. Crick presented his ideas about the genetic code in London in 1957, in a scientific paper called 'On Protein Synthesis'.

Ongoing studies on the human genome continue to shed more light on how genes, and the rest of the DNA molecule, work.

DID YOU KNOW?

Other information helped Crick and Watson to work out the structure of DNA.

The X-ray data of Rosalind Franklin and Maurice Wilkins helped Crick and Watson deduce that DNA had a helical structure.

Explaining enzymes

Learning objectives:

- describe what enzymes are and how they work
- explain the lock-and-key theory.

KEY WORDS

biological catalyst
active site
denatured
lock-and-key theory
metabolism
substrate
optimum

Chemical reactions happen all the time. *Metabolism* **describes all the reactions in a cell or the body. The energy transferred by respiration in cells is used for the continual enzyme-controlled processes of metabolism that synthesise new molecules.**

A special catalyst

A catalyst is a chemical that speeds up a reaction without being used up itself. This means it can be reused. Different reactions need a different catalyst.

Enzymes are **biological catalysts**. Enzymes catalyse most chemical reactions that happen in cells, for example, respiration, protein synthesis and photosynthesis. Enzymes help to:

- break down large molecules into smaller ones
- build large molecules from smaller ones
- change one molecule into another molecule.

1 **What is an enzyme?**

2 **Explain what enzymes do in a living organism.**

How do enzymes work?

Enzymes are large protein molecules made from folded, coiled chains of amino acids. Each enzyme has a unique sequence of amino acids. The **active site**, the area that attaches to the substrate (reactant), has a very specific shape that fits its substrate exactly.

Only one type of substrate can fit into the active site of an enzyme, like a key fits into a lock. Once the substrate is attached to the active site, it is changed into a product. Each enzyme catalyses one type of reaction This is called enzyme specificity.

If the shape of the active site changes, the enzyme is **denatured** and cannot catalyse the reaction. This is an irreversible change. The enzyme cannot work because the substrate cannot fit into the active site.

3 **What is an enzyme made from?**

4 **What happens when an enzyme is denatured?**

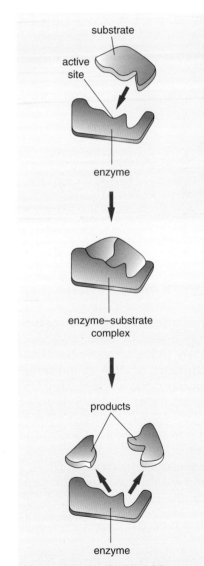

Figure 1.23 The **lock-and-key theory** is a simple explanation of how enzymes work

Changing enzyme reactions

Enzyme-controlled reactions are affected by:

- pH
- temperature – As the temperature is increased, the number of successful collisions between the enzyme and substrate will increase. The rate of reaction therefore increases.
- **substrate** concentration – the rate of reaction will increase as the concentration of substrate increases – up to a point. At lower substrate concentrations, not all the active sites will be occupied by substrate, but as the concentration of substrate increases, so does the rate of reaction until all of the active sites become occupied with substrate.
- enzyme concentration – similarly, as the amount of enzyme increases, there will be more collisions between the enzyme and substrate; the rate of reaction therefore increases.

> **KEY INFORMATION**
>
> Enzymes are chemicals. They are not living and, therefore, cannot be killed. They are denatured.

Every enzyme has an **optimum** pH and an optimum temperature. Above or below these levels, the rate of reaction will slow down. Extremes of pH or temperature can denature an enzyme.

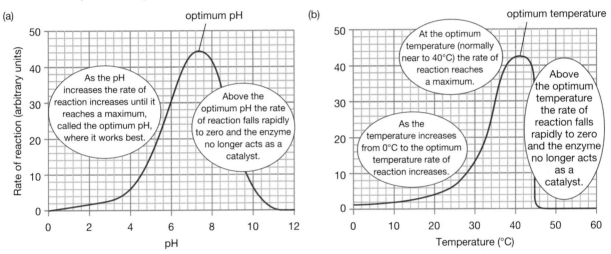

Figure 1.24 Graphs to show how (a) pH and (b) temperature affect the rate of an enzyme-catalysed reaction. What is the optimum pH for the reaction in (a)?

Both pH and temperature will affect the shape of the enzyme's molecular structure, and therefore the active site.

Many of the amino acids that make up the enzyme carry a charge. If the pH changes, the charge on these amino acids may change. Amino acids that previously attracted or repelled each other may, no longer, or begin to attract or repel. The shape of the active site may change. Temperature will denature enzymes because high temperatures disrupt the intermolecular forces between the amino acids that make up the enzyme. Denaturation of an enzyme is, almost always, irreversible.

5. **Biological washing detergents contain enzymes. Explain why clothes washed at 60°C will not be as clean as those washed at 40°C.**

6. **How does the lock-and-key theory explain the specificity of enzymes?**

PRACTICAL

Investigate the effect of pH on the rate of reaction of amylase enzyme

Learning objectives:

- describe how safety is managed, apparatus is used and accurate measurements are made
- explain how representative samples are taken
- make and record accurate observations
- draw and interpret a graph from secondary data using knowledge and observations.

Amylase is an enzyme that controls the breakdown of starch in our digestive systems. Starch turns a blue-black colour when iodine (an orange solution) is added.

These pages are designed ❶ to help you think about aspects of the investigation rather than to guide you through it step by step.

Making accurate measurements and working safely

In this investigation digestion is modelled, using solutions of starch and **amylase** in test tubes, to find the optimum pH required for the reaction. Amylase and **starch** solution are each added to a separate test tube and put in a water bath or a beaker of hot water at 25°C and left for 5 minutes. The pH buffer solution is added to the amylase, before adding the starch. To carry out this method small volumes of chemicals and enzymes (less than 10 cm³) must be accurately measured. To do this a 10 cm³ measuring cylinder or a 10 cm³ calibrated dropping pipette could be used.

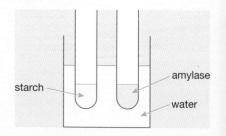

starch — amylase — water

The investigation also involves taking samples from the mixture at timed intervals and adding them to **iodine solution** in a spotting tile. To do this a glass rod or a dropping pipette could be used. The time at which the solution no longer turns a blue-black colour with iodine solution (the iodine solution remains orange) is recorded.

The procedure is repeated for different values of pH buffer solution.

❶ Which piece of apparatus would you use to:

a measure small volumes accurately?
b add drops of solution to the iodine?

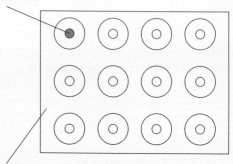

Drop of starch/amylase mixture added at zero time

Spotting tile containing drops of iodine solution

2 To calculate the time taken for the reaction to occur, the teacher has told the students to count up the drops of iodine solution used. Explain how this is an accurate measurement of the time taken.

3 Give two safety precautions that should be taken when doing the investigation.

Planning your sampling

A student carries out a trial run of the procedure before starting his investigation. He found that at pH7 the colour change took 40 seconds to happen. He then decided when to take samples of the solution.

4 What colour will the student see in the spotting tile when all the starch has been broken down by the amylase?

5 Explain why the student will need to take continuous samples throughout his investigation.

6 Why did he carry out a trial before starting the investigation?

7 From the result of the trial run, suggest suitable time intervals for the student to take the continuous samples in his investigation.

Using results to draw and interpret a graph

The student completed the investigation. They sampled the test solutions every ten seconds. This is the data.

pH of solution	Time for colour change to occur (seconds)		
	Test 1	Test 2	Test 3
5	150	160	160
6	70	70	80
7	40	50	40
8	80	80	60
9	130	90	140

The student decided to draw a graph of the data in a table to make it easier to see trends in the data.

8 Should the student draw a bar chart or a line graph?

9 The student repeated each pH test three times.

   a Why did they repeat the tests?
   b The student thought they had an anomalous result. Which result do you think it was?
   c What should the student do with the anomalous result?

10 Calculate the mean time for the colour change to happen at each pH.

11 Plot the graph of the student's data.

12 Use the graph to calculate the rate of reaction at each pH.

13 Use your knowledge of enzymes to help you identify patterns, make inferences and draw conclusions.

Cells at work

Learning objectives:

- explain the need for energy
- describe aerobic respiration as an exothermic reaction.

KEY WORDS

active transport
respiration
aerobic respiration
exothermic

This runner is using energy to run a marathon. But we all need a continuous supply of energy – 24 hours a day – just to stay alive.

We need energy to live

Organisms need energy:

- to drive the chemical reactions needed to keep them alive, including building large molecules
- for movement
- for keeping warm.

Energy is needed to make our muscles contract and to keep our bodies warm. It's also needed to transport substances around the bodies of animals and plants.

In other topics of the book, you will also find out that energy is needed:

- for cell division
- to maintain a constant environment within our bodies
- for **active transport**. Plants use active transport to take up mineral ions from the soil, and to open and close their stomata
- to transmit nerve impulses.

Figure 1.25 An average runner uses around 13 000 kJ of energy for a marathon

1. List four uses of energy in animals.
2. List four uses of energy in plants.

Aerobic respiration

Respiration is the continuously occurring process used by all organisms to release the energy they need from food.

Respiration using oxygen is called **aerobic respiration**. This type of respiration takes place in animal and plant cells, and in many microorganisms.

Glucose is a simple sugar. It is the starting point of respiration in most organisms. The food that organisms take in is, therefore, converted into glucose.

This chemical reaction is **exothermic**. A reaction is described as exothermic when it releases energy.

The energy released during respiration is used to build a high energy compound called **adenosine triphosphate**, or **ATP**. ATP is an energy carrier; it carries energy to the part of the cell where it's needed. On reaching this, the ATP breaks down, releasing its stored energy.

Energy from respiration that is not transferred to ATP is released as heat.

Figure 1.26 Birds and mammals use heat energy to maintain a constant body temperature

Figure 1.27 Insect flight muscles have huge numbers of well-developed mitochondria

3 What is the purpose of respiration?

4 How do birds and mammals make use of the waste heat energy?

Bioenergetics

This is the equation for aerobic respiration:

glucose + oxygen → carbon dioxide + water (energy released)

$$C_6H_{12}O_6 + 6O_2 \rightarrow 6CO_2 + 6H_2O$$

This equation describes the overall change brought about through each of a series of chemical reactions. A small amount of energy is actually released at each stage in the series.

The first group of steps occurs in the cytoplasm of cells, but most of the energy is transferred by chemical reactions in mitochondria. A maximum of 38 molecules of ATP can be synthesised for each molecule of glucose.

5 When and where does respiration occur?

6 Give one characteristic feature of actively respiring cells.

7 What is the maximum number of molecules of ATP that can be produced from one molecule of glucose?

DID YOU KNOW?

The muscle an insect uses to fly is the most active tissue found in nature.

COMMON MISCONCEPTIONS

Don't forget that *all* organisms respire. The equation is the reverse of photosynthesis, but don't confuse the two. Photosynthesis is the way in which plants make their food.

Living without oxygen

Learning objectives:

- describe the process of anaerobic respiration
- compare the processes of aerobic and anaerobic respiration.

KEY WORDS

anaerobic
respiration
fermentation

Stewart is a brewer. He adds yeast to a mixture of malted barley and hops in water.

Figure 1.28 Yeast converts sugar into alcohol, or ethanol. The process is completed in around 3 days

Anaerobic respiration

The yeast respires using the sugary liquid. The yeast cells divide rapidly. After a few hours there are so many yeast cells that the oxygen runs out. The yeast is able to switch its respiration so that it can obtain energy *without* oxygen. Many microbes such as yeast can respire successfully without oxygen.

This is **anaerobic respiration** – respiration without oxygen.

Anaerobic respiration in yeast cells and certain other microorganisms is called **fermentation**.

Anaerobic respiration occurs in the cytoplasm of cells.

1. **What is meant by anaerobic respiration?**
2. **Why do yeast cells switch from aerobic to anaerobic respiration in the process of making ethanol?**

Baking

Yeast is also economically important in baking bread. Yeast is mixed with flour and some sugar. The ingredients are mixed together thoroughly and the dough is left to rise before baking it.

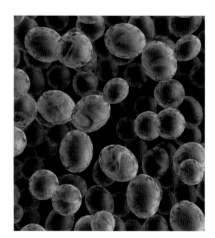

Figure 1.29 Yeast cells divide rapidly by mitosis. Many of the cells do not separate from each other

Figure 1.30 Dough is kneaded to mix the ingredients

3 Explain why sugar is added to dough.

4 Why does the dough rise?

5 What happens to the alcohol made during bread production?

The biochemistry of fermentation

The equation for fermentation is:

glucose → ethanol + carbon dioxide (energy released)

Anaerobic respiration is much less efficient than aerobic respiration. Only two molecules of ATP are produced per molecule of glucose that's respired. That's only a nineteenth as much energy as aerobic energy. But in situations where there's little oxygen, it means that cells can stay alive, and the amount of energy produced is still enough to keep single cells running.

Certain plant cells can also use alcoholic fermentation to obtain their energy. These include plants that grow in marshes, where oxygen is in short supply. Pollen grains can also respire anaerobically.

Without oxygen, we would die. But when actively contracting, our muscles run short of oxygen. They are able to respire anaerobically for short periods of time. Lactic acid, and not ethanol, is produced.

glucose → lactic acid (energy released)

6 Explain why it is helpful for pollen grains to respire anaerobically.

7 Write down the equation for fermentation.

8 For anaerobic respiration in muscle:
- write down the word equation
- work out the symbol equation.

9 Compare the reactants, products and the amount of energy produced for anaerobic respiration with those for aerobic respiration.

DID YOU KNOW?

Yeast is unable to use the starch in barley for respiration. Maltsters germinate the barley grains first to break down the starch into sugar.

KEY SKILLS

You must be able to compare aerobic and anaerobic respiration: the need for oxygen, the products and the amount of energy transferred.

Enzymes at work

Learning objectives:

*   explain how enzymes break down fats, proteins and carbohydrates
*   name the sites of production and action of specific digestive enzymes
*   interpret data about digestive enzymes.

In 1822, Alexis St. Martin was shot. Dr William Beaumont saved his life, but the wound did not heal. Dr Beaumont used the hole to watch what happened in Alexis's stomach after he ate food!

Physical or chemical digestion?

In the mouth, teeth are used to cut and grind food into smaller pieces. This is physical digestion. It allows food to pass through the digestive system more easily. It increases the surface area of the foods to speed up chemical digestion.

Muscles in the stomach wall also help to physically digest food by squeezing it. Muscles in other parts of the digestive system also squeeze the food to keep it moving by peristalsis.

Even small pieces of food cannot pass into the blood. Enzymes are produced in some parts of the digestive system. Enzymes break down food into very small soluble molecules, so they can be absorbed by the blood. This is chemical digestion.

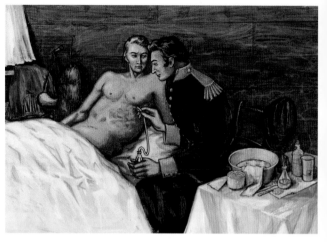

Figure 1.31 Alexis St. Martin with Dr Beaumont in 1822. Pieces of meat in the stomach were much smaller after a few hours. What had happened?

1. Why is physical digestion important?
2. How is chemical digestion different from physical digestion?

Digestive enzymes

Enzymes break down fats, proteins and carbohydrates into their constituent parts.

Most enzymes work inside cells, but the digestive enzymes work outside cells. They are produced by cells in glands and in the lining of the gut. The enzymes pass into the gut to mix with the food. There are three groups of enzymes in digestion:

*   Carbohydrases break down carbohydrates **(polymers)** into simple sugars **(monomers)**. Amylase is a carbohydrase that breaks down starch.
*   Proteases break down proteins (polymers) into amino acids (monomers).
*   Lipases break down fats into fatty acids and glycerol.

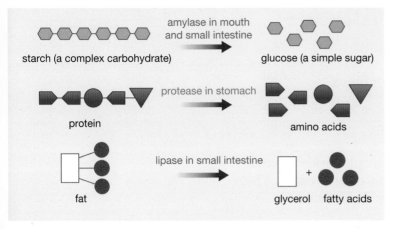

Figure 1.32 Why is chemical digestion important?

Different parts of the gut produce different enzymes, as shown in the table.

Enzyme	Site of production	Reaction
amylase	salivary glands, pancreas	starch → sugars
protease	stomach, pancreas, small intestine	proteins → amino acids
lipase	pancreas	lipids (fats) → fatty acids + glycerol

3 **Where are proteases produced and what reaction do they catalyse?**

4 **Suggest why digestive enzymes do not work inside cells.**

Speeding up digestion

Enzymes are affected by temperature and pH. Our body temperature is kept nearly constant at 37°C. That is the optimum temperature of enzymes in our body.

Enzymes also have an optimum pH. Salivary amylase in the mouth works best at pH 6.7–7.0 The protease enzyme in your stomach works best in acidic conditions, so the stomach produces hydrochloric acid. The stomach also produces mucus which coats the stomach wall to protect it from the acid and enzymes. Protease enzymes that are made in the pancreas and small intestine need alkaline conditions. Bile, made in the liver, neutralises the stomach acid so that these enzymes can work effectively.

5 **Look at Figure 1.33. What does this graph tell you about pepsin and trypsin enzymes?**

COMMON MISCONCEPTION

Bile is not an enzyme and it does not *digest* fat molecules. Bile *emulsifies* fat droplets to increase their surface area to speed up their digestion by lipase enzyme.

DID YOU KNOW?

Your stomach produces about 3 litres of hydrochloric acid a day.

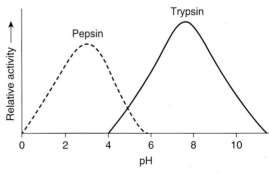

Figure 1.33

Looking at photosynthesis

Learning objectives:

- explain the importance of photosynthesis
- explain how plants use the glucose they produce.

Plants make carbohydrates (for example, sucrose and glucose) and oxygen when they photosynthesise. The plants release the oxygen that they do not need.

Learning about photosynthesis

Photosynthesis is a series of reactions that require energy. Reactions that need energy are called **endothermic** reactions. You will learn more about endothermic reactions in chemistry. In photosynthesis, energy is transferred from the environment to the chloroplast by light.

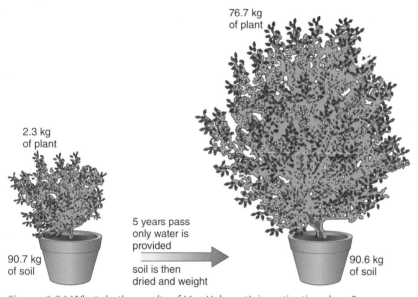

76.7 kg of plant

2.3 kg of plant

5 years pass only water is provided

soil is then dried and weight

90.7 kg of soil

90.6 kg of soil

Figure 1.34 What do the results of Van Helmont's investigation show?

Early scientists thought that plants grew just by using minerals in the soil.

In 1600, Jan Baptist van Helmont showed that the increase in the mass of a willow tree was not just due to the soil minerals.

In 1771, Joseph Priestley put a plant in a glass container with a lit candle (to use up the oxygen). He then left the investigation for 27 days. Priestley found the candle then burned again. This showed that oxygen was present again.

1. What did Van Helmont's investigation show?

2. How could you investigate whether plants need light to photosynthesise?

Using sugars

Glucose and sucrose molecules produced by photosynthesis are used in a number of ways. Sugars are soluble molecules that dissolve to be transported to wherever they are needed. Veins transport glucose to parts of plants shown in Figure 1.35 that do not photosynthesise.

Glucose is used by cells for respiration. Plants cannot make glucose at night so it is converted into insoluble starch for when it is needed. Starch is the main energy store in plants. It is found in every cell, where it is used for respiration in low light levels or the dark.

Plant cells respire sugars to provide energy, and produce carbon dioxide and water. The energy released is used for chemical reactions in cells, for example:

- building glucose into starch for storage
- building sugars into cellulose, which strengthens cell walls
- combining sugars with nitrate ions and other minerals to make amino acids for protein synthesis
- building fats and oils for storage.

3 **When and why do plants respire?**

4 **List five ways that plants use glucose.**

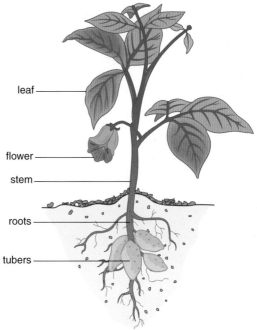

Figure 1.35 Why do plant organs need glucose?

leaf
flower
stem
roots
tubers

Plant respiration

Oxygen is a waste product of photosynthesis. When plant cells respire they use some of this oxygen. Plants respire continually because they need a constant supply of energy to keep them alive.

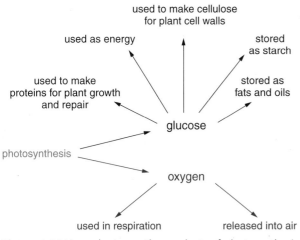

used to make cellulose
for plant cell walls

used as energy

used to make
proteins for plant growth
and repair

stored
as starch

stored as
fats and oils

glucose

photosynthesis

oxygen

used in respiration

released into air

Figure 1.36 How plants use the products of photosynthesis

starch is insoluble
and is made up of
many glucose
molecules joined
together

glucose
molecules
are soluble

Figure 1.37 Starch is a large molecule and glucose is a small molecule

DID YOU KNOW?

Some sea slugs eat algae but do not digest it fully. The algae photosynthesise inside the slugs to give them more food and energy.

The rest of the oxygen is released through the stomata, back into the air.

5 **Explain the relationship between photosynthesis and respiration in leaves.**

6 **Explain what is incorrect about the statement 'plants make oxygen for us to breathe'?**

Explaining photosynthesis

Learning objectives:

- identify the reactants and products of photosynthesis
- describe photosynthesis by an equation
- recall that photosynthesis is a two-stage process that takes place in chloroplasts
- explain gaseous exchange in leaves.

KEY WORDS

chlorophyll
chloroplast
carbohydrate

Plants and algae are amazing organisms. They transfer energy from outer space into chemical energy in glucose. Without plants, there would be no life! How do plants harness this energy?

Describing the process

Photosynthesis is the chemical reaction that plants use to produce glucose, so essentially they are able to make their own food. Photosynthesis needs two raw materials. These reactants are:

- carbon dioxide (absorbed through leaves)
- water (absorbed through roots and transported to leaves).

The reaction also needs light and **chlorophyll** in the leaves. The equation is:

$$\text{carbon dioxide} + \text{water} \xrightarrow{\text{light} + \text{chlorophyll}} \text{glucose} + \text{oxygen}$$

$$6CO_2 + 6H_2O \longrightarrow C_6H_{12}O_6 + 6O_2$$

This is an endothermic reaction. It requires energy in the form of light.

The products of photosynthesis are **carbohydrates**, for example glucose and starch. When iodine is added to a leaf, it will turn blue/black if starch is present. If starch is present, it shows that photosynthesis has happened.

DID YOU KNOW?

Some leaves have green parts and yellow/white parts. They are called variegated leaves. Variegated leaves only photosynthesise in the green parts where the chlorophyll is found.

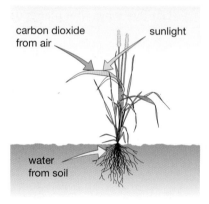

Figure 1.38 A plant needs light, water and carbon dioxide for photosynthesis

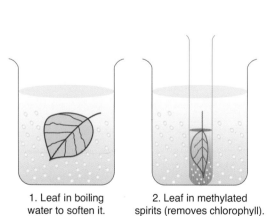

1. Leaf in boiling water to soften it.

2. Leaf in methylated spirits (removes chlorophyll).

3. Leaf washed. Few drops of iodine added.

4. Blue/black colour indicates starch produced byphotosynthesis.

Figure 1.39 Testing a leaf for starch

Oxygen is made during photosynthesis and released into the air. It is a waste product on which animals depend.

1. Which raw materials (or reactants) are used in photosynthesis and what are the products of the reaction?

2. A leaf was tested for starch. The iodine stayed orange.

   a What does this tell you about the leaf?
   b What conditions was it kept in?

There are actually two main stages in photosynthesis:

1. Light energy splits the water molecule, releasing oxygen (as a gas) and hydrogen ions.

2. Hydrogen reacts with carbon dioxide to make glucose.

Gaseous exchange in leaves

Leaves take in carbon dioxide from the air and release oxygen when they photosynthesise. This is called gaseous exchange.

Some students investigated gaseous exchange in leaves. They used the same size leaf in Tubes 1 and 2 and left them in a rack in bright light for an hour. Look at their method in the table.

Tube	Control	Tube 1	Tube 2
Set up	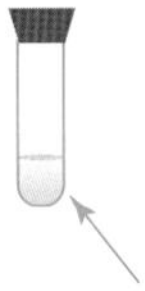	aluminum foil 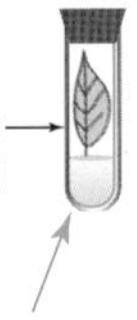	
	2 cm^3 hydrogencarbonate indicator		
Results	no change in colour	turns yellow	turns red

Figure 1.40 Investigating gaseous exchange in leaves.

Hydrogencarbonate indicator is an orange solution.

- In more acidic conditions it turns yellow.
- In less acidic conditions it turns red.

Carbon dioxide dissolves in water to form an acidic solution.

> **REMEMBER!**
>
> Light does not make food, but light is needed for the reactions to occur.

3. Describe the results of the investigation and explain why a control was used.

4. Explain what the results tell you.

5. Why are light and chlorophyll needed for photosynthesis?

6. Predict what would happen to the hydrogencarbonate indicator if you removed the aluminium foil? Explain your answer.

PRACTICAL

Investigate the effect of light intensity on the rate of photosynthesis using an aquatic organism such as pondweed

KEY WORDS

photosynthesis
hypothesis
chloroplasts

Learning objectives:

- use scientific ideas to develop a hypothesis
- use the correct sampling techniques to ensure that readings are representative
- present results in a graph.

Photosynthesis is the process by which green plants produce food. When plants photosynthesise they absorb light energy to power the reaction. The equation for photosynthesis is:

carbon dioxide + water $\xrightarrow{\text{light + chlorophyll}}$ glucose + oxygen

$$6CO_2 + 6H_2O \longrightarrow C_6H_{12}O_6 + 6O_2$$

These pages are designed ❗ to help you think about aspects of the investigation rather than to guide you through it step by step.

Developing a hypothesis

Two students are investigating how light intensity affects the rate of **photosynthesis** in pondweed. They will measure how much gas is released by the pondweed in 1 minute when they put a lamp at 10 cm, 15 cm, 20 cm, 25 cm and 30 cm away from the beaker containing the pondweed.

Before they begin the investigation they are going to make a **hypothesis**. Hypotheses are developed using previous knowledge or observations. The students know that:

- photosynthesis produces glucose and oxygen
- the oxygen will be released as bubbles of gas in the water
- light energy is absorbed by chlorophyll found in the **chloroplasts** in the mesophyll cells
- photosynthesis can be limited by different factors.

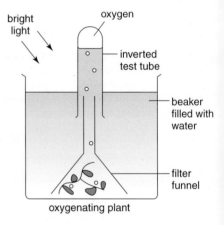

Figure 1.41 An oxygenating plant photosynthesising

1. **When will the light intensity be greatest?**

2. **How will increasing the light intensity affect the rate of photosynthesis?**

3. **When the rate of photosynthesis increases what will happen to the amount of oxygen produced?**

④ Could any other variable affect this investigation?

⑤ Suggest a hypothesis for the investigation that the students are going to do.

Planning your sampling

Two students decided that they would make their sampling representative by taking repeat readings at each light intensity. Look at their results.

Distance of lamp from pondweed (cm)	Number of bubbles per minute		
	Test 1	Test 2	Test 3
10	105	121	124
15	58	50	54
20	26	30	32
25	15	17	16
30	12	13	14

⑥ What do you notice about the results in Test 1 compared to the results in tests 2 and 3?

⑦ Suggest why this happened.

⑧ Suggest what the students should do with the Test 1 results.

⑨ Why is it important to take repeat readings when carrying out investigations?

Presenting results

Two students used a table to record their results because it was quick and the results were organised, but they found it hard to analyse them in this form. Their teacher said that they should think of a better way to present their results to help them. One student thought that using a bar chart would be the best method but the other disagreed. She presented her results as a line graph.

⑩ Which would be the best way to present these results? Explain why.

⑪ Plot the graph of the student's results using only Test 2 and 3 data.

Increasing photosynthesis

Learning objectives:

- identify factors that affect the rate of photosynthesis
- interpret data about the rate of photosynthesis
- explain the interaction of factors in limiting the rate of photosynthesis.

KEY WORDS

limiting factor

Plants grow faster in summer than in winter. This means that they must produce more food to allow them to grow in summer. Some factors can increase the rate of photosynthesis.

Plants in different habitats

Plants are found in every ecosystem, but their size, appearance and adaptations mean that they look very different. Tropical rainforests have dense plant life. In contrast, few plant species grow in tundra (Arctic regions with permanently frozen subsoil) and desert regions.

Figure 1.42 What are the environmental conditions of these habitats?

1 **How would you describe environmental conditions in tropical forest, tundra and desert ecosystems?**

2 **Suggest how the conditions you have described affect photosynthesis in each habitat.**

Limiting factors

Some students investigated the effect of light on the rate of photosynthesis. Look at their results (Figure 1.43). The students found that:

- Between A and B, the rate of photosynthesis increases as the light intensity increases. Because the rate depends on the light intensity, light intensity is called the **limiting factor**.
- Between B and C, increasing the light intensity has no effect on the rate of photosynthesis. Another factor is now the limiting factor.

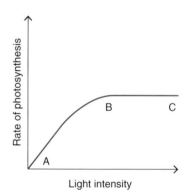

Figure 1.43 Can you explain the shape of the graph between B and C?

KEY INFORMATION

Remember that enzymes denature at temperatures greater than 40°C.

3 **What other factors might limit the rate of photosynthesis between B and C?**

Plants need carbon dioxide to photosynthesise but there is only 0.04% in the atmosphere. It is often the limiting factor controlling the rate of photosynthesis.

Carbon dioxide levels around plants rise when there is no light. This is because the plants are respiring but not photosynthesising. As light levels increase the plants use the carbon dioxide up.

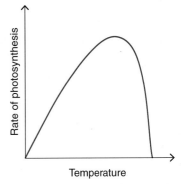

Figure 1.44 Explain what this graph shows

HIGHER TIER ONLY

Interacting limiting factors

Over one day, light, temperature and carbon dioxide levels change. Carbon dioxide may be the limiting factor when plants are crowded on a sunny day. Temperature may be the limiting factor in cooler months. Light may be the limiting factor at dawn.

Plants living in continual shade can adapt. They have a higher ratio of leaves to roots than other plants. The leaves are thinner, have a larger surface area and contain more chlorophyll to absorb light. A shortage of chlorophyll can limit the rate of photosynthesis.

DID YOU KNOW?

Pine trees grow in a cone shape to expose more needles to the sun, increasing the rate of photosynthesis.

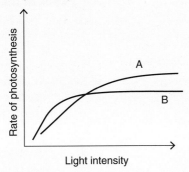

Figure 1.45 Photosynthesis in normal (A) and shade-adapted (B) leaves

The graph shows that shade-adapted leaves (B) are more efficient at absorbing low intensity light than normal leaves (A).

4 **Suggest the limiting factors for photosynthesis over one complete warm summer's day.**

5 **Describe and explain adaptations for photosynthesis shown by some shade-tolerant plants.**

6 **Suggest an advantage of a tree having needles rather than flat, broad leaves.**

MATHS SKILLS

Extracting and interpreting information

Learning objectives:

- to extract and interpret information from tables, charts and graphs
- understand and use inverse proportion – the inverse square law and light intensity in the context of factors affecting photosynthesis.

KEY WORDS

correlation
trend
inverse square law

Tables, charts and graphs give a lot of information in a small space. Extracting and interpreting data from graphics is a vital skill for all scientists.

Looking at tables

Tables allow us to classify and compare data. To read a table and extract information from it, you must first read the headings carefully.

Light intensity (units)	Rate of photosynthesis (number of bubbles per minute)
1	2
3	11
6	26
9	48
11	47
14	48

The headings of each column help us to read the table.

Column 1 tells us that this table is about light intensity, and column 2 tells us that the data collected was the rate of photosynthesis, which was measured by counting the number of bubbles released in a minute.

Looking at charts and graphs

The most commonly used statistical diagrams in science are line graphs, bar graphs and pie charts. Pie charts are used to show proportions and the relative importance of different data sets. The relative size of the angle at the centre of each sector represents the size of the data set. Different sectors can be compared without even knowing the numbers in the different groups.

DID YOU KNOW?

Correlations prove a relationship but do not prove cause and effect.

Look at the table.

1. **a** What was the light intensity when 26 bubbles were released in a minute?
   b What happened to the rate between 9 light intensity units and 14 light intensity units?

2. **a** At what light intensity was the rate of photosynthesis highest?
   b What trends do you notice in the data?

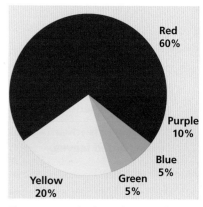

Figure 1.46 Pie chart showing the amount of time that hummingbirds spent at different coloured feeders.

In a bar graph each bar represents the number of a specific data set. The height of the bars allow us to compare the quantity of each sub-group within a data set.

Plot one data set against another to show whether or not there is a relationship, or correlation, between them. When the points are more or less in a straight line, it is said that there is a good **correlation** between the two data sets. Correlations can be positive, negative, or zero. Positive correlation shows that as one set of values increases, so does the second set (a 'more:more' relationship). Negative correlation shows that as one set of values increases, the other data set decreases (a 'more:less' relationship). Zero correlation shows that one data set increasing or decreasing has no effect on the other.

Another type of graph is the pictogram, which uses pictorial forms to represent data, for example, statistical data.

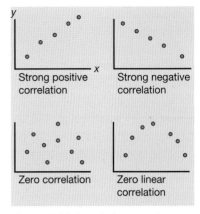

Figure 1.47 Correlations can be positive, negative, or zero.

Line graphs

To interpret or read a line graph:

- Look at the labels, scales and units on each axis. What are they telling you?

- Look at the general **trend** or trends on the graph. As factor × increases, what happens to factor Y?

- Pick out specific points of interest. Follow the line along the graph until you find the data point that corresponds with a value on the other axis.

3 What does the graph in Figure 1.48 tell you?

HIGHER TIER ONLY

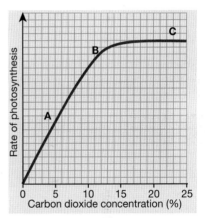

Figure 1.48 This line graph gives information about a factor that is relevant to plants

KEY INFORMATION

Remember to read table headings and graph axes carefully.

Inverse square law

You know that as the distance between the light source and a photosynthesising plant increases, the light intensity will decrease. This is described as being an inverse relationship. Light intensity obeys the **inverse square law**. The inverse square law states that if the light distance is doubled, the light intensity decreases by the square of the distance. For example, if the distance between the light source and the plant is doubled, the light intensity is quartered.

So, for example:

If the distance is doubled (i.e. it is 2× the original distance):

light intensity $= \frac{1}{2^2} = \frac{1}{4}$ of the light intensity.

If the distance is trebled (i.e. it is 3× the original distance):

light intensity $= \frac{1}{3^2} = \frac{1}{9}$ of the light intensity.

Check your progress

You should be able to:

calculate magnification used by a light microscope using eyepiece and objective lens magnifications	→ calculate the magnification of a light or electron micrograph	→ explain limitations of light microscopy and advantages of electron microscopy
describe the structure of a prokaryotic cell	→ describe the differences between eukaryotic and prokaryotic cells	→ explain why scientists have now separated organisms into three domains using evidence from chemical analysis
recall that DNA is the molecule that carries genetic information	→ describe DNA as a polymer of repeating units	→ describe the structure of DNA as a double helix
know that enzymes catalyse reactions in cells	→ describe how pH and temperature affect enzymes	→ explain how pH and temperature affect enzyme activity
understand that substrate molecules fit into active sites of enzymes	→ describe the lock and key theory	→ explain how carbohydrates, proteins and fats are broken down by digestive enzymes
recall that organisms can respire with oxygen (aerobic respiration) or without oxygen (anaerobic respiration)	→ use word equations to describe the processes of aerobic and anaerobic respiration	→ use symbol equations for aerobic and anaerobic respiration and be able to compare the two processes
use the word equation to describe photosynthesis	→ recall and use the symbol equation for photosynthesis	→ recall and use the balanced symbol equation for photosynthesis
describe photosynthesis as a two-stage process that occurs in chloroplasts	→ describe the use of light and chloroplasts in photosynthesis	→ explain that chloroplasts absorb energy to drive chemical reactions
name the factors that affect photosynthesis	→ describe how the rate of photosynthesis can be increased	→ explain the effects of interacting limiting factors on photosynthesis

Worked example

Laura is growing tomatoes in her greenhouse.

Laura knows that to increase her crop of tomatoes, she must increase photosynthesis.

1 **Laura heats her greenhouse. She wants to know the best temperature to grow the tomatoes in. Look at the graph.**

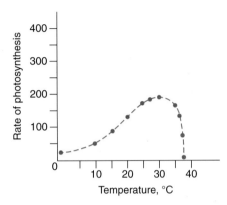

Explain what the graph shows

The rate increases from 5-30°C and then decreases to 0 at 37°C because the enzymes denature

2 **What is the best temperature for Laura to grow the tomatoes?**

30°C

How does water for photosynthesis get to the leaves?

Through the xylem by osmosis.

3 **Laura notices that when she turns the heaters up, she needs to water the plants more often. Explain why.**

More water evaporates

4 **Complete the equation for photosynthesis**

$$6CO_2 + H_2O \rightarrow C_6H_{12}O_6 + H_2O$$

The pattern has been given (increases and then decreases) and the explanation for the decrease in rate is correct.

A better answer would be to explain that the rate increases from 5–30°C as the enzymes gain more energy or collide more often.

Correct answer given.

One correct answer is given (xylem).

A better answer would be '…by transpiration'.

One correct answer is given

A better answer would be: Transpiration increases because more water evaporates through the stomata.

More detailed responses would give a higher mark.

Water (H_2O) has been correctly identified as a reactant, but has also been given as the product. The equation has not been balanced. The correct answer is:

$6CO_\mathbf{2} + 6H_2O \rightarrow C_6H_{12}O_6 + 6O_2$

End of chapter questions

Getting started

1 The diagrams below show an animal cell and a bacterial cell.

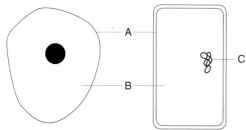

  i Parts of the cell labelled A and B are found in both animal cells and bacterial cells. Name cell parts A and B.   `1 Mark`

    a cell membrane   **d** nucleus
    b cell wall   **e** vacuole
    c cytoplasm

  ii What is the name of chemical C?   `1 Mark`

    a cellulose   **c** DNA
    b chlorophyll   **d** protein

2 Explain how you know that the cell shown is a plant cell.   `2 Marks`

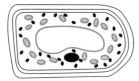

3 The diagrams below show some different cells. The length of each is included on the diagram. Arrange them in order of size.   `1 Mark`

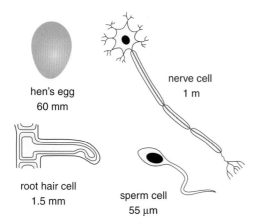

4 **a** Why do plants photosynthesise?   `1 Mark`

    b A student wants to test whether a leaf she has collected contains starch. Describe a test she could carry out.   `2 Marks`

5. **Gemma is using Feulgen stain to stain some dividing cells. The label on the bottle of stain is shown.**

IRRITATING TO EYES,
RESPIRATORY SYSTEM
AND SKIN

Explain two safety precautions she should take when using the stain.   `2 Marks`

Going further

6. **Draw one line from each cell structure to match it with its function.**   `1 Mark`

Cell structure	**Function**

Controls what enters and leaves cells

Mitochondrion

Respiration

Ribosome

Protein synthesis

7. **Use words from the box to complete the word equation for aerobic respiration.**   `1 Mark`

alcohol	carbon dioxide	glucose	lactic acid

.... + oxygen → .... + water (+energy)

8. **Write a word and balanced symbol equation for photosynthesis.**   `2 Marks`

9 A scientist is investigating the effect of different sugars on the anaerobic respiration of yeast.
She measures the volume of carbon dioxide produced over a 2-hour period.
She investigates two types of sugar, sucrose and lactose.

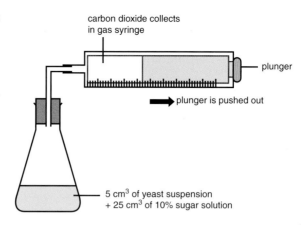

a Suggest ways in which she can be sure that the readings she takes are the result of using the two different types of sugar and not from other factors. **4 Marks**

b Her results are shown below.

Type of sugar	Volume of carbon dioxide produced (cm³)						
	Time (min)						
	0	20	40	60	80	100	120
sucrose	0	0.2	1.8	5.6	7.6	7.9	7.9
lactose	0	0	0	0	0	0	0

Suggest reasons for the scientist's results. **2 Marks**

More challenging

10 What structures inside plant cells absorb energy from light? **1 Mark**

11 Some students investigated how light intensity affects the rate of photosynthesis. The graph shows their results.

a Describe the pattern show by the graph. **1 Mark**

b Explain what is happening at A and B. **2 Marks**

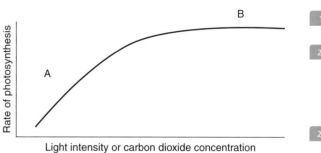

c Predict what would happen if the temperature was increased from 25 °C to 35 °C. Give reasons for your prediction. **2 Marks**

d Describe how you could measure the effect of light intensity on the rate of photosynthesis in pondweed. Draw a diagram to show what equipment you would need and how you would set it up. **4 Marks**

Most demanding

12 Explain how anaerobic respiration differs from aerobic respiration.

2 Marks

13 The graph shows the effect of temperature on the enzyme amylase.

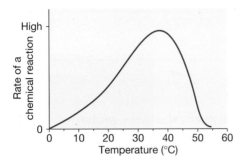

Use your knowledge of enzyme action to describe and explain the graph.

4 Marks

14 Lindsay wants to measure the effect of pH on the rate of reaction of amylase enzyme. She wants to find out the time taken to completely digest a starch solution at a range of pH values.

Describe an experiment Lindsay could carry out. Include the solutions she should use, and how she should make sure her results were accurate and representative.

4 Marks

Total: 40 Marks

SCALING UP

IN MULTICELLULAR ORGANISMS, CELLS HAVE TO DIVIDE

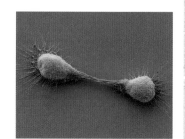

- In multicellular organisms, specialised cells are organised into tissues, tissues into organs, and organs into body systems.
- Cells divide as we're growing, and to replace cells that are injured, worn out or have died.
- This type of cell division is called mitosis.
- When a cell divides by mitosis, two daughter cells are produced, each are genetically identical to each other and to the mother cell.

MOLECULES MOVE BY DIFFUSION

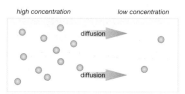

- Molecules in gases and liquids move from a high concentration to a lower concentration until all areas have an equal concentration.
- Different factors can affect the rate of diffusion.
- The steepness of a concentration gradient affects the rate of diffusion.

ANIMALS AND PLANTS TRANSPORT SUBSTANCES TO WHERE THEY ARE NEEDED

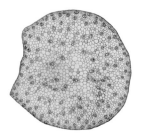

- There are two transport systems in plants: xylem transports water up the plant from the roots to the leaves, and phloem transports substances up and down the plant.
- The circulatory system of animals moves substances around the body in the blood.

BLOOD IS USED TO TRANSPORT OXYGEN TO BODY TISSUES

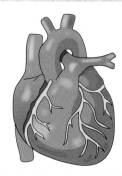

- Oxygen is taken from the lungs to the body. Carbon dioxide is returned from the body to the lungs.
- The function of the heart is to pump blood around the body.
- Blood is made up of red blood cells, white blood cells, plasma and platelets.

IN THIS CHAPTER YOU WILL FIND OUT ABOUT:

DO ALL MATERIALS MOVE BY DIFFUSION?

- In living tissues, water moves from a high water potential to a lower water potential by osmosis.
- The movement of water can affect the turgidity of living cells.
- Some substances that living cells need can be moved against a concentration gradient.

WHY SOME ORGANISMS NEED ORGAN SYSTEMS

- Size affects the ability and efficiency of diffusion alone to supply cells with nutrients.
- Some membrane surfaces and organ systems are specialised for exchanging materials to ensure that all body cells get the nutrients that they need.
- An example of an efficient exchange surface is root hair cells in plants.

DO ALL ORGANISMS MOVE MATERIALS IN THE SAME WAY?

- Small organisms do not have specialised organs for gaseous exchange or transport of some materials.
- Fish and and mammals have evolved specialised exchange surfaces for gaseous exchange.
- Fish and mammals have specialised transport systems.
- The heart is an efficient pump for the transport system.

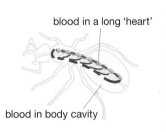

blood in a long 'heart'

blood in body cavity

WHICH SUBSTANCES DIFFUSE INTO PLANTS?

- Different factors affect the rate of diffusion in plant systems.
- Concentration gradients can affect the rate of photosynthesis.
- Substances move in and out the leaf during different processes, for example, photosynthesis, respiration and transpiration.

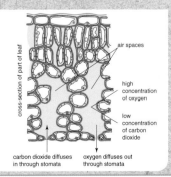

cross-section of part of leaf

air spaces

high concentration of oxygen

low concentration of carbon dioxide

carbon dioxide diffuses in through stomata

oxygen diffuses out through stomata

KEY CONCEPT

Diffusion in living systems

Learning objectives:

- describe the conditions needed for diffusion to occur
- calculate and compare surface area to volume ratios
- explain how materials pass in and out of cells.

KEY WORDS

diffusion
concentration gradient

In all living organisms, the transfer of many materials occurs by the process of *diffusion*. Diffusion is essential in living systems in the supply of important substances and in the control of certain processes.

Diffusion in living systems

Diffusion is sometimes called passive transport. This is because it happens due to the random motion of particles. No energy is required.

All that is needed for diffusion to happen is a **concentration gradient**. Diffusion can be defined as the net movement of particles from an area of high concentration to an area of lower concentration due to the random movement of particles, until **equilibrium** is reached.

1. **What effect do you think increasing the concentration gradient will have on the speed of diffusion?**

2. **What other factors will affect the speed of diffusion?**

Photosynthesis and diffusion

Leaf cells need carbon dioxide for photosynthesis and oxygen for respiration. The waste products of these processes must leave the leaf cells too.

Carbon dioxide diffuses into leaves through the stomata. During photosynthesis, the palisade cells use carbon dioxide; the concentration of carbon dioxide in the leaf is low but the concentration outside the leaf is relatively high. This results in a large concentration gradient, and carbon dioxide diffuses into the leaf.

The rate of diffusion in living systems can be increased by:

- increasing the surface area
- decreasing the distance the particles have to travel
- increasing the concentration gradient.

External conditions can also affect the rate of diffusion.

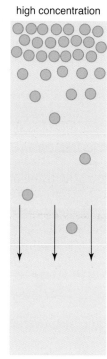

high concentration

low concentration

Figure 2.1 In diffusion, particles move from a higher concentration to a lower concentration

- Wind increases the concentration gradient of carbon dioxide between inside and outside, and the rate of diffusion increases.
- High humidity decreases the concentration gradient of water vapour between the inside and outside of the leaf, and diffusion slows down.

3 **Explain how oxygen produced during photosynthesis passes out of the leaf.**

4 **How does external temperature affect the rate of diffusion from a leaf?**

Diffusion and cells

Cells are made largely of water containing many dissolved substances. These substances and water enter and leave the cells through cell membranes. Cell membranes allow some particles through, but block others. They are called *partially (or selectively) permeable membranes.*

Cells need continual supplies of dissolved substances, for example, oxygen and glucose, for cellular activities. Waste products, for example, carbon dioxide, need to be removed. To enter or leave a cell, dissolved substances have to be small enough to pass through the partially permeable cell membrane. Diffusion allows this to happen.

Cell membranes are similar to football nets. Large footballs cannot pass through the netting, but small golf balls easily pass through. In the same way, large particles, for example starch, cannot pass through the cell membrane. However, small glucose particles can easily pass through the membranes. Cell membranes are very thin to allow substances to easily diffuse through them.

5 **Explain how materials pass in and out of cells. Use a diagram to help you.**

6 **Will diffusion ever stop completely? Explain your answer.**

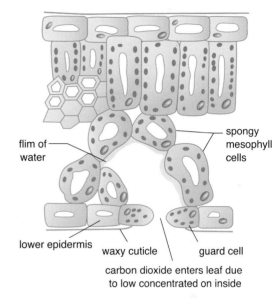

flim of water — spongy mesophyll cells

lower epidermis — waxy cuticle — guard cell

carbon dioxide enters leaf due to low concentrated on inside

Figure 2.2 Why are the stomata spaced out?

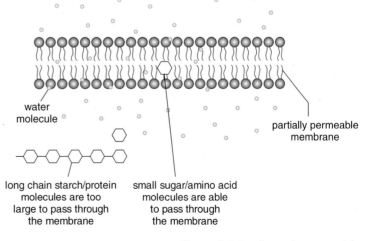

water molecule

partially permeable membrane

long chain starch/protein molecules are too large to pass through the membrane

small sugar/amino acid molecules are able to pass through the membrane

Figure 2.3 A cell membrane model. What is happening to the particles?

Explaining water movement

Learning objectives:

- describe how water moves by osmosis in living tissues
- identify factors that affect the rate of osmosis
- explain the term 'partially permeable membrane'.

KEY WORDS

osmosis
partially permeable
  membrane
water potential

Some examples of substances that are transported in and out of cells by diffusion are carbon dioxide and oxygen. Living cells contain a lot of water. How does water move in and out of cells?

The diffusion of water

Osmosis is the diffusion of water through a **partially permeable membrane**. Partially permeable membranes have tiny holes in them.

A solution is dilute when there is a high water potential. A dilute sugar solution has a high water potential (water is the solvent) and a low sugar concentration (the solute). A solution is concentrated when there is a low water potential. Most solute particles are too large to pass through the partially permeable membrane, but water molecules can pass through. Osmosis is the diffusion of water molecules from a dilute solution to a concentrated solution through a partially permeable membrane.

1. How does water move in and out of living cells?

2. Suggest why potatoes become soft when boiled.

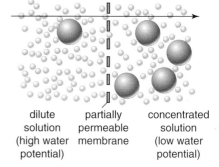

dilute solution (high water potential)   partially permeable membrane   concentrated solution (low water potential)

Key ○ water molecule   ● solute

Figure 2.4 Describe the movement of water particles

Osmosis and cells

Solutions containing lots of water molecules have a high water potential. Pure water has the highest water potential.

Look at the diagram.

In (a) the cell has a concentrated solution. Water molecules enter by osmosis from the surrounding dilute solution.

In (b) the cell has a dilute solution and a high water potential. Water molecules move out to the surrounding concentrated solution.

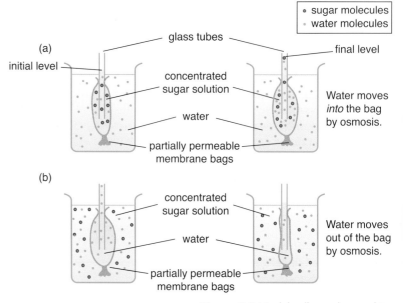

Figure 2.5 Model cells can be used to investigate osmosis

Living cells must balance their water content to work efficiently. Chemical reactions in cells use water. If the cytoplasm becomes concentrated, water enters by osmosis. If the cytoplasm becomes too dilute, water leaves the cell by osmosis.

Problems occur in animal cells when the external solution is more dilute than that inside the cell. Water enters; the cells swell and may burst.

When the external solution is more concentrated than that inside the cell, water moves out by osmosis. The cell shrinks and shrivels.

Plant cells have inelastic cell walls. Water enters the cell by osmosis and fills the vacuole. This pushes against the cell wall, making the cell turgid.

If water moves out the cell by osmosis, the vacuole shrinks and the cell becomes flaccid.

If too much water leaves the cell, the cytoplasm moves away from the cell wall.

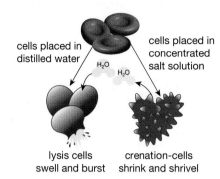

cells placed in distilled water

cells placed in concentrated salt solution

H_2O H_2O

lysis cells swell and burst

crenation-cells shrink and shrivel

Figure 2.6 What will happen if red blood cells are placed in a very dilute or a very concentrated solution?

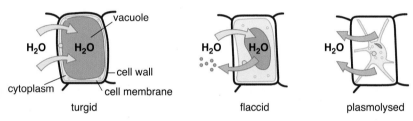

vacuole

H_2O H_2O

cell wall

cytoplasm   cell membrane

turgid

H_2O H_2O

flaccid

H_2O

plasmolysed

Figure 2.7 Explain the movement of water in these plant cells

3 **How are osmosis and diffusion similar and different?**

4 **Describe how osmosis affects animal cells.**

Explaining osmosis

Water molecules and sugar molecules in a solution move around randomly. When a sugar molecule hits the membrane, it bounces away. When a water molecule hits the membrane, it can pass through a hole to the other side.

In Figure 2.8, there are more water molecules on the left, so more water molecules can pass through the membrane to the right-hand side than can pass in the opposite direction. The water molecules move both ways, but the net movement is from left to right.

5 **Explain why there are differences in the effects of water on plant and animal cells.**

6 **Explain osmosis.**

> **REMEMBER!**
>
> **Osmosis is only the movement of water across a partially permeable membrane. No other molecules move by osmosis.**

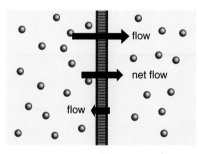

flow

net flow

flow

Figure 2.8 Water particles move both ways across the membrane

> **DID YOU KNOW?**
>
> Giant redwood trees grow over 90 m tall. The water pressure in the cells and the strong, lignified cell walls keep the plant upright.

Learning about active transport

KEY WORDS
....
active transport

Learning objectives:

- describe active transport
- explain how active transport is different from diffusion and osmosis
- explain why active transport is important.

Diffusion and osmosis explain how gases and water move down a concentration gradient to enter (and sometimes exit) living things. Minerals are taken up into the root hair cells of a plant by another method.

Active transport

Cells can absorb substances that are at low concentration in their surroundings by **active transport**. These substances move *against* the concentration gradient, for example, when plants absorb nitrate ions through their root hairs from the soil water. The concentration of nitrate ions in soil water is usually less than the concentration of nitrate ions inside the root hair cells.

Nitrate ions naturally diffuse down their concentration gradient, out of the cell and into the soil, but plants transport the nitrates *into* their cells using active transport.

Active transport moves substances from a more dilute solution to a more concentrated solution (against a concentration gradient). This requires energy from respiration.

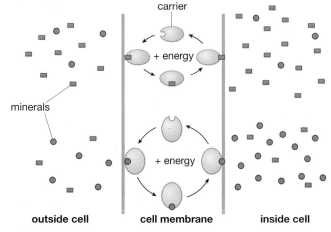

Figure 2.9 Why does active transport need energy?

1 **Describe how minerals are absorbed by plants.**

2 **How is active transport different to diffusion and osmosis?**

More active transport

Investigations have shown that a plant can absorb different minerals in different amounts. The plant can select which minerals it needs. Look at the graph. Algae absorb a lot of chlorine, but only a little calcium in comparison.

In 1938, scientists discovered that an increase in mineral uptake by a plant happened at the same time as an increase in its respiration rate. This shows that the process needs energy – because the minerals are absorbed against the concentration gradient.

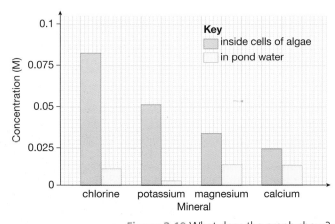

Figure 2.10 What does the graph show?

The greater the rate of cellular respiration, the more energy is available for active transport to happen.

Different cells use active transport for different purposes:

- Marine fish have cells in their gills that can pump salt back into the salty sea water.
- Cells in the thyroid gland take in iodine to use in the production of hormones.
- Cells in the kidney reabsorb sodium ions from urine.
- The villi in the small intestine absorb glucose from the gut (higher sugar concentration) into the blood (lower sugar concentration).
- Crocodiles have salt glands in their tongues that remove excess salt from their bodies.

3 **Suggest how cells that carry out active transport are adapted to do this.**

4 **Explain why it is important for a plant to transport actively only the minerals that it needs.**

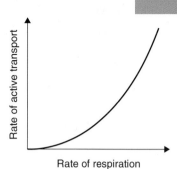

Figure 2.11 Explain the relationship between active transport and respiration

KEY INFORMATION

Active transport needs energy from respiration to move substances from a low concentration to a high concentration.

How does active transport work?

Look at the diagram. Special carrier molecules take mineral ions and other substances across the cell membrane. Different carriers take different substances. A carrier that moves glucose will not move calcium ions.

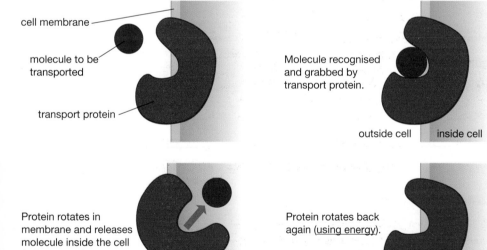

Figure 2.12 Each carrier molecule is specific to a certain mineral

5 **Describe how molecules are transported across a membrane in active transport.**

6 **Explain the similarities and differences between diffusion, osmosis and active transport.**

DID YOU KNOW?

Many animals that live in the sea have salt glands near their eyes. These excrete a salt solution that is six times stronger than urine.

Cell division

Learning objectives:

- describe the process of mitosis in growth, and mitosis as part of the cell cycle
- describe how the process of mitosis produces cells that are genetically identical to the parent cell.

As an adult, we are made up of 37 trillion (3.7×10^{13}) cells. To produce these cells, the fertilised egg needs to undergo many cell divisions.

Chromosomes

As we grow, the cells produced by cell division must all contain the same genetic information.

The genetic information of all organisms is contained in the nucleus, in chromosomes, made of DNA. The DNA in resting cells is found in the nucleus as long, thin strands. For cell division, these strands form condensed chromosomes.

Human body cells have 46 chromosomes, or 23 pairs. Each chromosome in a pair has the same type of genes along its length.

1. **How many chromosomes are found in human body cells?**

2. **How are the chromosomes arranged in a karyotype?**

Mitosis

New cells have to be produced for growth and development, and to replace worn out and damaged body cells.

When new cells are produced they must be identical to the parent cell. Cells divide to produce two new ones. This type of cell division is called **mitosis**. Two daughter cells are produced from the parent cell.

For some cell types, new cells are produced by the division of **stem cells** (discussed later in the chapter). In plants, cell division occurs in regions called meristems.

3. **When are new cells produced?**

4. **In this type of cell division:**
   a **how many chromosomes do daughter cells have?**
   b **how many daughter cells are produced?**

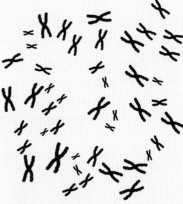

A photograph is taken of a dividing cell.

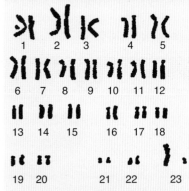

The chromosomes in the photograph are cut out and arranged into pairs. The pairs are arranged so that Pair 1 has the longest chromosomes; Pair 22 the shortest Pair 23 is the sex chromosomes.

Figure 2.13 A profile of a set of chromosomes, called a karyotype

So that the daughter cells produced are identical to the parent cell, the DNA must first copy itself. Each of the 46 chromosomes then consists of two molecules of DNA.

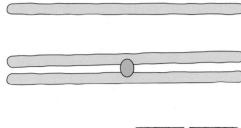

DNA molecule in the nucleus

The DNA replicates to form a double chromosome
Each half has an identical set of genes

The DNA condenses to form a recognisable chromosome. The DNA is now compacted to 1/50 000 of its original length

Figure 2.14 It is these 'double' chromosomes that we always see in micrographs or illustrations of chromosomes

During mitosis, the double chromosomes are pulled apart as each new set of 46 chromosomes moves to opposite ends of the cell (Figure 2.15). Two nuclei then form. The cytoplasm and cell membrane then divides and two identical cells are produced.

5 **Why do chromosomes appear double, or X-shaped, in micrographs?**

The cell cycle

A cell that is actively dividing goes through a series of stages called the **cell cycle**. The cycle involves the growth of the cell and the production of new cell components and division.

DID YOU KNOW?

Using radioactive carbon (^{14}C) dating of a cell's DNA, researchers in Sweden have been able to estimate the lifespan of different types of cells.

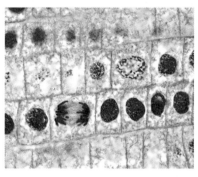

Figure 2.15 Mitosis in an onion cell

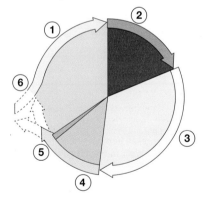

1 The cell grows. The number of sub-cellular structures, e.g. mitochondria and ribosomes, increases.

2 The DNA replicates.

3 Further growth occurs and the DNA is checked for errors and any repairs made.

4 Mitosis – the chromosomes move apart and two nuclei form.

5 The cytoplasm divides into two and the new cell membrane separates off to give two new, identical cells.

6 Temporary cell resting period, or the cell no longer divides, e.g. a nerve cell.

Figure 2.16 The cell cycle in actively dividing human cells, the whole cell cycle lasts 1 hour

6 **Using Figure 2.16, calculate the proportion of the cell cycle spent in mitosis. You will need a protractor.**

7 **If the cell cycle lasts 2 hours, estimate the time spent in mitosis.**

8 **Mitosis occurs rapidly in a newly formed fertilised egg. Suggest another situation in the body where you might expect cells to be actively dividing by mitosis.**

Cell differentiation

Learning objectives:

- explain the importance of cell differentiation
- describe how cells, tissues, organs and organ systems are organised to make up an organism
- understand size and scale in relation to cells, tissues, organs and organ systems.

KEY WORDS

differentiation
organ
organ system
specialised cells

Cell division makes up only part of our growth and development.

For the first four or five days of our lives, the cells produced as the fertilised egg divides are identical. Then, some of our cells start to become *specialised* to do a particular job.

Cell adaptations

In a multicellular organism, many different types of cell take on different roles to ensure that the organism functions properly and as a whole.

As cells divide, new cells acquire certain features required for their specific function. This is **differentiation**. A cell's size, shape and internal structure are adapted for its role. Most animal cells differentiate at an early stage.

Figure 2.17 By this stage in its development, this human embryo has developed many of the 200 different cell types in the human body

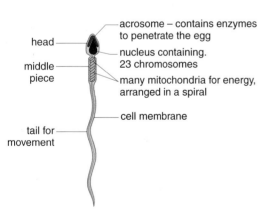

Figure 2.18 The function of a sperm cell is to swim in the female reproductive system with the aim of fertilising an egg. (Cell length 55 μm; width at widest point 3 μm)

- head
- middle piece
- tail for movement
- acrosome – contains enzymes to penetrate the egg
- nucleus containing. 23 chromosomes
- many mitochondria for energy, arranged in a spiral
- cell membrane

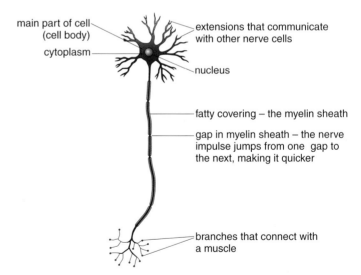

Figure 2.19 Nerve cells carry messages, or electrical impulses, from one part of the body to another. This type of cell brings about movement of the skeleton. (Motor nerve cell length: up to 1 m or more; diameter 1–20 μm)

- main part of cell (cell body)
- cytoplasm
- extensions that communicate with other nerve cells
- nucleus
- fatty covering – the myelin sheath
- gap in myelin sheath – the nerve impulse jumps from one gap to the next, making it quicker
- branches that connect with a muscle

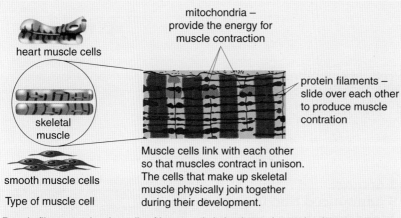

heart muscle cells

skeletal muscle

smooth muscle cells

Type of muscle cell

mitochondria – provide the energy for muscle contraction

protein filaments – slide over each other to produce muscle contration

Muscle cells link with each other so that muscles contract in unison. The cells that make up skeletal muscle physically join together during their development.

Protein filaments give the cells of heart and skeletal muscle a striped appearance. In smooth muscle, found, for instance, in the circulatory system, there are fewer filaments, which are thinner and less well-organised.

Figure 2.20 Muscle cells contain protein filaments which move as the muscle contracts. (Skeletal muscle length: average 3 cm; maximum 30 cm)

1 **How are the following cells adapted to their functions:**

  a **a sperm cell**
  b **a muscle cell**
  c **a nerve cell?**

2 **Cells of the pancreas produce the hormone insulin. Insulin is a protein. Suggest how pancreatic cells are adapted for their function.**

Cells, tissues and organs

Some cells work in isolation, like sperm cells. Others are grouped as **tissues** and work together.

A tissue is a group of cells with a particular function. Many tissues have a number of similar types of cell to enable the tissue to function.

Tissues are grouped into **organs**. Organs carry out a specific function.

Different organs are arranged into **organ systems**, for example the circulatory system, digestive system, respiratory system, and reproductive system.

3 **Arrange the following in ascending order of size:**

  system   cell   human body   organ   tissue

4 **Name two other types of cell and one other type of tissue in the circulatory system.**

5 **Red blood cells have a bioconcave shape which gives them a large surface area. How is this shape related to its function?**

KEY INFORMATION

You can work out how the structure of a cell is related to its function, even if you are not familiar with the type of cell in the question. Look at the size, shape and surface area of the cell, and what it contains, for example mitochondria, ribosomes or a food store.

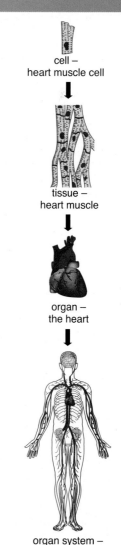

cell – heart muscle cell

tissue – heart muscle

organ – the heart

organ system – the circulatory system

Figure 2.21 The organisation of the human circulatory system

Stem cells

Learning objectives:

- describe the function of stem cells in embryonic and adult animals
- discuss potential benefits and risks associated with the use of stem cells in medicine.

KEY WORDS

adult stem cell
embryonic stem cell
meristems

**The UK has a shortage of blood donors.
In the summer of 2015 the NHS announced that it planned to start giving people blood transfusions using artificial blood by 2017.**

What are stem cells?

Stem cells are unspecialised cells that can produce many different types of cells.

Stem cells are found in the developing embryo and some remain, at certain locations in our bodies, as adults. They divide to produce a range of cells for development, growth and repair.

Figure 2.22 Embryonic stem cells

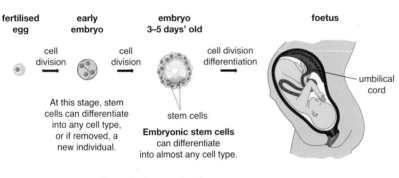

Figure 2.23 Stem cells in the human body

1. **What is the function of adult stem cells?**

2. **Which type of stem cell can differentiate into more cell types?**

Stem cell transplants

Transplanting stem cells, or transplants of specialised cells grown from stem cells, could help people with:

- injuries, e.g. spinal injuries leading to paralysis
- conditions in which certain body cells degenerate, e.g. Alzheimer's disease, diabetes and multiple sclerosis
- cancers, or following treatments for cancer such as chemotherapy or radiation, e.g. people with leukaemia.

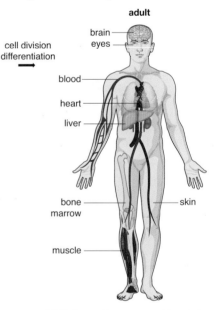

Adult stem cells are rare and found at certain locations only. Their role is to replace body cells that die through injury and disease.
They can differentiate only into cells from the type of tissue where they are found, e.g. blood, muscle.

Stem cell transplants also enable chemotherapy patients, who have had their bone marrow destroyed, to produce red blood cells.

The hope is that we will be able to culture stem cells in limitless numbers. Stem cell lines produced from patients with rare and complex diseases could transform the health service.

(3) **Name two conditions that could be treated with stem cell transplants.**

(4) **Why are stem cell transplants important for people who have had chemotherapy?**

Meristems

Like animals, plants have undifferentiated cells that can divide to produce new cells. In animals, these cells are called stem cells. In plants, these cells are found in regions called **meristems**.

Figure 2.24 The red blood cells in the artificial blood will be produced using stem cells

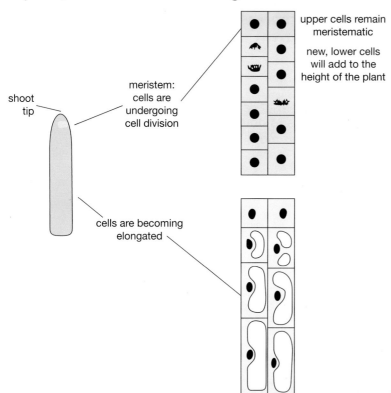

upper cells remain meristematic

new, lower cells will add to the height of the plant

meristem: cells are undergoing cell division

shoot tip

cells are becoming elongated

Figure 2.25 One meristem in plants is found towards the tip of the shoot; one towards the tip of the root

When cells from the meristems of plants are removed, scientists are able to grow them in tissue culture. Tissue culture is used to produce clones of plants quickly. It means that plants that are useful to us, and are genetically identical, can be grown economically.

(5) **Where are stem cells found in plants?**

(6) **How is the tissue culture of plant cells used?**

DID YOU KNOW?

Stem cell transplants are not new. Transplants of bone marrow, which contain stem cells, have been carried out since 1968. But there are very few stem cells in bone marrow (only 1 in 10 000 bone marrow cells). We currently isolate these from blood, rather than bone marrow.

KEY INFORMATION

Current potential for adult stem cell use in therapies is restricted to certain cell lines, but it may be greater than once thought. Scientists are trying to induce them to differentiate into a wider range of tissues, a process called transdifferentiation.

KEY CONCEPT

Cell development

Learning objectives:

- give examples of where mitosis is necessary to produce identical daughter cells
- understand the need for the reduction decision, meiosis
- describe the use and potential of cloned cells in biological research.

KEY WORDS

differentiation
gamete
meiosis
mitosis

Cell development involves the processes of cell growth, division and differentiation. These processes are closely linked, and are a key focus for current biological research.

Cells

The cell is the basic unit of life. You will have looked at cells with a microscope in school, probably cheek cells and onion skin cells. These illustrate the basic cell pattern, but most cells in all but the simplest of organisms are much more varied in their structure.

red blood cells absorb oxygen
ciliated cells line the windpipe. their cilia sweep away a covering layer of mucus
ovum (egg) – the female sex cell
bone cells produce bone
white blood cells help defend the body against disease

Figure 2.26 The structure of different types of cell is adapted to their function.

Cell division

Human life begins as a fertilised egg cell, or zygote. This cell develops into an adult with trillions of cells. As new cell components are added, and the cell reaches a certain size, it divides by mitosis. Mitosis occurs in several other situations:

- to replace cells when they die or become damaged
- when single-celled, eukaryotic organisms reproduce by **asexual reproduction**, for example yeast
- when cancer cells divide
- when eukaryotic cells are cloned.

When an organism reproduces sexually, the sex cells, or **gametes**, cannot be produced by mitosis. If they were, the number of chromosomes in our cells would double every generation! We need another type of cell division, called **meiosis**.

1 Give three examples of situations in which mitosis occurs.

2 Name one type of cell that does *not* divide by mitosis.

Cell differentiation

Cells must become specialised for the development of complex, multicellular organisms.

Cells that can differentiate into other cell types are called stem cells. Embryonic stem cells, found after four to five days, can develop into *almost* any cell type. We can't say *'all'*, as they can't develop into cells of the placenta.

Stem cells have the potential to produce an unlimited amount of tissue for transplants. They are also important in medical research such as on how cells differentiate, and in the testing of drugs.

Stem cell research and treatments will require the cloning of cells. Some people object to the idea of these techniques for moral and ethical reasons.

Cancer cells divide uncontrollably by mitosis and do not normally differentiate into mature, specialised cells. Cancer cells early in the development of the disease can look almost normal, but in advanced cancers, differentiation in most cells is very limited.

3 Why are some news articles that suggest that embryonic stem cells can differentiate into all cell types, strictly speaking, incorrect?

4 Stem cells are being used to test new drugs. What are the advantages of using human stem cells over using rats to test drugs?

KEY SKILLS

For each chapter in the book, map out how different concepts you have learnt link with each other. Use a large sheet of paper or computer software.

Investigating the need for transport systems

Learning objectives:

- describe the need for transport systems
- describe how the effectiveness of an exchange surface can be increased
- explain, in terms of surface area to volume ratios, the need for transport systems.

> **KEY WORDS**
>
> surface area
> exchange surfaces

Many chemical reactions happen inside living cells. Substances must enter the cell to fuel these reactions and the waste products of the reactions need to be removed. Larger cells have greater chemical activity, so need more substances, for example, nutrients and oxygen, and more substances have to be removed, for example, carbon dioxide.

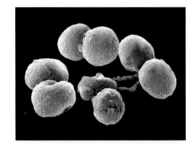

Size matters

Most cells are no more than 1 mm in diameter. This is because in small cells nutrients, oxygen and waste substances can diffuse quickly in and out. As the volume of a cell increases, the distance increases between the cytoplasm at the centre of the cell and the cell membrane. In cells bigger than 1 mm diameter, the rate of exchange with the surrounding environment may be too slow for diffusion to meet the cell's needs. The cell would probably not survive.

1 How does the size of a cell affect the chemical activity inside the cell?

2 Describe one chemical activity that takes place in cells.

Figure 2.27 Which will have the faster diffusion rate?

Looking at surface area to volume ratio

The surface area of a cell affects the rate at which particles can enter and leave the cell.

The volume of the cell affects the rate of chemical reactions within the cell (how quickly materials are used in reactions and how fast the waste products are made).

Look at the diagram. The cubes represent cells.

- cubes have 6 sides, so the surface area = length × width × 6
- the volume of a cube = length × width × height
- surface area to volume ratio = surface area ÷ volume

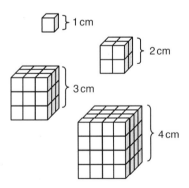

Figure 2.28 Cubes of increasing size

Calculate the surface area, volume and surface area to volume ratio (SA:V) for each of the cubes. Cube A has been done for you.

Cube	Number of internal cubes	Surface area (cm²)	Volume (cm³)	SA:V
A	1	6	1	6
B	8			
C	27			
D	64			

KEY INFORMATION

The feathery projections in a fishes gills are used to increase surface area. Water is continually taken in through the mouth and forced over the gills to maintain the concentration gradient.

3 What happens to the surface area and volume as the size increases?

4 What happens to the surface area to volume ratio as the size increases?

5 What does a decrease in surface area to volume ratio make it more difficult to do?

Transport systems and exchange surfaces

With a small surface area to volume ratio, multicellular organisms need surfaces and organ systems specialised for exchanging materials. Once an organism is multicellular and has several layers of cells, the oxygen and nutrients take longer to diffuse in and are all used up by the outer layers of cells. Exchange systems allow transport into and out of all cells for the organism's needs. As well as exchanging substances, cells also have to lose heat fast enough to prevent overheating.

To function efficiently, exchange surfaces need the following features:

- a large surface area to maximise exchange
- a thin membrane to provide a short diffusion path
- a method of transporting substances to and from the exchange site, for example, a blood supply to carry nutrients around the body, and lungs to take oxygen into the body.

Organism		SA:V
bacterium		6 000 000
amoeba		60 000
fly		600
dog		6
whale		0.06

6 How are efficient exchange surfaces adapted to carry out their function?

7 Explain why large organisms need transport systems but small organisms do not.

Learning about the circulatory system

Learning objectives:

- identify the parts of the circulatory system
- describe the functions of the parts of the circulatory system
- explain how the structure of each part of the circulatory system relates to its function.

KEY WORDS

double circulation
lumen
valves

Very small animals have no need for a transport system. But as the distance from the internal cells to the animal's surface increases, a transport system becomes vital to supply cells with oxygen and nutrients, and to take away waste materials.

Transport systems

The circulatory system carries essential and waste materials around the body. For example, it works with the gaseous exchange system to:

- carry oxygen from the lungs to all body cells
- carry carbon dioxide from all body cells to the lungs.

Insects have an open circulation system with no blood vessels. The blood flows slowly round the body cavity.

In closed circulatory systems, blood flows in vessels. There are two types of closed circulatory systems:

- a single circulation (for example, in fish); the blood flows in one circuit around the body
- a **double circulation** (for example, in humans); the blood flows in two circuits around the body:
  - › from the heart to the lungs
  - › from the heart to the rest of the body.

Blood is pumped out of the heart into arteries under high pressure. As the blood flows from the arteries, through capillaries and then veins, the pressure decreases.

1. What is a double circulation system?

2. Why do closed circulation systems need a heart?

How does the system work?

Each type of blood vessel is adapted to carry out slightly different functions.

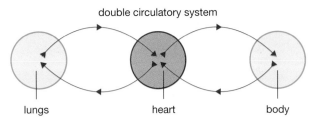

double circulatory system

lungs   heart   body

Figure 2.29 Representation of blood flow in humans. Blood travels from the heart around the body, back through the heart, and on to the lungs. What happens to the blood in the lungs?

KEY INFORMATION

Arteries carry blood away from the heart.

DID YOU KNOW?

Every cell in your body is 0.05 mm away from a capillary, so substances have a very short distance to diffuse.

Arteries	Veins	Capillaries
thick, elastic wall, small lumen	thin wall, large lumen, valve	single cell wall
carry blood from the heart	carry blood to the heart	carry blood from arteries to veins
blood under high pressure with a pulse	blood under low pressure, flows smoothy	pressure falls and pulse disappears
thick walls, not permeable	thinner walls, not permeable	walls are one cell thick and permeable
small **lumen**	large lumen	
no valves	valves along their length prevent backflow of blood	no valves
carry oxygenated blood (except pulmonary artery)	carry deoxygenated blood (except pulmonary vein)	blood slowly loses its oxygen

Blood flows from the heart to arteries, arterioles (small arteries), capillaries, venules (small veins), veins and then back to the heart.

3 **Describe how blood is transported around the body.**

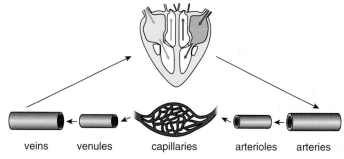

Figure 2.30 The sequence of blood flow

Explaining adaptations

Mammals are very active animals. They need a double circulation system because:

- blood pressure is higher, especially to the body tissues, so blood is pumped faster than with a single circulation.
- there is a higher blood flow to body tissues. This means that more oxygen can be carried to body cells for respiration to supply the energy needed and waste products can be removed quickly.
- oxygenated blood is separate from deoxygenated blood.

Adaptations of the blood vessels include:

- the thick elastic walls of arteries withstand the high pressure of the blood
- capillary networks have a large exchange surface area
- the thin permeable walls of capillaries mean that substances have only a short distance to diffuse
- large lumen in the veins gives the least flow resistance
- valves in the veins prevent the backfow of blood.

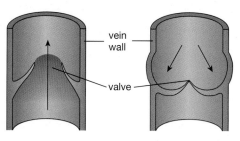

Figure 2.31 How do valves prevent backflow?

4 **Explain how the structure of blood vessels is adapted to their function.**

5 **Why is a double circulation an advantage to an active animal?**

Investigating gaseous exchange

Learning objectives:

- identify the parts of the human gaseous exchange system and know their functions
- explain how gaseous exchange occurs in humans
- explain the adaptations of the gaseous exchange surfaces.

KEY WORDS

alveolus (plural: alveoli)

Our body needs a constant supply of oxygen for cellular respiration. Mammals have evolved a specialised exchange surface to provide a continuous supply of oxygen and to remove carbon dioxide.

The breathing system

The lungs are in the thorax. They are surrounded by the ribcage to protect them. Between the ribs are the intercostal muscles. These help to **ventilate** (move air into and out of) the lungs. Gaseous exchange happens in the **alveoli**.

COMMON MISCONCEPTION

Breathing is gaseous exchange and respiration is the release of energy from food.

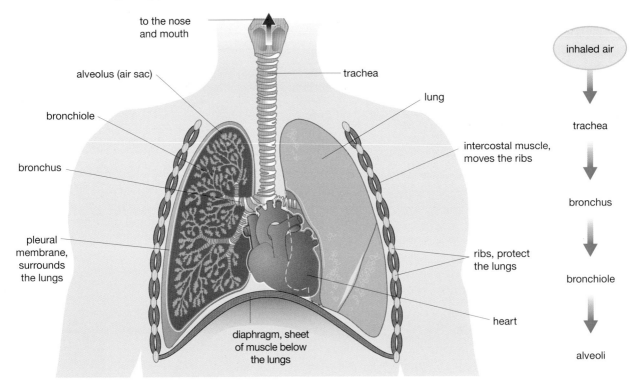

Figure 2.32 The respiratory system

Air is filtered, warmed and moistened in the mouth and nasal passages. It passes into the trachea, through one of the bronchi into the lungs. In the lungs, air passes through the many bronchioles until it reaches an **alveolus** (air sac). Oxygen then passes across the specialised cell membrane of the alveolus into the blood.

1. Describe how air reaches the alveoli.

2. What is gaseous exchange and where does it happen?

Gaseous exchange

Oxygen is used to release energy from food during respiration. Carbon dioxide is a waste product of the reaction. Gaseous exchange is:

- taking in oxygen
- releasing carbon dioxide.

Gaseous exchange happens in the alveoli. Blood transports the gases to and from the surface of each alveolus through the capillaries that cover the alveoli.

Air entering the alveoli has a greater oxygen concentration than the deoxygenated blood flowing through the lungs. This steep concentration gradient allows efficient diffusion to happen.

Deoxygenated blood contains a greater concentration of carbon dioxide, so it diffuses out of the blood and into the alveoli to be breathed out.

3 **Explain how gaseous exchange happens in the alveoli.**

4 **What is the difference between breathing and respiration?**

Why are alveoli good exchange surfaces?

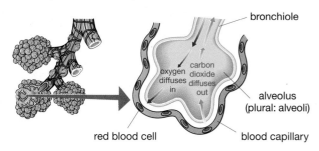

Figure 2.33 Gaseous exchange in the alveoli

Alveoli are efficient exchange surfaces. They have evolved adaptations to ensure maximum gaseous exchange:

- The large number of alveoli in the lungs provides a large surface area resulting in efficient diffusion of gases.
- The exchange surface at the alveoli wall is very thin (just one cell thick). This means that the diffusion distance for the gases is very short.
- Each alveolus is surrounded by blood capillaries to ensure a good blood supply. Oxygen is constantly moved into the blood and carbon dioxide is constantly taken to the lungs to be removed. This means that gaseous exchange happens at the steepest concentration gradients possible.
- The alveoli surfaces are moist. Gases dissolve to allow efficient diffusion across the exchange surface.

5 **Describe and explain how alveoli are adapted to their function.**

6 **Explain how cells located deep in our body can receive the oxygen they need and dispose of carbon dioxide efficiently.**

DID YOU KNOW?

The lungs have over 300 million alveoli and the left lung is slightly smaller than the right, so there is room for your heart.

Exploring the heart

Learning objectives:

- describe the structure and function of the heart
- identify the functions and adaptations of the parts of the heart
- explain the movement of blood around the heart.

KEY WORDS

aorta
atrium (plural: atria)
cardiac muscle
vena cava
ventricle

Active or larger animals need a transport system with a pump. This is to maintain a constant supply of materials to meet the demand of all cells throughout the body, and to remove waste.

The heart

The heart is made of muscle (**cardiac muscle**). Heart muscle continually contracts and relaxes. It uses a lot of energy. Heart muscle receives oxygen and glucose for respiration from the blood brought by the coronary arteries.

The heart has two pumps (a double circulation) that beat together about 70 times every minute of every day.

Each pump has an upper chamber (**atrium**) that receives blood and a lower chamber (**ventricle**) that pumps blood out. Both **atria** fill and pump blood out at the same time, as do both ventricles. The natural resting heart rate is controlled by a group of cells located in the right atrium that act as a pacemaker.

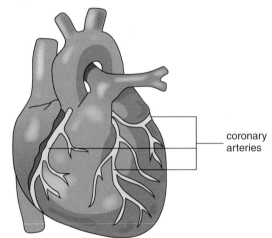

Figure 2.34 Why does the heart need an oxygen supply?

coronary arteries

Blood from the lungs contains oxygen and enters the heart at the left atrium. It passes into the left ventricle and is pumped out to the body.

Blood from the body contains very little oxygen and enters the heart at the right atrium, passes into the right ventricle and is pumped to the lungs to be oxygenated.

1 **What is the function of the heart?**

2 **Describe how blood flows through the heart.**

The parts of the heart

The heart has four main blood vessels:

- The pulmonary vein transports oxygenated blood from the lungs to the left atrium.
- The **aorta** (main artery) transports oxygenated blood from the left ventricle to the body.

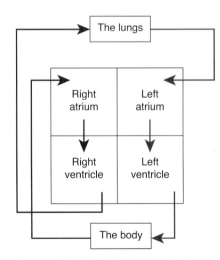

Figure 2.35 Blood flow through the heart

- The **vena cava** (main vein) transports blood from the body to the right atrium.
- The pulmonary artery transports deoxygenated blood from the right ventricle to the lungs.

Ventricles have thicker walls than atria because they pump blood further. The left ventricle pumps blood around the body. It has a thicker wall than the right ventricle, which only pumps blood to the lungs. Valves between the atria and the ventricles prevent the backflow of blood. They open to let blood through and then shut.

3 **Describe the functions of the different chambers of the heart.**

4 **Describe how the atria and ventricles move blood through the heart.**

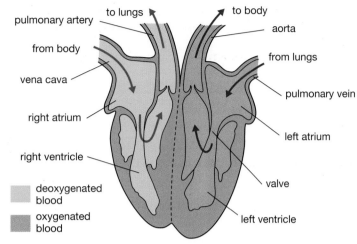

Figure 2.36 Why does the heart need two pumps?

Explaining blood flow

In the second century, Galen thought the heart sucked blood out of the veins. In the seventeenth century, Galen's ideas were disproved by William Harvey, who explained heart structure and described the blood vessels.

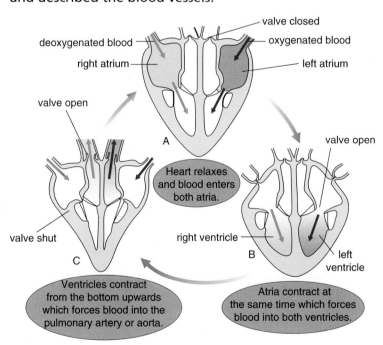

Figure 2.37 The cardiac cycle

KEY INFORMATION

Atria receive blood, ventricles pump it out.

DID YOU KNOW?

The complete cardiac cycle normally takes 0.8 seconds.

5 **Explain the sequence of contractions and valve openings as blood passes through the heart.**

6 **If a coronary artery supplying the left ventricle becomes blocked, what effect does this have on the functioning of the heart? Explain your answer.**

Studying blood

Learning objectives:

- identify the parts of the blood and their functions
- explain the adaptations of red blood cells
- explain how red blood cells and haemoglobin transport oxygen efficiently.

Effective exchange systems in animals need a method of transporting substances to and from the exchange site, for example, mammals have an efficient circulatory system.

What is blood?

Blood is a tissue. It is a mixture of cells, solutes and a liquid. The liquid part of blood is **plasma**. It is straw coloured.

Red blood cells, white blood cells and platelets are suspended in the plasma. Each part of the blood has a specific function:

- Plasma transports substances around the body, for example, carbon dioxide.
- Red blood cells carry oxygen from the lungs to body cells.
- White blood cells help to protect the body against infection.
- Platelets are cell fragments which help the clotting process at wound sites.

There are millions of red blood cells in the plasma. This is why blood looks red.

Figure 2.38 Why does blood look red?

1. **Look at the scanning electron micrograph of blood (Figure 2.37). Identify which cells are present.**

2. **What is the function of:**

   a red blood cells
   b white blood cells?

Looking closer

The blood parts can be separated by spinning them very fast in a machine called a centrifuge. About 55% of blood is plasma; plasma consists of roughly 90% water and 10% solutes. It is very important because it transports many substances, for example:

- hormones
- antibodies
- nutrients, such as glucose, amino acids (proteins), minerals and vitamins
- waste substances, like carbon dioxide and urea.

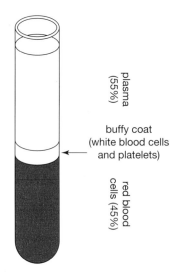

plasma (55%)

buffy coat (white blood cells and platelets)

red blood cells (45%)

Figure 2.39 Blood looks like this if it is separated in a centrifuge

Red blood cells transport oxygen from the lungs two tissues all over the body. Blood is able to transport oxygen efficiently because in 1 mm³ of blood there are about 5 million red blood cells. Red blood cells:

- are tiny, allowing them to pass through the narrow capillaries
- have a biconcave disc shape, giving them a large surface area to volume ratio which increases the efficiency of diffusion of oxygen into and out of the cell, and reduces the diffusion distance to the centre of the cell
- contain **haemoglobin** which binds to oxygen to transport it from the lungs to the body tissues
- have no nucleus, increasing the space available for haemoglobin.

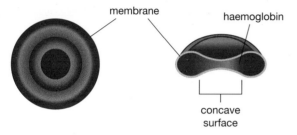

Figure 2.40 Red blood cells are adapted to carry oxygen

3 Describe the role of plasma.

4 How are red blood cells adapted to their function?

How the blood carries oxygen

Haemoglobin binds with oxygen at high concentration to form a bright red compound called oxyhaemoglobin. The bonds between the haemoglobin and oxygen are weak, and oxyhaemoglobin dissociates to haemoglobin and oxygen in low oxygen concentrations.

oxygen + haemoglobin $\rightleftharpoons$ oxyhaemoglobin

5 Describe how haemoglobin transports oxygen.

6 Use SA:V to explain how red blood cells are adapted to their function.

Sickle cell anaemia is a serious inherited blood disorder where the red blood cells develop abnormally and contain defective haemoglobin.

7 Explain why somebody with sickle cell anaemia is likely to feel very tired and breathless while exercising.

KEY INFORMATION

Red blood cells transport oxygen; plasma transports many substances including carbon dioxide.

DID YOU KNOW?

Crabs have blue blood, earthworms and leeches have green blood and starfish have clear or pale yellow blood!

Investigating leaves

Learning objectives:

- identify the internal structures of a leaf
- explain how the structure of a leaf is adapted for photosynthesis
- recall that chloroplasts absorb energy from light for photosynthesis.

KEY WORDS

epidermal tissue
vascular bundle

Leaves work to manufacture glucose. Chloroplasts in leaves absorb the light needed for photosynthesis. How do the organelles inside the leaf work together to do this?

The structure of a leaf

Leaves of green plants are plant organs that are adapted to allow them to photosynthesise efficiently. Most leaves:

- are broad, with a large surface for light to be absorbed
- are thin, so that carbon dioxide has a short distance to diffuse
- have vascular bundles (veins). These support the leaf and transport
  - › water to the leaf
  - › glucose away from the leaf.

1 **How does the shape of a leaf help photosynthesis to happen?**

2 **What is the function of vascular bundles?**

Inside the leaf

The diagram shows the internal structure of a leaf. Each part has a specific function

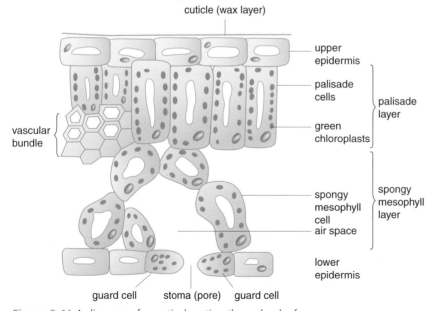

Figure 2.41 A diagram of a vertical section through a leaf

The upper surface is covered by a cuticle to protect it. Under the cuticle are layers of different cells:

- **epidermal tissues** cover the leaf, letting light penetrate
- palisade mesophyll carry out photosynthesis, absorbing most of the light
- spongy mesophyll has air spaces for diffusion of gases
- lower epidermal tissue protects the underside of the leaf.

Chloroplasts in the mesophyll are where light is absorbed for photosynthesis.

The lower epidermis has small pores called stomata. Each stoma allows gases to diffuse in and out of the leaf.

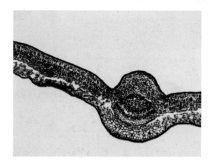

Figure 2.42 A micrograph of a section through a leaf. Compare what you can see here with the diagram in Figure 2.41.

3 Describe the function of mesophyll cells.

4 Why do leaf cells contain chloroplasts but root cells do not?

5 Why is the cuticle thin, transparent and waxy?

Adaptations for effective working

Using a microscope, look at a slide of a section through a leaf.

Identify the layers of cells. Calculate the magnification you used.

Each type of leaf cell has features that make it adapted for its function.

> **DID YOU KNOW?**
>
> Meristem tissue is found at the growing tips of roots and shoots. It differentiates into different types of plant cells.

Layer	Adaptation	Function
upper epidermal tissue	thin and transparent waxy cuticle	allows light to pass to the mesophyll to protect the leaf and stop water loss
palisade mesophyll	regular-shaped cells, arranged end-on, near upper surface; most chloroplasts at the top of the cells	absorb the maximum amount of light possible
spongy mesophyll	irregular-shaped cells; many air spaces	increases surface area for CO_2 absorption; allows gases to diffuse
lower epidermal tissue	many stomata; surrounded by guard cells	allow gases to diffuse; guard cells open and close stomata
vascular bundles	contain xylem and phloem tubes	transport substances around the plant

6 Suggest why stomata are found on the lower epidermal tissue.

7 Explain how the adaptations of the palisade mesophyll allow it to photosynthesise efficiently.

Learning about plants and minerals

Learning objectives:

- describe how mineral ions from the soil are taken up by plants
- explain how root hair cells are adapted for efficient osmosis
- describe the function of different mineral ions in a plant.

Like animals, plants also need to exchange materials. Leaves are exchange surfaces that are specialised for photosynthesis. Plants also need minerals and water. The root hair cells are adapted for the uptake of these materials.

Roots and minerals

Root hair cells are found on plant roots, just behind the root tip. Root hair cells help to anchor the plant, and absorb water and **mineral ions** from the soil.

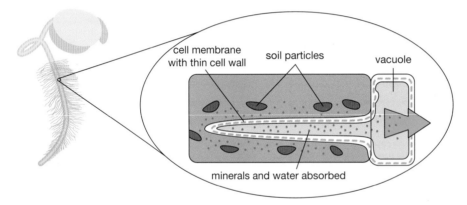

Figure 2.43 Root hair cells are specialised exchange surfaces

Fertilisers containing minerals can be added to the soil to improve plant growth. Fertilisers contain nitrates, phosphates, potassium and magnesium. It is the root hairs that absorb the water and the minerals.

Each root hair cell has a long thin exchange surface reaching out between the soil particles. Water is absorbed by osmosis and mineral ions are absorbed by active transport.

1 **What are the functions of root hairs?**

2 **How do plants absorb the minerals they need?**

Root hair cells

Plants need water to maintain the shape of their cells and for photosynthesis. Minerals are needed to make proteins and other chemicals to help the plant grow.

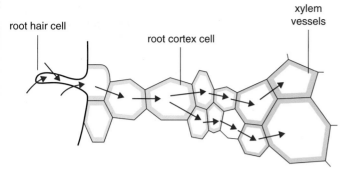

root hair cell

root cortex cell

xylem vessels

Figure 2.44 Roots are adapted for the transport of water and minerals

Root hair cells are an efficient exchange surface for osmosis because they:

- provide a large surface area for absorption of water
- have no cuticle, just a thin membrane to allow absorption
- have a thin cell wall to reduce the distance for osmosis
- have a large permanent vacuole to absorb as much water as possible
- are close to the xylem, so that materials can be moved around the plant.

These adaptations mean that a lot of water and mineral ions can get into the cell very quickly and then pass around the plant efficiently.

3 **How are root hair cells adapted for osmosis?**

4 **Why do plants need minerals?**

Looking at minerals

Mineral ions are only found in low concentrations in the soil, compared to the concentration inside the root hair cell. They need to be taken in by active transport. Root hair cells contain many mitochondria to supply the energy needed for this.

The table lists some of the minerals that you might hear about. You only need to remember about nitrates and magnesium for your examinations.

Mineral	Use in the plant
nitrates, containing nitrogen (N)	to make amino acids for protein synthesis
phosphates, containing phosphorus (P)	in respiration to make DNA and new cell membranes
potassium (K)	in respiration in photosynthesis to make enzymes
magnesium (Mg)	needed for photosynthesis

5 **Why are enzymes important in plants?**

6 **A farmer adds fertiliser to the soil to make his plants grow better. It is a warm, windy day. Describe how the plants take in and transport the fertilisers, and why this happens more quickly on a windy day.**

Looking at stomata

Learning objectives:

- describe transpiration in plants
- explain the structure and function of stomata
- explain the relationship between transpiration and leaf structure.

KEY WORDS

transpiration
xylem

Gases continually pass in and out of leaves through tiny openings found on the lower surface of each leaf. The openings are called stomata. They control the exchange of gases in plants. Do all leaves have the same concentration of stomata?

Water movement in plants

Plants absorb water from soil through root hairs. The water passes into the root, up the stem and into the leaves. Water on the surface of the spongy mesophyll evaporates and diffuses out of leaves via the stomata. This movement of water through the plant and leaves is called **transpiration**.

Transpiration rate is affected by temperature, light availability, wind and humidity.

1. What is transpiration?

2. Describe the path of water through a plant.

3. Predict what conditions will cause the rate of transpiration to increase.

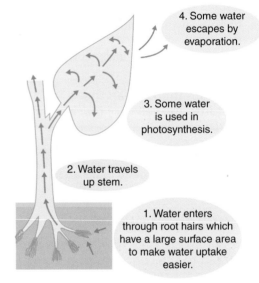

4. Some water escapes by evaporation.

3. Some water is used in photosynthesis.

2. Water travels up stem.

1. Water enters through root hairs which have a large surface area to make water uptake easier.

Figure 2.45 Where does the water in the leaf come from

Transpiration

Plants need a constant flow of water. Water is transported in tubes called **xylem** in the veins. Evaporation of water from the leaf causes water to be drawn up the plant, just like a child sucking through a straw. Transpiration is important because:

- evaporation of water cools leaves
- water is a reactant in photosynthesis
- cells full of water support the plant
- water carries dissolved materials around the plant.

If too much water is lost through the stomata, plants may wilt and die. Surrounding each stoma are two guard cells. The guard cells are attached to each other at both ends. When it is light, guard cells take in water and become turgid (swollen). The inner walls are thickened and rigid, so they pull apart and the pore opens.

In the dark, guard cells lose water and become flaccid (limp). The inner walls move together and close the pore.

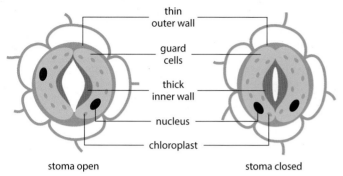

thin outer wall
guard cells
thick inner wall
nucleus
chloroplast

stoma open   stoma closed

Figure 2.46 Explain how stomata open and close

4 **Explain how stomata open and close.**

5 **Predict why stomatal density may differ for different species.**

KEY INFORMATION

Water evaporates from the cell surfaces and the water vapour diffuses out of the leaf.

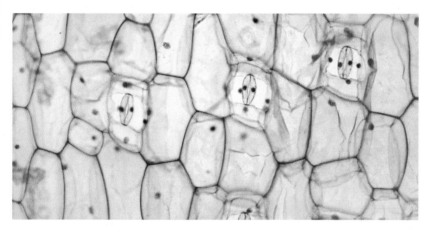

Figure 2.47 Make stomatal impressions of two different leaves using clear nail varnish. Use a microscope to calculate the stomatal density of each leaf

DID YOU KNOW?

Water lilies have stomata on the upper leaf surface so that they are not under water.

The effect of adaptations

A disadvantage of stomata is that while they are open for gas exchange, water loss occurs. Leaves are broad and thin to increase surface area. Water only has a short distance to diffuse out.

Marram grass grows on beaches. It has rolled leaves with thick cuticles and stomata are sunk into pits. Interlocking hairs hold water vapour. These features all reduce water loss.

6 **Explain how water loss in plants is a result of the adaptations for photosynthesis.**

7 **Explain how marram grass is adapted to prevent water loss.**

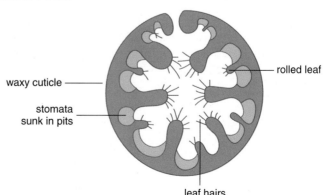

waxy cuticle
stomata sunk in pits
rolled leaf
leaf hairs

Figure 2.48 Marram grass grows on exposed sand dunes. What conditions have the greatest effect on transpiration?

Google search: 'transpiration in plants'   **85**

Moving water

Learning objectives:

- describe the structure and function of xylem and roots
- describe how xylem and roots are adapted to absorb water
- explain why plants in flooded or waterlogged soil die.

KEY WORDS

lumen
phloem
translocation
xylem

Plants do not have a heart or blood, but they still need a transport system to move food, water and minerals to every cell. The roots, stem and leaves form a plant organ system for the transport of substances.

Transport systems

Plants have two transport systems:

- **xylem** cells carry water and minerals from the roots around the plant, especially to the leaves
- **phloem** cells transport dissolved sugars made in the leaves around the plant. This is called **translocation**.

Xylem and phloem tubes are found in continuous vascular bundles.

Water enters plants through the roots. Root hair cells near the root tip have hair-like projections that grow between soil particles to absorb water.

1 Why is water needed in the leaves?

2 What are the functions of xylem and phloem?

3 State what is meant by translocation.

COMMON MISCONCEPTION

Many students confuse xylem and phloem. Remember phloem carries food.

Adaptations for transport

Roots are narrow tubes with a large surface area. Root hair cells also increase the surface area for water absorption. The water has only a short distance to travel to the xylem to be moved up and around the plant (Figure 2.49).

Xylem tubes are made from long cells with thick, reinforced walls containing lignin. This makes them strong. The cell walls are waterproof, which makes the cells die. The contents and end walls break down to form a vessel with a hollow centre or **lumen**. Water and minerals flow through the tubes. Xylem cells form the wood in a tree.

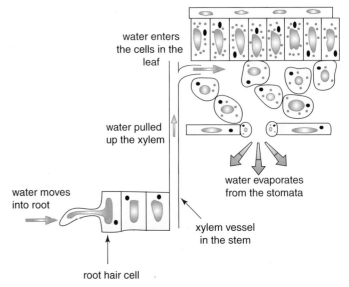

water enters the cells in the leaf

water pulled up the xylem

water moves into root

water evaporates from the stomata

xylem vessel in the stem

root hair cell

Figure 2.49 Use a microscope to observe root hair cells

Figure 2.50 shows the vascular bundles (xylem and phloem) in the different parts of the plant.

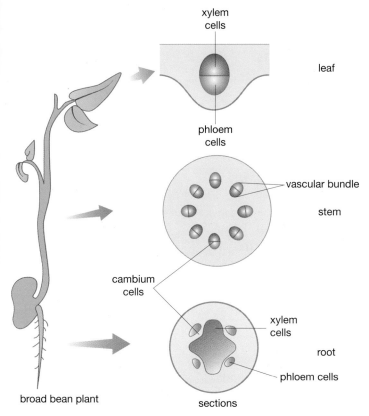

Figure 2.50 Use a microscope to draw sections through a root, stem and leaf to show xylem and phloem

4 **How are root hairs adapted to absorb water?**

5 **How is xylem adapted for its function?**

Water effects

Healthy plants balance water uptake and loss. If plants lose water faster than it is replaced, they wilt. Wilting protects the plant. Leaves droop and hang down to reduce the surface area for water loss by evaporation. The stomata close and photosynthesis stops to prevent water loss. The disadvantage is that the plant may overheat. Plants stay wilted until they get water, the temperature drops or the sun is not shining on them.

Plants can have too much water. Waterlogged soil contains very little air. This means that the root cells do not receive the oxygen they need for respiration. They die and rot if the waterlogging lasts a long time.

6 **Describe the changes in a plant that help to prevent water loss.**

7 **A plant grown in a pot with no drainage is prone to dying. Explain why this might happen.**

Figure 2.51 Why has this plant wilted?

DID YOU KNOW?

Plant transport systems are found in the bark of trees. Some animals chew this away, causing the tree to die because it cannot transport water and glucose to where it is needed.

Moving sugar

Learning objectives:

- describe the movement of sugar in a plant as translocation
- explain how the structure of phloem is adapted to its function in the plant
- explain the movement of sugars around the plant.

Sugars are needed by all cells for respiration. They are transported from the leaves for immediate use or storage. Amino acids are needed by all growth areas.

Phloem vessels

Phloem cells are elongated, thin-walled living cells that form columns or tubes.

The movement of sugars in plants is called **translocation.** Translocation happens in the phloem. Cell sap containing sugars and amino acids is moved from where these substances are produced to where they are needed.

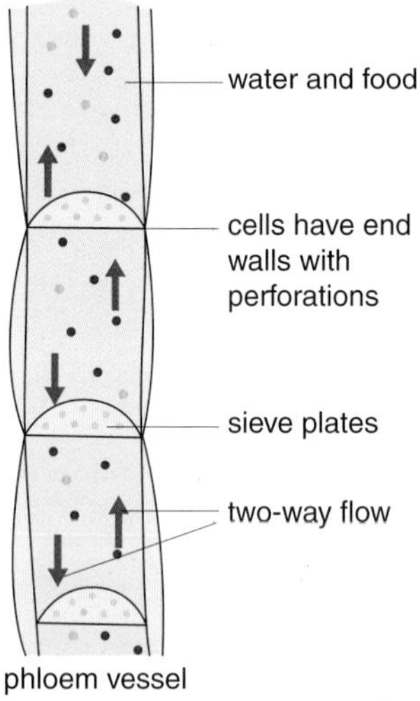

① Why are carbohydrates and proteins transported as sucrose and amino acids in the phloem vessels?

② What is translocation?

③ Design a diagram to show how the plan uses the glucose made in photosynthesis.

water and food

cells have end walls with perforations

sieve plates

two-way flow

phloem vessel

Figure 2.52 How is phloem different to xylem? Make a model of phloem cells

The structure of phloem vessels

The end cell walls of phloem cells do not break down, but they do have many small pores in them. These perforated walls are called **sieve plates**.

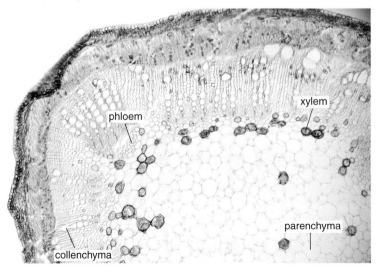

xylem

phloem

parenchyma

collenchyma

Figure 2.53 Use a microscope to observe and draw phloem vessels

Phloem cells contain cytoplasm but have no nucleus. They have a companion cell next to them. The companion cell controls the activities of the phloem but does not help with translocation. Substances in phloem vessels are moved by a process that requires energy.

Substances are transported in any direction in the phloem. Glucose made by photosynthesis is converted into a complex sugar called sucrose. Sucrose and amino acids are transported to all tissues in the plant. Different tissues use the substances in different ways.

4 Describe the structure of phloem cells.

5 How is the structure of phloem cells different to xylem cells?

KEY INFORMATION

Phloem is living, has thin walls and has sieve plates. Xylem is dead, has strengthened walls and no sieve plates.

How are phloem vessels adapted for their function?

Phloem vessels have:

- companion cells with a nucleus and many mitochondria, which provide the energy needed to move substances in the phloem
- limited amounts of cytoplasm and no nucleus to allow efficient movement of substances
- perforated sieve plates to allow the movement of substances through the phloem
- two-way flow of substances so that they are transported all over the plant.

6 Why do phloem vessels have companion cells?

7 Explain the function of the sieve plates.

DID YOU KNOW?

The strings that go up and down the length of bananas are phloem vessels.

Investigating transpiration

KEY WORDS

potometer

Learning objectives:

- describe how transpiration is affected by different factors
- describe how a potometer can be used to investigate factors that affect water uptake.

Water is an essential constituent of all plant tissues. Plants absorb large amounts of water but only use 2–5% of it for metabolic processes. Why do plants lose so much water?

Environmental factors and transpiration

Water for photosynthesis is transported to leaves in xylem vessels. Diffusion out of the spongy mesophyll causes a film of water to cover the cell surfaces. Water evaporates into the spaces between cells and the water vapour moves along the concentration gradient towards the stomata, and escapes from the leaf. When transpiration increases, water uptake by the plant increases.

Factors that increase the rate of transpiration are:

- an increase in temperature
- an increase in wind speed
- a decrease in humidity.

When plants photosynthesise, the stomata are open to allow carbon dioxide to diffuse into the leaf. Factors that increase photosynthesis will increase transpiration.

Some students investigated how light intensity affected the rate of transpiration (Figure 2.55).

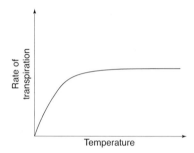

Figure 2.54 How does temperature affect transpiration rate?

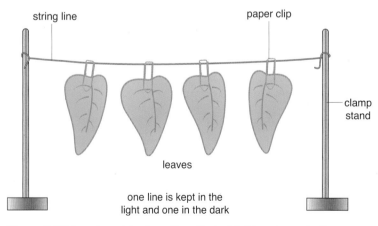

Figure 2.55 Experiment to show the effect of light on transpiration

① **In Figure 2.55, why were leaves put in the dark and the light?**

② **What measurements could the students take?**

③ **Predict what you think would happen to the leaves put in the dark and the light.**

How plants control water loss

Potometers are used to measure the uptake of water by plants in different conditions. The movement of the air bubble in the tube shows how much water is taken up.

Different plants control water loss in different ways:

- waxy cuticle: in hot environments it can be very thick
- most stomata are on the underside of leaves, protected from environmental factors
- needle-like, spiny or rolled up leaves
- stomata in pits on the leaf surface.

4. Describe an experiment to show that transpiration rate is affected by air movement.

5. Describe what happens to transpiration rate as humidity decreases.

6. Describe how a leaf is adapted to reduce water loss.

Explaining changes in transpiration

On still days when water vapour diffuses out of the leaf, the diffusion and evaporation concentration gradients decrease until the water vapour concentration inside and outside the leaf are equal and transpiration stops.

On windy days, water vapour is blown away. The concentration gradients are maintained and the transpiration rate increases.

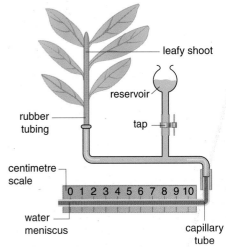

Figure 2.56 A potometer

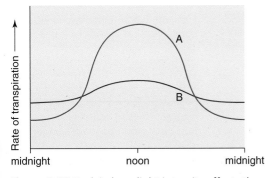

Figure 2.57 Explain how light intensity affects the rate of transpiration for plant A and plant B

7. Explain how the structure of a leaf is adapted to reduce water loss.

8. Why is water uptake rate not the same as transpiration rate?

9. Predict and draw graphs to describe and explain how transpiration rate is affected by:

   a cold conditions   b windy conditions

   c dull cloudy conditions   d still, humid conditions.

10. 'Plants grow best in cooler, cloudy and humid conditions because they lose less water.' Discuss this statement. Do you agree with it? Explain why.

KEY INFORMATION

Remember that water diffuses out of cells and evaporates to form water vapour that can escape from the leaf.

DID YOU KNOW?

Transpiration keeps plants cool. Some trees lose hundreds of thousands of litres of water in one day through transpiration.

MATHS SKILLS

Surface area to volume ratio

Learning objectives:

- be able to calculate surface area and volume
- be able to calculate surface area to volume ratio
- know how to apply ideas about surface area and volume.

In science, we use mathematical skills to help us understand what is happening. Surface area to volume ratio is very important in living things.

Finding the area of a surface

Alveoli provide a large surface area for gaseous exchange between the air and the bloodstream. If our lungs were smooth on the inside, like balloons, the surface area would be much less and materials would not be exchanged fast enough.

We can calculate surface area in different ways. For a rectangular shape, we multiply the length by the width. For example, an area of skin 4 cm long and 7 cm wide has a surface area of $(4 \times 7) = 28\,cm^2$.

Living things are not generally made up of regular shapes, such as rectangles, so we have to use other ways of finding the area. One way is to use squared paper and to count how many squares are covered (or are largely covered) by the specimen.

Figure 2.58 Elephants have wrinkled skin to increase their surface area.

KEY INFORMATION

Note that both the length and the width have to be measured in the same units and that the answer is in those units, squared.

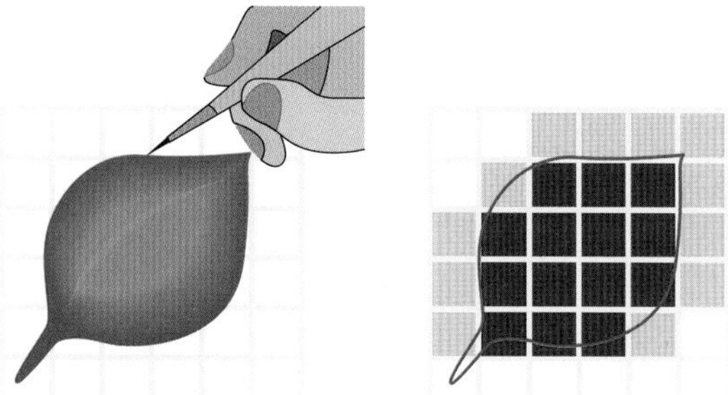

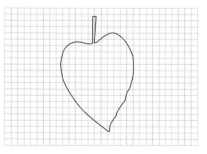

1 square = 1 cm²   1 square = 1 cm²

Figure 2.59 Counting squares that are largely covered is (approximately) balanced by not counting squares that are slightly covered.

1   **Estimate the surface area of the leaf in Figure 2.60.**

2   **Calculate the surface area of:**
  a   a piece of tree bark that is 30 cm long and 3 cm wide
  b   a razor shell that is 50 mm long and 8 mm wide.

Figure 2.60 One square is 1 cm².

Working out the volume

It is easier for warm-blooded animals to keep warm on cold days if their volume is large, but then it is harder for these same animals to lose heat on a hot day. We calculate the volume of a cube by multiplying length by width by height. A die with a side of 2 cm has a volume of (2 cm × 2 cm × 2 cm) = 8 cm³. Again, all the distances need to be in the same units and the volume is also in those units, cubed.

3 What is the volume of:

    a a science laboratory 10 m wide, 15 m long and 3 m high?
    b a block of wood 2 cm wide, 3 cm long and 4 cm high?

4 Finding the volume of a tree branch is tricky, but one way is to immerse the branch in a tank full of water. Suggest how the volume is measured.

Surface area to volume ratio

In science it is useful to compare the surface area with the volume. We do this by finding the ratio of one compared with the other. To find the ratio, divide the surface area by the volume. For example, for a cube with sides 2 cm long:

surface area = 2 × 2 × 6 = 24 cm²;
volume = 2 × 2 × 2 = 8 cm³;
surface area to volume ratio = 24:8 = 3:1

The shape of an organism also affects its surface area to volume ratio. Spheres have the smallest surface area compared with their volumes. Many small mammals have a shape that is almost spherical – for example, a mouse – and puppies and kittens curl up into a ball to sleep. As small animals, they want to minimise their surface area to volume ratio so as to minimise heat loss.

5 Compare how surface area, volume, and surface area to volume ratio change as the size of a cube increases. Use cubes with sides of 1, 2, 3, 4, 6 and 8 cm.

6 Compare and contrast phloem and xylem cells. Look at A, B and C in Figure 2.61.

Which animal will have problems keeping:

    a cool? Explain your answer.
    b warm? Explain your answer.

7 Devise a method to measure the volume of the air you breathe out in one breath.

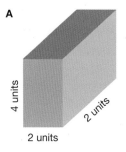

A
4 units
2 units
2 units

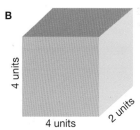

B
4 units
4 units
2 units

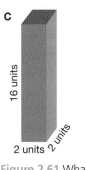

C
16 units
2 units 2 units

Figure 2.61 What do you notice about the surface area to volume ratios of these 'animals'?

DID YOU KNOW?

Arctic foxes have much smaller ears than desert-dwelling fennec foxes. Arctic foxes must reduce heat loss but fennec foxes must increase heat loss to their environment.

Check your progress

recall that cells must divide for growth and replacement of cells → describe how chromosomes double their DNA and are pulled to opposite ends of the cell, before the cytoplasm divides, during mitosis → describe the events of the cell cycle and explain the synthesis of new sub-cellular components and DNA

recall that organism development is based on cell division and cell specialisation → explain the importance of differentiation and explain how cells are specialised for their functions → understand size and scale in the components of organ systems

recall where stem cells are found → understand the potential of stem cell therapies → evaluate scientific and ethical issues involved with stem cell therapies

identify the parts of a leaf and their function → describe how leaves are adapted for efficient photosynthesis → explain how the leaf's structure is adapted for photosynthesis

know the definition of diffusion → explain diffusion using the idea of particles → explain how substances pass in and out of cells

describe how water travels in plants → describe adaptations in xylem and phloem → explain adaptations of xylem and phloem

describe experiments on the rate of transpiration → describe how different factors affect transpiration → explain how different factors affect transpiration

recall that the movement of sugars is called translocation → describe how proteins and carbohydrates are transported in plants → explain how concentration gradients affect processes

recall that osmosis describes water movement in and out of cells → explain osmosis as the movement of water through a partially permeable membrane → predict water movement during osmosis

explain the words flaccid, plasmolysed and turgid
describe the effect of SA:V on the diffusion of substances → describe the features of a range of exchange surfaces in plants and animals → explain the features of exchange surfaces

describe the functions of different parts of the circulatory system → describe how the circulatory system transports substances → explain how the circulatory system is adapted to its function

Worked example

The diagram shows the human heart.

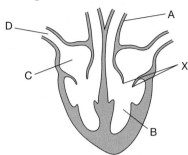

1 **Label parts A–D on the diagram.**

A Artery

B Left ventricle

C Right atrium

D Vena cava

2 a **What is the name of part X?**

Valve

b **Part X can become damaged or may leak. What effect will this have?**

Person will have a lack of energy and breathlessness.

c **How can a damaged or leaky part X be treated?**

Transplant a valve from another person.

d **Give an advantage and a disadvantage of the treatment.**

It will not be rejected.

3 **The heart pumps blood to the lungs so that gaseous exchange can happen.**

Why are alveoli an efficient exchange surface?

They have a large surface area compared to volume to give a large area for gaseous exchange. Good blood supply to take oxygen to body cells where it is used for respiration for energy for growth.

B–D correctly identified. Giving 'artery' for A is insufficient.

'Aorta' is a better answer.

Valve is correctly identified.

Two symptoms correctly identified.

One treatment has been identified.

Artificial valves are another treatment.

The student has correctly identified an advantage of one treatment but they have only answered half the question for this. The failure to identify two treatments has lost marks.

Two correct answers are identified. Then the student forgets the question being asked and moves away from the topic of alveoli.

Overall, this student shows a good understanding of the topic but does not give complete answers. Careful reading of the questions, and consideration of exactly what is being asked for, in addition to more detailed responses, would help the student achieve a much higher mark.

End of chapter questions

Getting started

1 What is the function of the heart? `1 Mark`

2 Describe the difference between respiration and breathing. `1 Mark`

3 Explain why mitosis is important in plants and animals. `2 Marks`

4 Jenna is investigating the effect of light on leaf growth. To do this she needs to calculate the surface area of each leaf.

a Estimate the surface area of this leaf: `1 Mark`

Jenna's results are shown on the right:

b Calculate the mean area for the north facing tree. `1 Mark`

c Explain the difference in the results. `2 Marks`

Leaf	South facing tree (most sun)	North facing tree (most shade)
	Area (cm³)	
1	14.0	29.0
2	18.0	19.5
3	13.5	28.0
4	21.5	29.5
5	15.5	23.0
Mean	16.5	

5 Explain why the alveoli are an efficient exchange surface. `2 Marks`

Going further

6 In plants, what is the name of the vessel that transports water? `1 Mark`

7 What is the function of valves in the circulatory system? `1 Mark`

8 Explain how the features of a sperm cell help it to fertilise an egg. `2 Marks`

9 How are plant roots adapted for the exchange of materials? `2 Marks`

10 *Amoeba* is a single-celled organism that lives in fresh water. It has a vacuole that fills with water, moves to the outside of the cell and bursts. A new vacuole starts to form. Use osmosis to explain why *Amoeba* needs a vacuole. `4 Marks`

More challenging

11 A scientist measured water uptake and transpiration in a tree over 18 hours. The graph shows her data.

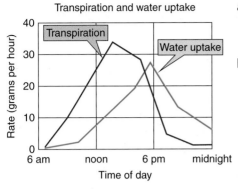

Transpiration and water uptake

a Transpiration is highest between 1–2 pm. When is water uptake highest? `1 Mark`

b Compare and explain the rate of transpiration with the rate of water uptake. `2 Marks`

12 A teenage girl had her heartbeat measured at 74 beats per minute. Each beat pumped 70 cm³ of blood. Calculate how much blood will be pumped in 10 minutes. Give your answer in litres. `1 Mark`

13 Which organism can absorb nutrients quicker?

Explain your answer.

a 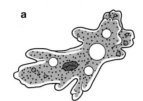   b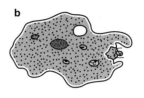
`2 Marks`

14 Explain how the structure of xylem and phloem are adapted to their functions in the plant. `4 Marks`

Most demanding

15 What is the disadvantage of having a large volume compared to surface area? `2 Marks`

16 We can calculate the length of time a cell is at a certain stage in the cell cycle using the formula:

$$\text{Length of time spent in phase} = \frac{\text{observed number of cells at the stage}}{\text{total number of cells observed}} \times \text{length of time for cell cycle}$$

The following data were obtained when observing stomach cells from two patients:

Type of cell	Number of cells observed		Time for cell cycle (min)
	Not dividing	Dividing by mitosis	
Patient 1: normal stomach cells	87	13	600
Patient 2: cancerous stomach cells	104	16	420

Suggest what conclusions can be drawn from the data. `4 Marks`

17 Carbon dioxide, needed for photosynthesis, moves into the leaf by diffusion. Suggest and explain two ways in which the structure of the leaf allows carbon dioxide to diffuse to the cells that require it. `4 Marks`

`Total: 40 Marks`

ORGANISM LEVEL SYSTEMS

ORGANS WORK TOGETHER AS SYSTEMS

- Organs are aggregations of tissues.
- Organ systems work together to form organisms.

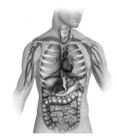

METABOLISM INVOLVES CHEMICAL SYNTHESIS AND BREAKDOWN OF SUBSTANCES

- Products of digestion are used to build carbohydrates, lipids and proteins.
- In animals, carbohydrate is stored as glycogen.
- Glucose is required by all cells for respiration; carbon dioxide and water are waste products.
- Carbon dioxide is excreted by the lungs.
- Excess protein is converted to urea.
- Other waste products from cells are transported in the blood and excreted by the kidneys.

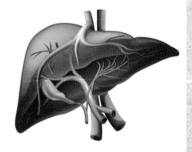

HOW HUMANS REPRODUCE

- The structure of the male and female reproductive systems.
- How gametes are produced and the processes of fertilisation, pregnancy and birth.
- Some diseases are transmitted sexually and this can be prevented by some forms of contraception.

IN THIS CHAPTER YOU WILL FIND OUT ABOUT:

HOW CONDITIONS IN THE BODY, PROCESSES AND ORGAN SYSTEMS ARE COORDINATED AND CONTROLLED

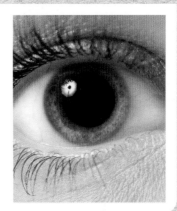

- Regulation of the internal conditions in the body is called homeostasis.
- The nervous and endocrine systems are involved in this coordination and control.
- The nervous system works using electrical impulses, transmitted using nerves; the endocrine system uses chemicals called hormones, which are secreted by endocrine glands.
- In the nervous system, receptors can be grouped into sense organs, such as the eye.

CONTROL OF METABOLISM AND LEVELS OF CHEMICALS IN THE BODY

- The concentrations of glucose, must be kept within strict limits.
- Glucose concentration is controlled by hormones.
- Lack of insulin, or a loss of sensitivity to it, causes a condition called diabetes, which must be controlled.
- The control of hormone secretion by many glands is by negative feedback.

CONTROL OF SEXUAL DEVELOPMENT AND HUMAN REPRODUCTION

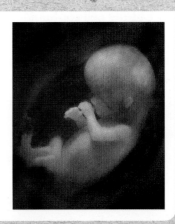

- Reproductive hormones cause secondary sexual characteristics to develop.
- Pituitary gland hormones regulate egg development and release, and along with reproductive hormones, prepare the body for a possible pregnancy.
- Different methods of contraception help to prevent unwanted births.
- Fertility drugs and *in-vitro* fertilisation are possible solutions to infertility.

The nervous system

Learning objectives:

- explain how the nervous system is adapted to its functions
- describe the structure of the central nervous system and nerves
- explain how the parts of the nervous system form a coordinated response.

Nerve cells communicate with each other and with muscles, glands and other structures. There are critical periods during our lives when nerve cells are able to make these connections with other nerve cells. That's why we're able to learn different skills at different times – usually early on – in our lives.

The structure of the nervous system

Our nervous system enables us to detect our surroundings, and coordinate our behaviour.

The structure of the nervous system is well adapted to these≈functions.

1. **What is the function of the nervous system?**

2. **What are the two parts of the nervous system?**

Nerves

The nervous system consists of nerve cells or **neurones**. Neurones are specialised for transmitting messages in the form of an electrical impulse.

The part of the cell containing the nucleus is called the cell body. The cell body of all neurones is found in the CNS. Neurones, however, have an extended shape so that they can carry nerve impulses from one part of the body to another. They also have fine branches at their tips to communicate with other neurones.

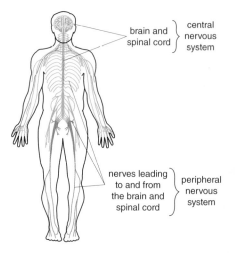

Figure 3.1 The nervous system is made up of the **central nervous system** (CNS) and the peripheral nervous system (PNS)

Figure 3.2 The projections that extend from a nerve cell communicate with other nerve cells

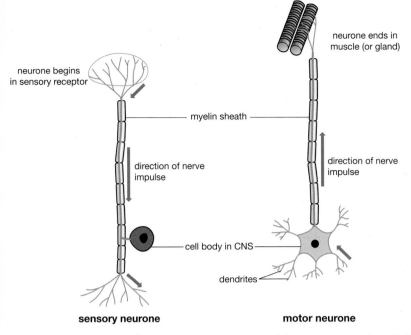

neurone ends in muscle (or gland)

neurone begins in sensory receptor

myelin sheath

direction of nerve impulse

direction of nerve impulse

cell body in CNS

dendrites

sensory neurone

motor neurone

Figure 3.3 Two types of neurone. The long regions of the neurones are bundled together as 'nerves'.

Receptors are cells that detect any changes in the environment. Receptors are sometimes grouped to form sense organs. Sensory neurones relay nerve impulses from these receptors to the CNS.

The CNS processes the information and coordinates how the body should respond.

Motor neurones relay impulses from the CNS to the effector – for instance, a muscle or gland.

The sequence of events is:

stimulus → receptor → coordinator → effector → response

3 What is the scientific name for a nerve cell?

4 Describe the pathway of a nerve impulse, beginning with the stimulus and ending with the response.

The transmission of a nerve impulse

The nerve impulse is electrical. It means that it can be transmitted quickly.

In vertebrates, neurones are covered with a fatty layer called the myelin sheath. The myelin sheath acts as an insulator and speeds up the transmission of the impulse. But the myelin sheath is not continuous. Periodically, there are small gaps in it – around 1 μm in size. These allow the nerve impulse to jump from one gap to the next, further increasing the speed of transmission.

5 Use your knowledge of nerve cells to predict what might happen if the myelin sheath around your nerve cells began to break down.

6 Explain how the nervous system is adapted to its function.

DID YOU KNOW?

If the myelin sheath does not develop properly, or becomes or inflamed or damaged – in conditions such as multiple sclerosis, and diseases such as leprosy – the transmission of nerve impulses can be seriously affected.

Reflex actions

Learning objectives:

- explain the importance of reflex actions
- describe the path of a reflex arc
- explain how the structures in the reflex arc relate to their function.

KEY WORDS

reflex action

reflex arc

Nasim's doctor tests his reflexes by tapping the tendon just below the knee cap. Nasim's leg kicks up.

Reflexes are related to survival

Reflex actions are rapid, automatic responses to a stimulus. We do not have to think about them. Reflex actions form the basis of behaviour in simpler organisms. In humans, they prevent us from getting hurt. In other animals, our human ancestors and babies they are also related to survival.

Some reflex actions include:

- removing our hand from a hot or sharp object
- the grasping reflex, in which a baby grips a finger
- blinking our eyes if an object approaches rapidly.
- the pupil reflex, whereby the pupil gets wider in dim light and narrower in bright light.

Figure 3.4 The knee jerk reflex. A normal reaction time is around 50 milliseconds (ms)

1 What is a reflex action?

2 Why are reflex actions important?

The reflex arc

Our spinal reflexes do not involve the brain. Or, at least, not to begin with. In a reflex action, the nerve impulse follows a pathway called the **reflex arc**.

Figure 3.5 shows the pathway taken by a nerve impulse when a person puts a hand on a hot object.

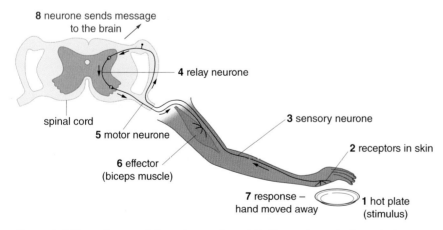

8 neurone sends message to the brain

4 relay neurone

spinal cord

5 motor neurone

6 effector (biceps muscle)

3 sensory neurone

2 receptors in skin

7 response – hand moved away

1 hot plate (stimulus)

Figure 3.5 The reflex arc. Follow the numbers 1–7. The pathway is through the spinal cord

The pathway includes:

- a sensory neurone – transmits nerve impulses from the receptor to the CNS
- a relay neurone, in the spinal cord – transmits the impulses from the sensory to the motor neurone
- a motor neurone – sends impulses from the CNS to the effector.

In this case, the effector is the biceps muscle, which moves the arm. The hand is moved away from the hot object.

Because other neurones in the spinal cord link via a synapses with those of the reflex arc, a message is sent to the brain *after* the hand has been removed (number 8 in figure 3.5). It tells us that the plate was hot.

③ **Name the nervous pathway that a nerve impulse takes during a reflex action.**

④ **Explain how the parts of this pathway relate to their function.**

Linking nerves

The three neurones in the reflex arc don't link together *physically*. There's a gap – called a synapse – between each pair. This means that *many* neurones can connect with each other. In the brain, neurones can link up with up to 10000 others.

Nerve impulses pass across a synapse with the help of chemical transmitter molecules.

3.2

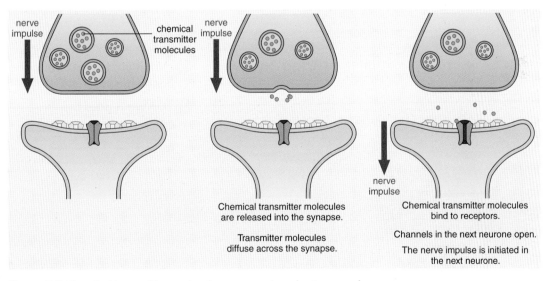

Chemical transmitter molecules are released into the synapse.

Transmitter molecules diffuse across the synapse.

Chemical transmitter molecules bind to receptors.

Channels in the next neurone open.

The nerve impulse is initiated in the next neurone.

Figure 3.6 Chemical transmitter molecules cause an impulse to move from one neurone to the next

⑤ **What is the gap between neurones called?**

⑥ **How does a nerve impulse travel from one nerve to the next?**

⑦ **Compose a flow diagram to describe and explain the sequence of events in a reflex arc.**

The endocrine system

Learning objectives:

- recall that the endocrine system is made up of glands that secrete hormones into the blood
- know the location of the major endocrine glands
- understand why the pituitary gland is the 'master gland'.

KEY WORDS

endocrine gland
endocrine system
hormone

The world's tallest man was Robert Pershing Wadlow (1918–1940). He was 2.72 m when he died at the age of 22. His height was caused by an excess of growth hormone, produced by the pituitary gland.

The endocrine system

Hormones are produced by glands of the **endocrine system**. **Endocrine glands** secrete hormones directly into the blood.

Hormones are often described as *chemical messengers*. They circulate in the blood and produce an effect on target organs. Many hormones are large molecules.

Like the nervous system, hormones work on effectors. But, unlike the nervous system, the effects they produce don't take milliseconds. With the exception of a hormone called adrenaline, effects of hormones take minutes, hours or, in the case of hormones involved in our development, they act for years.

Figure 3.7 We all produce growth hormone. Maximum production is during our youth

1. What is the function of the endocrine system?

2. On what does the endocrine system act?

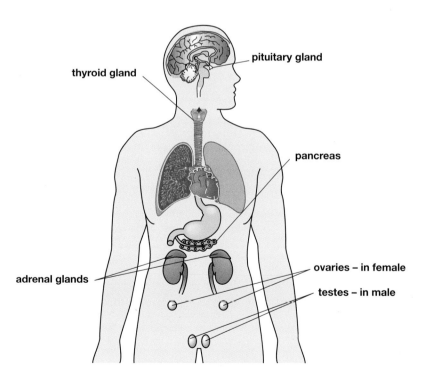

Figure 3.8 The location of the major endocrine glands in the body

Location of the endocrine glands

There are a number of endocrine glands situated in different parts of the body. Some of these are gender specific and some produce enzymes as well as hormones.

3 Which organ secretes hormones and also digestive enzymes?

4 Which endocrine glands are found in the female only?

The master gland

The pituitary gland is an outgrowth from the base of the brain.

Some of the hormones that it secretes, such as growth hormone, have a direct effect on their target organs. Other hormones have an indirect effect; they cause other glands to secrete hormones. It is, therefore, called the master gland as it regulates the secretion of other endocrine glands.

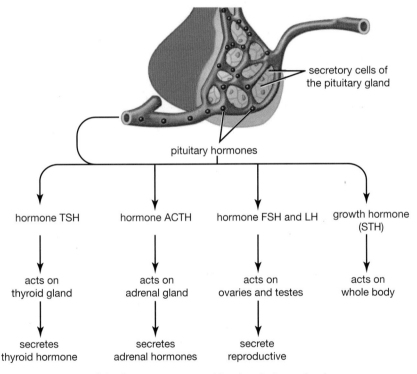

Figure 3.9 Some of the hormones secreted by the pituitary gland

DID YOU KNOW?

Some people do not produce enough growth hormone. In the 1960s, 27 000 people worldwide were given growth hormone extracted from the pituitary glands of dead people. A small number ended up with the brain disease, CJD, from infected brain tissue. Growth hormone is now produced by genetically modified organisms.

5 Explain why the pituitary gland is called the master gland.

6 Name one hormone that exerts its effects over the whole body.

REMEMBER!

You need to be able to label the major endocrine glands on a diagram of the human body.

Negative feedback

Learning objectives:

- explain the role of thyroxine in the body
- understand the principles of negative feedback, as applied to thyroxine.

KEY WORDS

basal metabolic rate

negative feedback

pituitary gland

thyroxine

Priya's tired and sluggish and is putting on weight. Her heart rate feels slow. She also feels the cold. It could be a problem with her thyroid gland.

HIGHER TIER ONLY

The thyroid gland

The thyroid gland affects our activity by producing the hormone **thyroxine**. Thyroxine stimulates the body's **basal metabolic rate** – it increases the metabolism of all the body's cells. Priya has an underactive thyroid. That explains her symptoms.

Under- or over-active thyroid glands are common. As adults, these conditions are fairly easily treated. But thyroxine also controls our growth and development – starting in the uterus. In the embryo, infant or child, mental and physical development is severely retarded by insufficient levels of thyroxine.

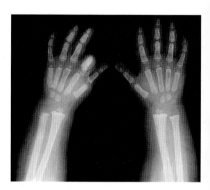

Figure 3.10 This 6-year-old's finger shows stunted development owing to lack of thyroxine. Children in the UK are tested at birth using a drop of blood from their heel.

1 **Suggest a symptom of an *overactive* thyroid.**

2 **What is the function of thyroxine?**

Control of thyroxine secretion

The **pituitary gland** controls secretions from other glands. One such gland is the thyroid gland.

Levels of thyroxine in the blood are increased when the pituitary gland secretes thyroid-stimulating hormone (TSH). The thyroid gland responds by secreting thyroxine. If levels of thyroxine become too high, TSH secretion is blocked.

Thyroxine increases the respiration rate of cells. In the process, heat energy is released. The body will secrete thyroxine when its temperature falls. The same is true of adrenaline, the hormone that is released when we are frightened or excited. Both hormones raise our body temperature, particularly with heat released by the liver. If our body temperature becomes too high, the thermoregulatory centre in the brain detects the temperature rise, and the hormones' secretion is blocked.

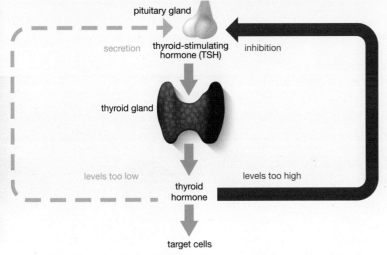

Figure 3.11 A simplified version of the negative-feedback system that controls thyroxine secretion

3 Which hormone regulates thyroxine production?

4 Which hormones help to control our body temperature?

The principles of negative feedback

The endocrine system keeps the conditions in the body constant using feedback systems.

A simple *negative*-feedback system is the central-heating system in your home. If the temperature falls in your living room, the thermostat detects this and switches on the heating. The room warms up.

When the thermostat temperature is reached, it detects this, and turns off the heating. This is **negative feedback** because when the desired effect is reached, the system is switched off.

Negative feedback within the endocrine system prevents a system from becoming overactive. The system is inhibited by its own products.

5 Give a definition of a negative feedback system.

6 Figure 3.12 illustrates a *simple* negative feedback system, but it's not a perfect comparison with thyroid secretion. Explain why.

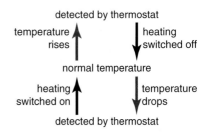

Figure 3.12 Negative feedback in a central-heating system

KEY CONCEPT

Systems working together

Learning objectives:

- describe the effects of adrenaline
- understand that automatic control systems may involve nervous responses and chemical responses
- understand that combinations of hormones work to produce a response.

KEY WORDS

adrenaline

Harry is frightened of having of having a flu vaccination. He screams. His heart begins to race. His skin goes pale.

HIGHER TIER ONLY

Adrenaline

Adrenaline prepares us – very quickly when we get a fright – for emergency action. It has a number of effects on the body.

Figure 3.13 These effects are the result of the release of a hormone called adrenaline.

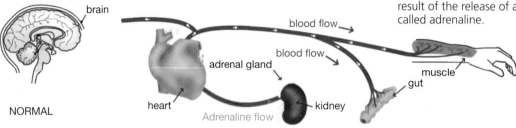

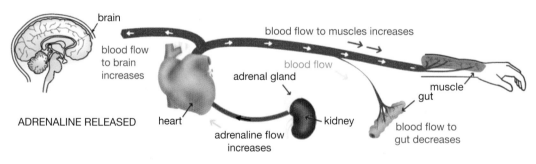

Figure 3.14 As the heart pumps more rapidly, more blood, with glucose and oxygen, is delivered to our muscles and brain.

Our muscles are being prepared for us to run, or maybe to fight. Adrenaline is called the 'flight-or-fight' hormone.

1. Which hormone is released when we become frightened?

2. There is only a set volume of blood in the body. Suggest how more blood can be pumped to the brain and muscles.

The nervous and endocrine systems interact

The release of adrenaline is a good example of how the nervous and endocrine systems interact.

Connections to and in the brain and to the adrenal glands are *nervous*. The part of the adrenal gland called the adrenal medulla responds to nervous stimulation by releasing the hormone adrenaline.

The adrenaline that is released – as you have seen previously – acts on various parts of the body, including the liver cells. In the liver, it promotes the breakdown of glycogen into glucose, and its release into the bloodstream.

Most of us do not use the flight-or-fight response on a regular basis. But it is there if we need it.

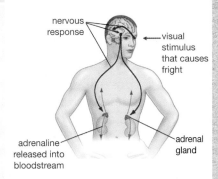

Figure 3.15 The nervous and endocrine systems produce our reaction to a fright.

3 Explain how the nervous and endocrine systems work together in times of stress.

4 Which other hormone stimulates the breakdown of glycogen in the liver?

Hormones working together

Several hormones are involved in glucose metabolism – insulin and glucagon (see topic 3.12), thyroxine (see topic 3.4) and now adrenaline (and also cortisol).

And a number of hormones work together to control our development and reproduction.

These hormones and many others work together in our bodies to ensure that our bodies *do* work as a coordinated whole.

5 Describe the action of three hormones on glucose metabolism.

6 Describe how two hormones affect our development.

7 Use your knowledge of the endocrine system to create a concept map, which links keys words that are covered in the topic, and explains how the words are linked.

DID YOU KNOW?

The brain's response to fear also leads to the release of a hormone by the pituitary gland. This hormone acts on a different part of the adrenal gland. A hormone called cortisol is released. Its release is not as quick as adrenaline – it sustains our response to possible danger.

REMEMBER!

This topic provides an illustration of how the body systems work together to produce a coordinated response.

Human reproduction

Learning objectives:

* describe the roles of hormones in sexual reproduction
* explain how hormones interact in the menstrual cycle.

Our first exposure to sex hormones is not at puberty, but as a foetus. In the presence of male sex hormones (which needs a Y chromosome), male characteristics develop; in their absence, the foetus becomes female.

Reproductive hormones

Secondary sex characteristics develop as our bodies produce reproductive hormones at puberty.

Oestrogen is the main female reproductive hormone that is produced at this time. It is produced by the ovaries. Eggs start to mature in the ovaries and are released, at approximately one every 28 days. This process is called ovulation.

In the male, **testosterone** is the main reproductive hormone. It is produced by the testes. It stimulates sperm production.

DID YOU KNOW?

Women produce a hormone called Human Chorionic Gonadotrophin during pregnancy. An early method of pregnancy testing was to immerse the African clawed toad, *Xenopus laevis*, in the urine of a patient. If the patient was pregnant, the toad would begin to ovulate.

1. Give the main reproductive hormones in males and females.

2. What happens in males and females under the influence of these hormones?

The menstrual cycle

The menstrual cycle is the reproductive cycle in women, which – by convention – starts with a period (menstruation), if the woman is not pregnant.

Hormones involved in the menstrual cycle include:

* follicle stimulating hormone (**FSH**), which causes eggs to mature in the ovaries
* oestrogen and **progesterone**, which maintain the lining of the uterus.

3. Name three hormones involved in the menstrual cycle.

4. Which hormones maintain the lining of the uterus?

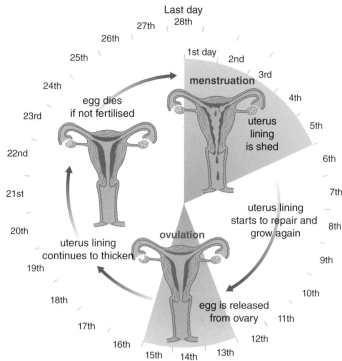

Figure 3.16 The menstrual cycle lasts approximately 28 days, but this is highly variable

Menstrual cycle hormones

The menstrual cycle is concerned with the maturation of an egg every month and preparing the uterus to receive that egg if it is fertilised, that is if the woman becomes pregnant.

These hormones interact with each other during the menstrual cycle.

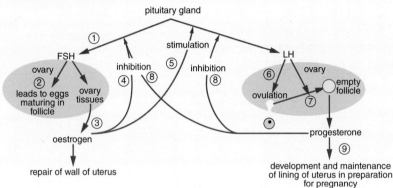

Figure 3.17 The roles of the hormones as the cycle progresses are:

1 FSH is secreted by the pituitary gland.

2 FSH causes the eggs to mature in the ovaries.

3 FSH stimulates the ovaries to produce oestrogen.

4 & 5 Oestrogen inhibits further release of FSH and stimulates release of luteinising hormone, LH.

6 LH triggers ovulation – the release of the mature egg from the ovary – and …

7 … leads to the secretion of progesterone by the empty follicle that contained the egg.

8 Progesterone inhibits the release of LH and FSH.

9 Progesterone maintains the lining of the uterus during the second half of the menstrual cycle, in readiness for receiving a fertilised egg.

5 **Which two hormones repair the uterus after menstruation and encourage its growth?**

6 **Suggest which hormones show:**
- **negative feedback**
- ***positive* feedback.**

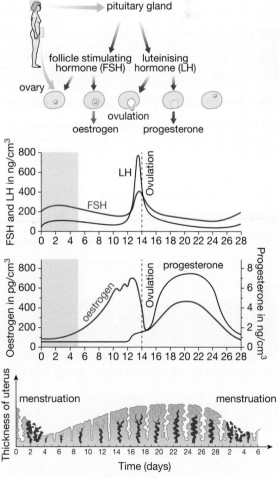

Figure 3.18 The menstrual cycle is controlled by four main hormones

Contraception

Learning objectives:

- understand that fertility can be controlled by different hormonal and non-hormonal methods of contraception
- evaluate the different methods of contraception.

KEY WORDS

cervix

combined contraceptive pill

progestogen-only pill

If the population continues to increase at the current rate, human life on Earth will not be sustainable. Efforts to bring down the birth rate need to continue.

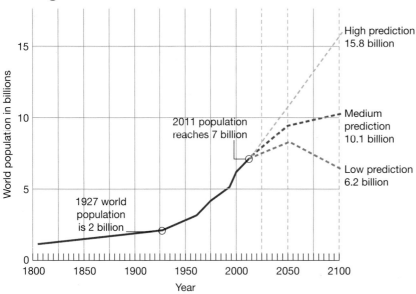

Figure 3.19 One prediction for world population growth

Contraceptive methods

Most contraceptive methods fall into one of two types:

- methods that use hormones
- non-hormonal methods, or barrier methods.

Some people choose *natural* planning methods. A woman's time of ovulation is linked with:

- her menstrual cycle, occurring at around 14 days
- a *slight* increase in body temperature
- thinning of mucus secreted from the **cervix**.

By estimating when ovulation occurs, it's possible to avoid having sexual intercourse when an egg might be in the oviduct. But eggs and sperm can live for several days, and women's cycles can be irregular.

Some people choose to have surgery. In the woman, the oviducts are cut, sealed or blocked by an operation. In the man, the sperm ducts are cut, sealed or tied. Surgical methods are designed to be permanent.

DID YOU KNOW?

Oral contraceptives were first approved for use in Britain in 1961. The hormone content was equivalent to seven of today's pills.

KEY SKILLS

You may be provided with new information or data on contraceptives that you have to analyse and interpret.

1. How can contraceptives be divided into broad categories?
2. List three indicators of ovulation.

Barrier methods

Barrier methods prevent sperm from reaching an egg.

Condom (male)	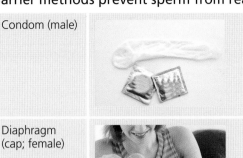	a rubber or polyurethane sheath that is rolled over the erect penis
Diaphragm (cap; female)	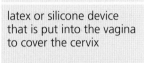	latex or silicone device that is put into the vagina to cover the cervix

Two commonly used barrier methods

A spermicidal cream is toxic to sperm. It can help with the effectiveness of other contraceptives, such as diaphragms. It should not be used on its own, or with condoms.

3. Give two examples of barrier methods of contraception.
4. When should a spermicidal cream be used?

Hormonal methods

Hormonal methods of contraception use reproductive hormones to prevent pregnancy. The **combined contraceptive pill** contains a synthetic oestrogen and progesterone.

For women for whom the combined pill isn't suitable, for instance, if they're older or have high blood pressure, there's also a **progestogen**-only pill (POP, mini pill).

These contraceptives inhibit the release of the pituitary hormones that control egg maturation and release. They also thicken cervical mucus which helps to prevent sperm reaching an egg. The combined pill is taken for 21 days, allowing periods to occur. The POP is taken every day.

Some other types of contraceptive can also include hormones. Intrauterine devices (IUDs) are placed in the uterus. They prevent a fertilised egg from implanting in the uterus.

Plastic IUDs also release progestogen. Copper versions have copper wound around plastic. Copper is toxic to sperm.

5. How do oral contraceptives work?
6. What is an IUD?
7. IUDs could be considered unethical because they do not prevent fertilisation of an egg. What do you think? Give reasons to justify your answer.

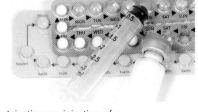

Injection: an injection of a progestogen is given.

Implant: a small flexible rod is implanted under skin of the upper arm. Progestogen is released slowly.

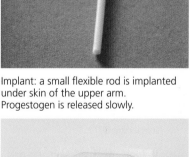

Patch: A sticky patch is put on the skin. It releases oestrogen and progestogen slowly.

Figure 3.20 Hormonal contraceptives can also be used as injections, implants or patches

Figure 3.21 An IUD.

Which contraceptive?

Learning objectives:

- discuss the effectiveness of different hormonal and non-hormonal methods of contraception
- evaluate data on the different methods of contraception.

KEY WORDS

condom

IUD

A microchip implant has been developed that can store and release regular, controlled doses of a contraceptive for up to 16 years.

The chip can be controlled wirelessly. It could be turned off at any time to start a family.

Reliability

People who are considering using contraceptives should look at their success rate.

Successful surgery is 100% effective but irreversible. Natural family planning methods *can* be effective if used correctly, with guidance and teaching. Computerised devices that monitor hormone changes improve reliability of natural methods.

1. **How can the reliability of natural family planning methods be improved?**

2. **Which method(s) is, or are, the most effective contraceptive?**

Advantages and disadvantages of different methods

With surgery, couples no longer need to think about contraception at all. But the decision should be carefully considered.

Hormonal contraceptives are convenient, although POPs do need to be taken at the same time every day to be effective. Implants last for 3 years, injections 12–13 weeks and patches 1 week. With injections, fertility may not return to normal straightaway.

With the combined pill, implant and patch, periods may be more regular, lighter and less painful. Oral contraceptives also reduce the risk of certain cancers, though those containing oestrogen slightly increase the risk of blood clots, and breast and cervical cancer.

Type of contraception	Percentage of pregnancies prevented
condoms	98
diaphragm	92–96
implants	99
IUD	>99
oral contraceptives	>99

The effectiveness of contraceptives when used *perfectly*

Method	Advantages	Disadvantages
condoms	• widely available • can protect against transmitted infections, e.g. HIV	• may slip off • must withdraw after ejaculation and not spill semen
diaphragm	• put in just before sex • no health risks	• needs to be left in for several hours after sex • some people are sensitive to spermicide
IUD	• works immediately • can stay in place for 10 years (copper); 3–5 years (hormonal)	• insertion may be uncomfortable • periods may be longer or more painful

Advantages and disadvantages of other methods

3 Suggest why oral contraceptives are affected by vomiting or diarrhoea, but injections, implants and patches are not.

4 Give one advantage and one disadvantage of using an IUD.

Wider issues

People must decide whether to use contraception or not. This could be influenced by religious factors.

If people do use contraception, they must choose a method.

Health factors are important in family planning, but for many people the decision to use contraception is *economic*, or can be a *lifestyle* choice:

- Can a couple afford to start a family?
- Is contraception likely to be needed every day?
- How soon would the woman like to become pregnant *after* using contraception?

A wider issue associated with contraception is one of world population and sustainability, although there are ethical issues with its use in population control. It can be seen as interfering with human rights and reproductive freedom.

5 Name the most widely used contraceptive method in the UK.

6 Discuss non-scientific questions around a need for contraception.

7 Some governments have considered compulsory sterilisation to control population growth. Evaluate the advantages and disadvantages of sterilisation.

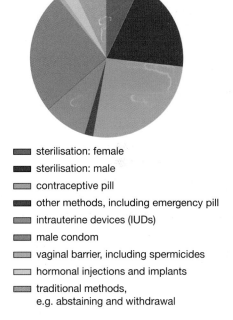

- sterilisation: female
- sterilisation: male
- contraceptive pill
- other methods, including emergency pill
- intrauterine devices (IUDs)
- male condom
- vaginal barrier, including spermicides
- hormonal injections and implants
- traditional methods, e.g. abstaining and withdrawal

Figure 3.22 Contraceptive use in the UK, 2008–9

DID YOU KNOW?

Fifteen types of contraceptive are used in the UK. Two are designed *specifically* for men; 13 for women.

KEY SKILLS

Be prepared to evaluate data on the use of different types of contraception.

IVF

Learning objectives:

- explain the use of hormones in technologies to treat infertility
- describe the technique of *in-vitro* fertilisation.

Louise Joy Brown was born on 25 July 1978 at Oldham General Hospital. She was the first 'test tube baby'.

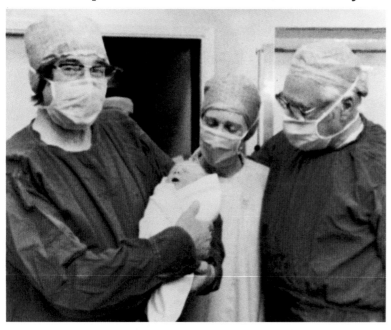

Figure 3.23 Louise was born following the pioneering technique of physiologist Dr Robert Edwards and gynaecologist Dr Patrick Steptoe

HIGHER TIER ONLY

Treating infertility

The NHS recommends that if a couple has been trying to conceive for a year – 6 months if the woman is over 35 – but with no success, it may be time to investigate.

For women whose levels of FSH are too low to conceive, combined hormones can be given as a **'fertility drug'**.

After treatment with a fertility drug, many women ovulate and become pregnant. They are warned of the possibility of multiple births.

If treatment is successful, it's usually within the first 3 months.

Figure 3.24 The women's ovaries are monitored with ultrasound to look at the number and size of developing follicles

1. **Explain why FSH and LH are given as fertility treatments.**

2. **Why are the ovaries monitored after treatment?**

In-vitro fertilisation

In-vitro fertilisation (IVF) may be an option to treat infertility. Here, eggs are fertilised outside the body. '*In vitro*' means, literally, 'in glass'. Eggs are removed from the mother and are fertilised, in the laboratory, with sperm collected from the father.

The technique is more successful if the woman:

- is younger
- has previously been pregnant
- has a BMI within the range of 19–30
- has low alcohol and caffeine intake, and does not smoke.

Counselling is important at this stage. The couple must be optimistic, yet prepared for failure.

3 What is *in-vitro* fertilisation?

4 Give two criteria that increase the possibility of successful IVF.

Stages of the process

The stages of IVF:

- The woman is given FSH and LH to stimulate the production of more eggs than normal in her ovaries.
- Eggs are then collected. The woman is sedated but conscious.
- Eggs are mixed with the father's sperm in the lab for 16–20 hours. They are monitored microscopically for fertilisation.
- Any embryos are allowed to develop for 5 days. They will contain around 100 cells.
- One or two embryos are selected and placed in the mother's uterus.

A number of **IVF cycles** – from stimulation of the ovaries to implantation – can be attempted. If a cycle is unsuccessful, a gap of 2 months is usually left as the treatment is emotionally and physically stressful.

5 If the father's sperm count is low, explain how the procedure is sometimes modified.

6 What is a cycle of IVF treatment?

7 Compare and contrast fertility treatment with IVF.

Figure 3.25 A *single* sperm is sometimes selected and injected into the egg. The procedure is carried out microscopically

COMMON MISCONCEPTION

Don't confuse *fertility treatment* and *IVF*. IVF is just one type of fertility treatment.

IVF evaluation

Learning objectives:

- describe the technique of *in-vitro* fertilisation
- evaluate the processes involved in fertility treatments.

KEY WORDS

IVF

Scientists in Oxford have devised a test that could improve the success rate of IVF. A clinical trial resulted in a pregnancy rate of 80%.

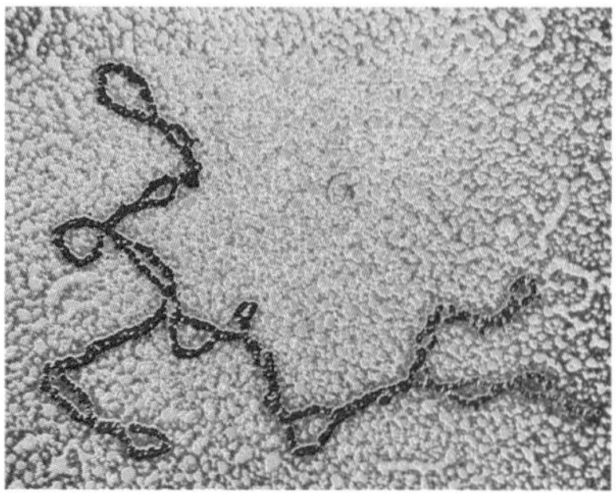

HIGHER TIER ONLY

The couple's perspective

IVF is available on the NHS – provided certain criteria are fulfilled. The National Institute for Health and Care Excellence (NICE) produces guidelines, but the final decision made by the woman's local NHS.

The process begins with counselling. This prepares the couple for the success, or the chance of failure. Emotional support is continuous through the process.

Figure 3.26 The test is based on mitochondrial DNA. Many IVF embryos had unusually high levels that prevented their implantation

1 Who determines the selection procedure for IVF on the NHS?

2 Why is counselling important for potential IVF couples?

Medical and scientific evaluation

Around half the embryos produced by IVF have an incorrect number of chromosomes. One-third of the normal embryos actually selected will not implant in the uterus.

Age of woman in years	Proportion of live births in %
Under 35	32.2
35–37	27.7
38–39	20.8
40–42	13.6
43–44	5.0
Over 44	1.9

The woman's age is one factor affecting success

Figure 3.27 Eggs or embryos are stored cryogenically. That way, they can be used later on. But does freezing and then thawing affect them?

The success rate is not high, but it *is* rising – by 1% per year. There are reports of higher incidences, among IVF babies, of premature births, stillbirths, low birth-weights and infant deaths. But rates are higher still in babies born to couples with infertility problems who eventually manage to conceive naturally.

One possible drawback of successful IVF is an increased possibility of multiple births, as more than one embryo is implanted. This increases the risk to the mother and babies.

3 The data in the table are based on NHS 2010 statistics. Estimate the *current* success rate for a woman under 35.

4 Describe three medical issues of IVF.

Ethical issues

Many people object to the technique and the treatment of embryos:

- One argument says that fertility treatments are just removing natural obstacles to fertility, but IVF is not natural. It's replacing the physical and emotional relationship of conceiving with a laboratory technique.
- Embryos that are not transplanted are eventually destroyed. Is a human embryo a mass of cells to be used, selected and discarded? Should we accept these losses as the price for success? Or does an embryo demand the *unconditional* moral respect given to any human being?

Modern microscopical and genetic techniques have enabled embryos to be screened for abnormalities. One serious concern is that couples with no fertility problems may use IVF as a technique to select a child, possibly using dubious selection criteria – a form of eugenics.

5 Discuss one ethical issue of IVF.

6 How could the screening of embryos be misused?

DID YOU KNOW?

Nobel Prize winner Professor, later Sir, Robert Edwards was aware that his work was controversial. After publication of a paper on producing embryos, he stopped research for 2 years while considering whether it was right to continue.

REMEMBER!

Use this topic to help you to evaluate the range of issues associated with IVF.

Homeostasis

Learning objectives:

- explain the importance of homeostasis in regulating internal conditions in the body
- recall that these control systems involve nervous or chemical responses
- describe how control systems involve receptors, coordination centres and effectors.

KEY WORDS

endocrine system
homeostasis
metabolic reactions
hormone
nervous system
receptor
target organ

Eve is running a marathon. While she is running, mechanisms in her body will try to keep internal conditions as constant as possible when external conditions change.

What changes in Eve's body?

As Eve is running, the rate at which her body cells respire increases. Her heart rate, breathing rate and breath volume increase during exercise to supply her muscles with more oxygenated blood. Her muscle cells break down glucose to release the energy she needs. Heat energy is also released.

The heat energy is carried around Eve's body by her blood. Normal body temperature is 37 °C, the optimum temperature for enzyme action and other **metabolic reactions**. These need to proceed at the appropriate rate.

Figure 3.28 Conditions in Eve's body will change during the marathon

Eve must control her body temperature within strict limits.

One way she does this, as she runs, is to sweat. But sweating will also affect the water level in her body. She takes in extra water from sports drinks during the race. The drinks also contain some glucose. Her stores of glycogen will decrease during the race and, as she suffers from fatigue at the end of the race, her blood glucose concentration falls.

1. **Why does body temperature need to be kept constant?**

2. **Name two other things that have to be controlled by the body.**

Homeostasis

Homeostasis is the regulation of internal conditions in the body. It is necessary to maintain the optimum conditions for body function. These internal conditions can change as a result of processes within the body and as external conditions change. Homeostasis is necessary to ensure that metabolic reactions in the body proceed at an appropriate rate.

The control systems involved in homeostasis are 'automatic' – they happen all the time or if conditions change – we don't have to think about taking any action. The nervous and endocrine systems work together to maintain, or at least try to maintain, a constant internal environment.

- the **nervous system** – uses electrical impulses to communicate
- the **endocrine system** – uses chemical molecules to communicate.

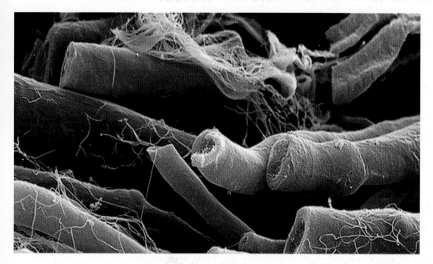

Figure 3.29 The long regions of nerve cells are bundled together as nerves

3 Write down a definition of homeostasis.

4 Which two body systems are responsible for homeostasis?

Control systems

All control systems in the body, whether nervous or endocrine, have the same pattern.

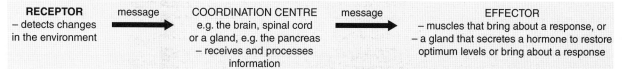

| RECEPTOR
– detects changes in the environment | message → | COORDINATION CENTRE
e.g. the brain, spinal cord or a gland, e.g. the pancreas
– receives and processes information | message → | EFFECTOR
– muscles that bring about a response, or
– a gland that secretes a hormone to restore optimum levels or bring about a response |

Figure 3.30 The components of the body systems that are responsible for homeostasis

The nervous system and endocrine system are different in nature but, in practice, the two systems interact with and regulate each other.

	Nervous system	Endocrine system
response	rapid and precise	slower but acts for longer
nature of message	nerve impulse – electrical	a **hormone** – chemical
action	carried in nerves to specific location, e.g. muscle	carried in blood to all organs, but affects the **target organ** only

5 How are changes detected by the body?

6 Compare and contrast the nervous system and the endocrine system.

DID YOU KNOW?

The squid has giant nerve cells, up to 1 mm in diameter. Study of these has been key to our understanding of how nerve impulses are transmitted.

REMEMBER!

Know the sequence of receptor → coordination centre → effector.

Controlling blood glucose

Learning objectives:

- recall that blood glucose is monitored and controlled by the pancreas
- explain how insulin controls the blood glucose level
- understand how insulin works with another hormone – glucagon – to control blood sugar level.

KEY WORDS

glucagon

insulin

Pao cannot produce enough of the hormone insulin to control her blood sugar. She has diabetes. She needs injections of insulin to stay alive.

Controlling blood sugar

The pancreas secretes enzymes that digest carbohydrates, proteins and lipids.

The pancreas also has another function. It produces hormones that control the concentration of our blood glucose. Glucose is needed by all cells for respiration to release energy. It is carried to cells in our blood. But its concentration must be strictly controlled within certain limits.

After a meal, the concentration of glucose in our blood increases. The hormone insulin causes glucose in the blood to move into our body's cells. Here, this glucose can be used for respiration. In cells of the liver and muscle, the glucose is also converted into glycogen so that it can be stored.

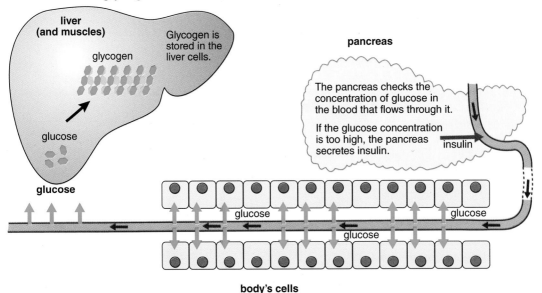

Figure 3.31 Insulin secreted into the bloodstream causes our body's cells to take up glucose

1 **Name a hormone that controls blood glucose.**

2 **What effect does this hormone have on our body's cells?**

Blood glucose concentration

Insulin restores the blood glucose concentration to its normal level. A little insulin is produced as you first smell or chew food. As you eat food and it's digested, the blood glucose level rises, which causes a surge in insulin. The insulin level reaches a peak, then gradually falls.

Figure 3.32 shows what happens to blood glucose on eating a meal and then with the effect of insulin.

3 Describe how a person's blood glucose concentration changes after a meal.

4 How long after having a meal did this person's blood glucose level start to fall?

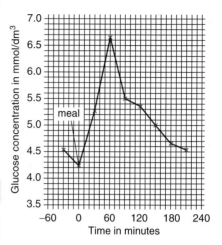

Figure 3.32 Blood glucose concentrations can rise to up to 10 mmol/dm³ after a meal or snack, before falling as insulin is secreted

HIGHER TIER ONLY

Glucagon

Blood glucose is normally regulated at about 4–7 mmol/dm³ of blood. To obtain this fine control, another hormone which is produced by the pancreas is also involved – **glucagon**.

Insulin and glucagon achieve this fine control by balancing glucose with carbohydrate stored as glycogen. This balance is maintained via a negative feedback cycle.

Insulin promotes the uptake of glucose by cells, and its conversion into glycogen in the liver and muscles.

Glucagon, which is secreted in response to low blood glucose concentration, promotes the conversion of stored glycogen into glucose, which is released into the bloodstream.

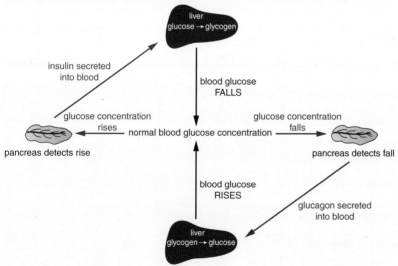

Figure 3.33 The control of blood glucose concentration by insulin and glucagon

5 What is normal concentration of blood glucose? Why is it important to maintain this level of blood glucose?

6 Explain how a constant level of blood glucose concentration is maintained.

DID YOU KNOW?

Until the discovery of insulin in 1921 by Frederick Banting and Charles Best, diabetes wasn't treatable.

Banting and Best carried out experiments on dogs and, later, themselves, before testing purified insulin on a teenager with diabetes in 1922.

REMEMBER!

Don't confuse the storage compound glycogen with the hormone glucagon.

Diabetes

Learning objectives:

- understand the causes of Type 1 and Type 2 diabetes
- compare Type 1 and Type 2 diabetes
- evaluate information on the relationship between obesity and diabetes, and make appropriate recommendations.

KEY WORDS
....
Type 1 diabetes
Type 2 diabetes

Diabetes, if poorly controlled, can damage circulation, nerves, and muscles in the feet and legs, that may then need amputating.

Type 1 diabetes

In **Type 1 diabetes**, the pancreas is unable to produce enough, or any, insulin.

Without it, the body's cells are unable to take up glucose. The blood glucose level becomes uncontrollably high, and glucose is excreted in the urine.

Without glucose, cells must use alternative energy sources. Fat and protein are used. The person will lose weight.

If the condition is not controlled, kidney failure and death will result.

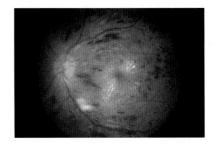

Figure 3.34 Diabetes causes damage to the retina of the eye. If left untreated, it may lead to blindness

1 **What is the cause of Type 1 diabetes?**

2 **Describe the sequence of events that will occur if a person has diabetes that isn't controlled.**

Type 2 diabetes

The main cause of **Type 2 diabetes** is that the body's cells lose their sensitivity – they no longer respond, or respond as effectively – to the insulin being produced.

One test for diabetes is the glucose tolerance test. After 8–12 hours of no eating or drinking, blood glucose is measured. The person is then given glucose and their blood retested 2 hours later. If the person's tolerance to glucose is lowered, the glucose will be above a certain level when retested.

3 **What is the cause of Type 2 diabetes?**

4 **Describe how the glucose tolerance test can help to diagnose Type 2 diabetes.**

5 **Use Figure 3.35 to describe the effects of insulin secretion in the three examples of people shown on the graph.**

What causes diabetes?

Only 10% of people with diabetes have Type 1. The cells that produce insulin have been destroyed. This can be an autoimmune condition – in which the immune system attacks the person's own body.

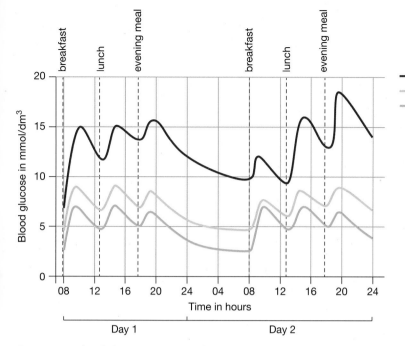

Figure 3.35 Blood glucose increases after a meal in a person with Type 2 diabetes and is not brought back to normal

Type 2 diabetes tends to cluster in families. But it's also associated with a Western lifestyle – one that includes high energy 'fast' food and an inactive life. There's a clear link with obesity.

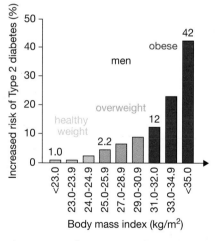

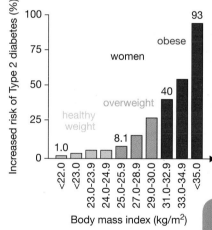

Figure 3.36 There is a correlation between increased risk of diabetes and obesity, as indicated by body mass index (BMI)

Type 2 diabetes is now emerging in young people. The first cases were in 2000, in children aged 9–16. Around three in ten children are now obese.

6 **Discuss links between genetics and the environment with Type 2 diabetes.**

7 **Compare the correlation between obesity and Type 2 diabetes in men and women.**

Diabetes recommendations

Learning objectives:

- explain how Type 1 and Type 2 diabetes are treated
- evaluate information on the relationship between obesity and diabetes, and make appropriate recommendations.

In 2014, 3.3 million people in the UK had been diagnosed with diabetes. Diabetic patients are currently costing the NHS about £10 billion a year. *That's £1 million per hour.*

Treatment

There's currently no cure for diabetes. **Type 1 diabetes** cannot be prevented. Patients with Type 1 diabetes *control* it with insulin injections.

For **Type 2 diabetes**, obesity accounts for 80–85% of the risk of developing it; so, it is preventable. The most important way of managing the condition is by modification of lifestyle. This involves exercise and diet. Carbohydrate-controlled diets are important for all people with diabetes. Foods that rapidly affect blood sugar level should be avoided.

1 **How can people with Type 1 diabetes control the condition?**

2 **What recommendations should be given to people with Type 2 diabetes?**

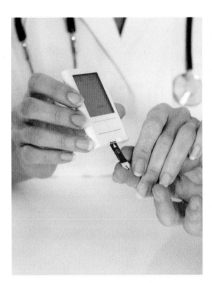

Figure 3.37 It's within our hands to control one type of diabetes – Type 2

Ethical considerations

Public guidelines and national programmes of weight management have been designed to help to prevent Type 2 diabetes.

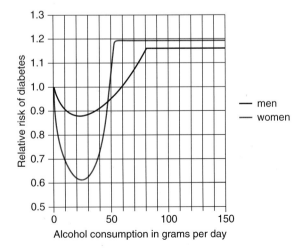

Figure 3.38 The intake of alcohol is one factor that affects the risk of developing diabetes. The risk is relative to that for people who have never drunk alcohol.

It's clear that a change in the lifestyle of many people would reduce the incidence of Type 2 diabetes. However, we can't *insist* that people do this. In any case, do we have a right to? And other factors, such as a person's ethnicity, affect the prevalence of the condition. Is it ethical for the authorities to make this type of distinction when giving guidance or making policy?

The sugary drinks and snacks produced by food manufacturers contribute to obesity. Do they have an ethical responsibility to manufacture healthier foods? And do restaurants and school canteens also have a responsibility to provide healthy food?

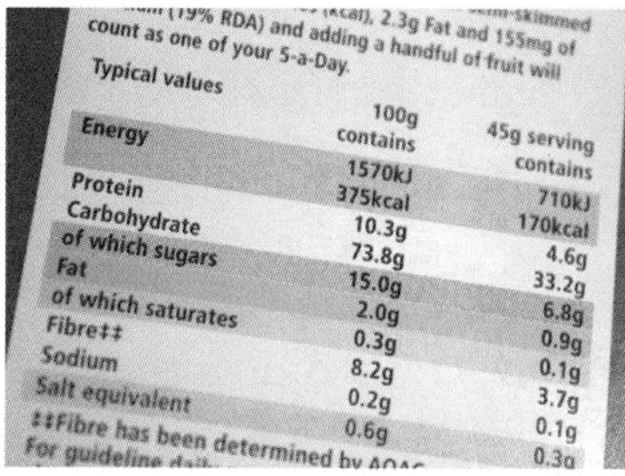

(3) **What measures could be taken to reduce Type 2 diabetes?**

(4) **What advice should be given to anyone who drinks alcohol about the risk of developing diabetes?**

Figure 3.39 A 'traffic light system' on food labels informs consumers of its nutritional content

Social considerations

A professor of food policy considers that some snacks, that are just sugar and flavouring, should not be termed 'foods' at all.

One possible solution is a 'sugar tax' – on the cost of sugary foods, or on food companies that continue to produce foods that contribute to poor health. But a tax might affect most the people who could least afford it. A Health Survey for England report found that the risk of diabetes was highest among the most deprived of the population.

> **REMEMBER!**
>
> Be prepared to make recommendations for control of diabetes, considering social and ethical issues and consequences.

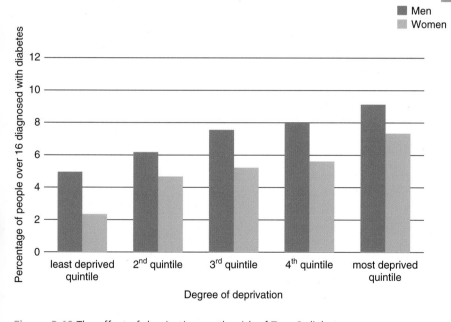

Figure 3.40 The effect of deprivation on the risk of Type 2 diabetes

(5) **Discuss what food manufacturers and caterers could do to reduce diabetes.**

(6) **Suggest explanations for the trend in the graph in Figure 3.40.**

MATHS SKILLS

The spread of scientific data

Learning objectives:

- be able to calculate means and ranges of data
- be able to use range bars on graphs
- understand how to estimate uncertainty from a set of measurements.

KEY WORDS

mean
estimate
range
repeatability
uncertainty

When results are collected, how they are spread out is important. It helps us to make judgements about the quality of the data we have collected. This is important when attempting to identify trends in data.

The spread of data

A person's blood glucose level was measured. The measurement was repeated three times on the same blood sample. The following values were obtained:

6.2 mmol/dm^3 6.1 mmol/dm^3 6.0 mmol/dm^3

If you carry out *any* experiment and then do it again, you often get a slightly different result. This may not be because you've used the equipment wrongly. In any measurement there are always random errors that cause measurements to be spread around the true value. This is why it's best to repeat measurements and find the mean.

A **mean** reduces the effect of random errors and gives you the best **estimate** of the true value.

The mean value of a set of measurements is the sum of the values divided by the number of values:

$$\text{mean} = \frac{6.2 + 6.1 + 6.0}{3} = 6.1 \text{ mmol glucose/dm}^3$$

The **range** is a measure of spread. It is calculated as the difference between the largest and smallest values

6.0 – 6.2 mmol/dm^3, or 0.2 mmol/dm^3.

The spread of data on graphs

Data that are consistent are said to be **repeatable**; the narrower the range of a set of data, the higher the degree of **repeatability**. We can be more confident of conclusions we draw from data with a high degree of repeatability.

1. **Another set of readings, using a blood sample from a different person, were:**

   9.6 mmol/dm^3
   9.5 mmol/dm^3
   9.8 mmol/dm^3

   What is the mean of these values?

2. **What is the range of this set of values?**

Estimating uncertainty in data

The best estimate of the true value of a quantity is the mean of repeated measurements. When calculating a mean, include all the values for data you have collected, unless you have any anomalous results (measurements that do not fit into the pattern of the other results). You could check if a result was an anomaly by repeating it. The more repeated readings you take, the better estimate you'll get of the true value. Three to five repeats are often suggested.

Table 4 shows the data collected on the effect of the hormone thyroxine on heart muscle tissue:

Time in minutes	Oxygen uptake, in cm^3 oxygen/g of heart muscle tissue					
	Experiment 1	Experiment 2	Experiment 3	Experiment 4	Experiment 5	Mean
10	3.3	3.9	3.6	3.8	3.9	3.7
20	7.8	8.3	8.0	7.8	8.1	8.0
30	11.7	11.2	11.5	11.6	11.5	11.5
40	14.6	14.8	15.1	14.9	14.6	14.8
50	17.7	17.2	17.5	17.6	17.5	17.5
60	26.7	26.0	26.5	27.4	26.9	

Table 4 The effect of thyroxine on heart muscle was measured by the oxygen uptake by the cell.

For the data collected after ten minutes:

The mean is 3.7 cm^3 oxygen/g of heart muscle.

The range *about* the *mean* gives an estimate of the level of **uncertainty** in the data collected

For this set of data, the upper limit is 3.9 cm^3/g; the lower limit 3.3 cm^3/g.

The range is 0.6 cm^3/g. So, according to our data, the true value could be up to 0.3 cm^3/g above the mean, or 0.3 cm^3/g below the mean.

Uncertainty is therefore calculated by:

$$uncertainty = \frac{upper\ limit\ of\ range - lower\ limit\ of\ range}{2}$$

So, as we have seen above, uncertainty $\frac{3.9 - 3.3}{2} = \frac{0.6}{2} = 0.3$

Uncertainty is written next to the mean. In this instance, it is:

3.7 cm^3/g ± 0.3 cm^3/g

Note that the units are written *both* after the mean and value of uncertainty. The value of uncertainty has the same units and number of decimal places as the measurements.

3 Calculate the mean for the set of data collected at 60 minutes.

4 Calculate the uncertainty in these measurements.

Check your progress

You should be able to:

describe the structure of the nervous system and location of the endocrine glands →	describe how neurones are adapted to their role and the transmission of an impulse in reflex arc →	explain how nerve impulses are transmitted across synapses
identify the reproductive hormones and their role in the development of secondary sexual characteristics →	describe the role of hormones in the menstrual cycle →	explain the roles and interactions of hormones in the menstrual cycle
identify different methods of contraception →	describe how different methods of contraception work →	evaluate the use of different methods of contraception
identify fertility drugs and *in-vitro* fertilisation as possible solutions to infertility →	describe the techniques involved in fertility treatments →	evaluate fertility treatments
recognise the need for homeostasis →	recall that the nervous and endocrine systems are responsible for homeostasis →	describe the components of body control systems and compare nervous and hormonal control
identify glucose concentration as a condition requiring control →	describe how these are controlled by the nervous and/or endocrine system →	explain how negative feedback is involved in homeostasis

Worked example

1 **Priya has an underactive thyroid gland. She does not secrete enough of the hormone thyroxine.**

Describe how secretion of thyroxine is controlled.

Secretion of thyroxine is controlled by the release of the hormone thyroid-stimulating hormone (TSH) by the pituitary gland. It is secreted when levels fall. If levels increase to above normal levels, secretion of TSH is shut down.

This is a good answer. The student has been careful to say that TSH is released by the pituitary gland, as it is not produced there.

The student has, however, omitted a key term to describe the process – negative feedback. An annotated diagram could have been used to illustrate the principle (see topic 3.4).

2 **Priya is given several injections of thyroxine over six days of treatment.**

The graph shows the effect of the hormone on her Basal Metabolic Rate (BMR).

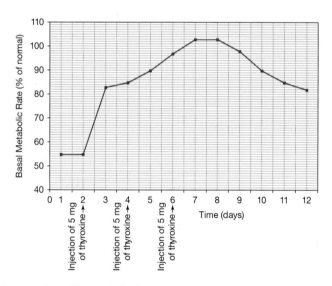

This is a part answer to the question.

The student has described the trend but could have illustrated the answer using data from the graph, e.g. after 2 days Priya's BMR increases from 55 to 83, after 4 days, … etc.

The student should have made clear that Priya's BMR attained its normal value after 6½ days, increased to slightly above normal (113%), and then, after eight days, decreased steadily.

Discuss the effect of the hormone injections.

The injection of the hormone after 2 days produces a sharp increase in Priya's metabolic rate. The next two injections only produce slight increases. After 8 days, her BMR starts to fall.

The student's answer is a description, but not really a discussion. It should have been stated that it is the role of thyroxine to act on the body's cells to increase their metabolism.

On the basis of the fall in BMR after 8 days, the student could have suggested that the treatment would be unlikely to be effective without repeated injections.

End of chapter questions

Getting started

1 The following diagram shows the location of the major endocrine glands.

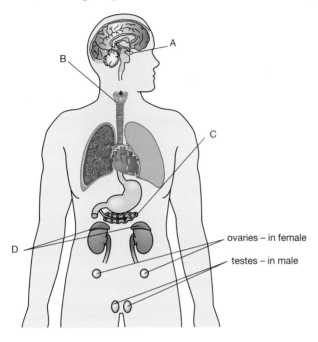

a Which letter labels the thyroid gland? **1 Mark**

b Which letter represents the gland where, if it produces insufficient hormone, diabetes results? **1 Mark**

c Which letter labels the pituitary gland? **1 Mark**

d Why is the pituitary gland described as the 'master gland'? **1 Mark**

2 How is glucose taken up into cells? **2 Marks**

3 Describe the recommendations a doctor would make to a patient diagnosed with Type 2 diabetes. **2 Marks**

4 The table gives some guidelines for the US army on recommended water intake and the type of light training during hot weather.

Temperature range in °C	Water intake in cm³/hour	Training time:rest time in minutes
25.5 – 27.9	500	60:0
28.0 – 29.4	500	60:0
29.5 – 29.9	750	60:0
31.0 – 31.9	750	60:0
>32.0	1000	50:10

Explain the recommendations fully. **2 Marks**

Going further

5 Compare the nervous and endocrine systems according to their:

- type of message
- speed of response.

`2 Marks`

6 Which hormone leads to oestrogen production by the ovaries?

`1 Mark`

7 Why does body temperature need to be kept constant?

`1 Mark`

8 Scientists have researched the relationship between the number of sugar-sweetened soft drinks consumed by a group of women and the relative risk of diabetes.

Their results are shown below.

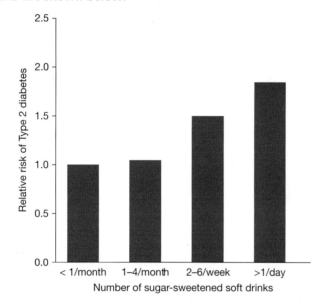

Explain what this suggests about the cause of Type 2 diabetes.

`2 Marks`

9 Explain how glucagon interacts with insulin to control blood sugar levels in the body.

`4 Marks`

More challenging

10 Give the name of a type of contraception that protects against sexually transmitted infections. `1 Mark`

11 What is a disadvantage of sterilisation as a method of contraception? `1 Mark`

12 Explain how hormonal methods of contraception work. `2 Marks`

13 The bar chart below records the success rate of *in-vitro fertilisation* (IVF) in Australia in 2013.

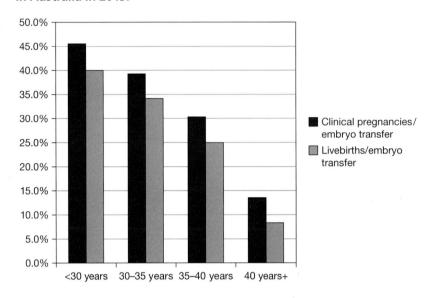

Describe the effect of the mother's age on the success rate of IVF. `2 Marks`

14 A mother places her finger on her baby daughter's palm. The baby grasps it. It is a reflex action.

Describe the process by which this reflex action occurs. You can use a diagram to help with your description. `4 Marks`

Most demanding

15 Explain how thyroxine is involved in a negative-feedback system to control body temperature.

2 Marks

16 This graph shows data relating to glucose concentration in the bloodstream.

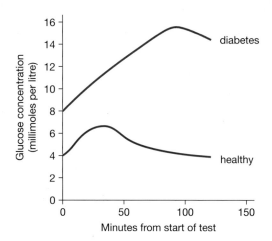

Explain what the graph shows about the difference in response of healthy and diabetic patients to increasing glucose levels.

4 Marks

17 Endometriosis is a condition where the type of cells that normally line the uterus are found 'trapped' in the pelvic area and lower tummy.

During the menstrual cycle the cells that have moved can react in the normal way to the hormones controlling menstruation.

This can cause a number of problems including abdominal pain and painful periods.

Using the information from the graph below, as well as your own knowledge, explain what happens to the cells that have moved and how doctors could treat the condition using sex hormones.

4 Marks

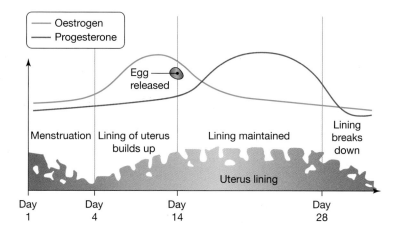

Total: 40 Marks

COMMUNITY LEVEL SYSTEMS

ALL ORGANSMS HAVE TO UNDERTAKE CERTAIN LIFE PROCESSES

- Plants use carbon dioxide from the atmosphere to photosynthesise and produce simple sugars, such as glucose.
- Plants and animals need to take in water from their habitat; water is needed for chemical reactions.
- Dead plant and animal material is broken down by microbes.

ORGANISMS IN AN ECOSYSTEM DEPEND ON EACH OTHER FOR SURVIVAL

- Food chains show how energy is transferred between living organisms.
- A change in the population of one organism affects other organisms in the food chain.
- Some organisms survive by living in or on another species.

ORGANISMS AFFECT AND ARE AFFECTED BY THE ENVIRONMENT

- Organisms can affect populations of other plants and animals in their habitat.
- Some animals feed on dead animal and plant matter.
- If one organism is removed from a food web, the whole food web can be affected.

IN THIS CHAPTER YOU WILL FIND OUT ABOUT:

HOW ARE MATERIALS IN A COMMUNITY CYCLED?

- Carbon is cycled from organisms to the atmosphere.
- Water is cycled to provide a constant source of fresh water.
- Microorganisms help in cycling materials through an ecosystem.
- We use the process of decay to produce compost.

WHAT FACTORS AFFECT LIVING ORGANISMS IN A HABITAT?

- There is a maximum size to food chains.
- Decomposers break down dead animal and plant matter.

HOW DO PLANTS AND ANIMALS WITHIN A COMMUNITY INTERACT?

- Changes in abiotic (non-living) factors affect a community.
- Changes in biotic (living) factors affect a community.
- Animals compete for limited resources in a habitat.

Cycling materials

KEY WORD

decomposers

Learning objectives:

- recall that many materials are recycled in nature
- explain the stages in the water cycle
- explain the role of microorganisms in decomposition.

All materials in the living world are recycled to provide the building blocks for future organisms.

Natural recycling

Water, carbon, oxygen and nitrogen are some of the materials that are recycled.

The water cycle provides fresh water for plants and animals on land. It describes how water moves on, above or just below the ground. Water molecules move between rivers, oceans and the atmosphere by precipitation, evaporation, transpiration and condensation.

Carbon is found in compounds that make up living organisms. Plants get carbon from air during photosynthesis. Animals get carbon from plants. The carbon in dead plants and animals is released by **decomposers** during the decay process.

Figure 4.1 Decomposers clean up the environment

1 **Give an example of a decomposer that breaks down carbon in dead animals and plants.**

2 **What is the role of decomposers?**

Explaining the water cycle

Water is continuously recycled by:

- precipitation: water droplets in clouds get bigger and heavier. they fall as rain, snow or sleet.
- evaporation: water evaporates as it is heated by the Sun's energy. water vapour is carried upwards in convection currents.
- transpiration: water vapour is released into the air through stomata in leaves.
- condensation: water vapour rises, cools and condenses back into water droplets that form clouds.

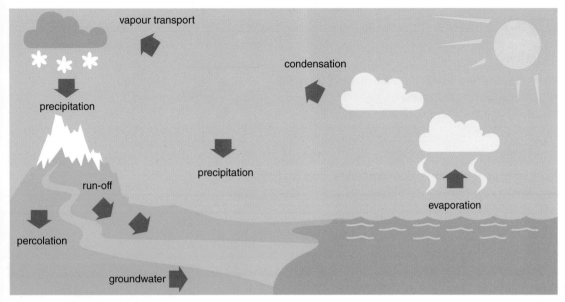

Figure 4.2 The water cycle

The water cycle is important because it circulates water that:

- maintains habitats
- maintains internal fluids and transport systems
- is needed for chemical reactions
- is a reactant in photosynthesis.

4.1

> **REMEMBER!**
>
> Learn the stages of the water cycle.

3 Explain the stages in the water cycle.

4 In what stage of the water cycle can water be:

    a a gas?
    b a solid?

Explaining decay

Worms, woodlice and maggots break down waste and dead material into smaller pieces for decomposers to digest.

Decomposers are microorganisms (bacteria and fungi). They break down the smaller pieces of dead material. Decomposers release waste carbon dioxide, water, heat and nutrients (that plants use).

5 Explain the role of microorganisms in cycling materials.

6 Why is the water cycle important?

Figure 4.3 Woodlice live on rotting wood and help to break it down for decomposers

Cycling carbon

KEY WORD

carbon cycle

Learning objectives:

- recall that plants take in carbon as carbon dioxide
- explain how carbon is recycled
- interpret a diagram of the carbon cycle.

Materials are cycled through ecosystems continually. As one process removes them, another releases them into the ecosystem again.

Looking at carbon

The amount of carbon on Earth is fixed. Most carbon is found combined with other elements, for example in fossil fuels and carbonate rocks. Carbon is also found dissolved in water in rivers, lakes and oceans. A small amount is in the air in carbon dioxide.

Producers use carbon dioxide to photosynthesise. The carbon is used to make carbohydrates, proteins, fats and DNA that form new biomass, which is eaten by consumers.

All organisms respire to release energy for cellular processes. They release waste carbon dioxide back into the environment, which is then used by plants.

1 **How do organisms cycle carbon dioxide?**

2 **Why is most carbon dioxide on Earth not available for photosynthesis?**

Figure 4.4 Burning fossil fuels releases carbon into the air

Explaining the carbon cycle

The atmosphere contains about 0.04% carbon dioxide, which is enough for every plant to produce biomass (food), by photosynthesis. This process transfers energy from the Sun into chemical energy.

When animals eat plants, they absorb carbon from them. Carbon passes along food chains, even when organisms die and decay. Energy is transferred along the food chain and to the environment at each trophic level.

Carbon dioxide is returned to the atmosphere by:

- Plants, animals and decomposers respiring:
     glucose + oxygen → carbon dioxide + water
- burning (combustion) of fossil fuels and wood:
     fossil fuel/wood + oxygen → carbon dioxide + water

The continual cycling of carbon is shown in Figure 4.5.

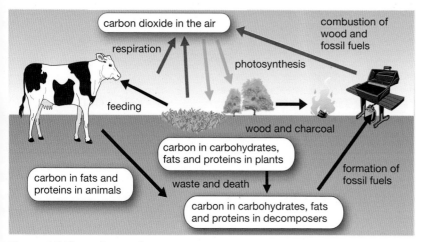

Figure 4.5 The carbon cycle

Burning fossil fuels and wood releases more carbon into the atmosphere. Scientists are unsure if the **carbon cycle** can still maintain the balance. Increased levels of carbon dioxide in the atmosphere cause global warming.

③ **Name two processes that release carbon dioxide.**

④ **Use Figure 4.5 to describe the carbon cycle.**

REMEMBER!

The carbon cycle returns carbon from organisms to the air for plants to use in photosynthesis.

Carbon stores

Shells of marine organisms contain carbonates. Corals and microscopic algae cover themselves with calcium carbonate. Shells of dead organisms fall to the sea floor. Over millions of years they are compressed to form limestone. Carbon dioxide reacts with rain to form carbonic acid. This acid rain weathers limestone and releases carbon dioxide.

Figure 4.6 What causes weathering of limestone statues?

Carbon dioxide can be absorbed by oceans and held in a carbon sink. During volcanic eruptions and forest fires, massive amounts of carbon dioxide are released into the atmosphere.

⑤ **Why is the carbon cycle important to all living organisms?**

⑥ **Explain the processes involved in the carbon cycle.**

DID YOU KNOW?

Between 1000 and 100 000 million metric tonnes of carbon pass through the carbon cycle every year.

KEY CONCEPT

Learning about ecosystems

Learning objectives:

* recall that many materials are recycled in nature
* explain the stages in the water and carbon cycles
* explain the role of microorganisms in decomposition.

Ecology looks at how organisms survive, how they relate to other organisms and their physical environment, and the features that make them successful in their habitat.

Ecosystems and biodiversity

Living organisms are affected by their environment. For example, if plants cannot absorb enough water for their needs, they wilt and may die. But plants also affect their environment. Plant roots hold soil particles together and stop the wind from blowing the soil away.

An ecosystem is defined as the interaction of a community (of living organisms) with the non-living parts of their environment. Ecosystems can be:

* natural, for example, oceans, lakes, puddles and the rainforest
* artificial, for example, fish farms and planted forests.

In every ecosystem there are different living organisms. Biodiversity is the range of different plant and animal species living in an ecosystem. The living organisms in an ecosystem are described as producers, consumers and decomposers. Decomposers break down dead organisms.

1 **What is an ecosystem?**

2 **Describe the biodiversity of the marine ecosystem in Figure 4.7.**

Exploring ecosystems

A population is the total number of one species in an ecosystem. A community is all the plants and animals living in an ecosystem. The place where a living organism lives in the ecosystem is its habitat.

Figure 4.7 A marine ecosystem

REMEMBER!

A community is all the different plants and animals in an ecosystem and a population is the total number of one species.

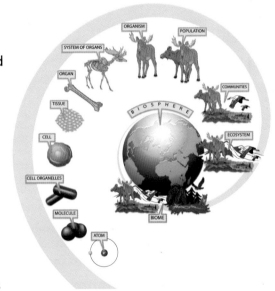

Figure 4.8 The levels of organisation in an ecosystem

High biodiversity is important in an ecosystem because:

- it allows a wide variation of food sources reducing the dependence of a species on a particular food source
- it provides us with food, medicines, the atmosphere and water.

Taking more of a species than we need from the environment (for example, by overhunting, deforestation and overfishing), and not replacing them, means that populations are not sustainable. This puts species in danger of extinction.

3 Explain the difference between

   a an ecosystem and a habitat
   b a community and a population.

4 Describe the ecosystems shown in Figures 4.7 and 4.9.

Ecosystem interactions

Some natural ecosystems have high biodiversity, such as the rainforest or shallow tropical coral reefs. They provide a wide variety of food throughout the year and shelter, above and below the ground or water. Other natural ecosystems, such as the Arctic tundra or deep-sea thermal vents, have low diversity, with species adapted to survive those extreme environments.

Artificial ecosystems have low biodiversity: the variety and number of plants is limited, so only a small number of animal species can survive.

All ecosystems are self supporting: all the requirements for living organisms to grow and survive are present. They do need an external energy source, which is usually the Sun.

All animals depend on plants for oxygen and food. Plants depend on animals for carbon dioxide, pollination and seed dispersal. This is called interdependence.

5 How is an ecosystem self supporting?

6 Explain how living organisms are interdependent.

7 Construct an argument putting forward reasons why we should protect areas of high biodiversity such as rainforests.

Figure 4.9 How are these ecosystems similar and different?

DID YOU KNOW?

Deserts are advancing and taking over fertile land. In Mali (West Africa) the Sahara advanced about 350 km in approximately 20 years.

Changing abiotic factors

Learning objectives:

- explain how abiotic and biotic factors can affect communities
- explain changes in the distribution of species in an ecosystem
- describe stable and unstable populations.

KEY WORDS

abiotic factor
biotic factor
distribution
competition

Living organisms are affected by many different factors as they grow and try to survive.

What are abiotic factors?

Many factors affect where an organism lives. **Abiotic factors** are physical (that is, non-living) conditions that affect the **distribution** of an organism. These factors include:

- temperature
- light intensity
- oxygen levels for animals that live in water
- carbon dioxide levels for plants
- moisture levels
- soil pH and mineral content for plants
- wind intensity and direction.

Biotic factors are caused by living organisms affecting other populations in their ecosystem. Biotic factors include:

- food availability
- new pathogens
- new predators
- **competition** between species.

Abiotic and biotic factors change over time. For example temperature varies daily, monthly, seasonally and over many years.

1 Choose one abiotic and one biotic factor. Explain how a lack of each factor would affect a plant and an animal.

2 Apart from blocking light, how else might trees affect the grass that grows beneath them?

Figure 4.10 What abiotic factors affect each of these organisms?

Looking at changes

The numbers and types of organisms can gradually change across a habitat. These changes are easy to see on the sea shore, where there are distinct zones of organisms due to changing tides (see Figure 4.11).

REMEMBER!

Abiotic factors are non-living. Biotic factors are living organisms. Changes in these factors cause changes in the distribution of organisms.

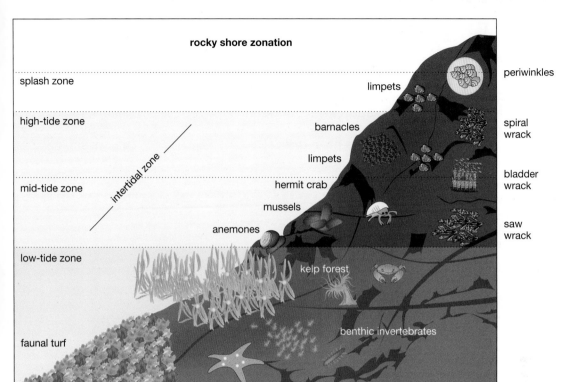

Figure 4.11 Zones on the sea shore

3 Name the abiotic factors that change on the sea shore. How can these factors affect distribution of seaweeds?

4 Suggest why limpets are found higher up the shore than anemones?

Looking at how distribution of species can change

Factors that affect the distribution of organisms do not work alone. Two or more factors can interact to form very different environments within a habitat.

Animals such as rabbits and sheep graze on plants. The amount of grazing affects the numbers of plant species found.

Little grazing allows a few plants to out-compete others. As grazing increases more plant species grow because dominant plants are controlled by the animals, allowing weaker species to grow. Only specially adapted plants can resist the effect of intensive grazing and survive.

A stable community is where the biotic and abiotic factors are in balance so that population sizes remain fairly constant.

5 What is a stable community?

6 Describe and explain the impact of grazing on plant species as shown in Figure 4.12.

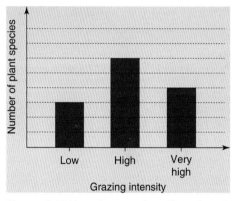

Figure 4.12 How does grazing affect plants?

DID YOU KNOW?

Plants are rare in deserts but after rain the distribution changes. Large numbers grow, flower and make seeds quickly while the water is available.

DID YOU KNOW?

Tropical rainforests and ancient oak woodlands are stable communities.

Investigating predator–prey relationships

Learning objectives:

- describe how changes in one population affect another
- explain interdependent relationships
- explain how predator–prey populations have cyclical changes.

KEY WORDS

consumer
producer
interdependence
mutualism
predators
parasitism
cycle

All species in a community depend on each other. This is interdependence.

A change in population size

Primary consumers (or herbivores) eat **producers** (plants). Primary consumers are eaten by secondary consumers (carnivores). Some animals are primary and secondary consumers, (they eat plants and animals). They are omnivores, for example, humans.

Consumers that hunt and eat other animals are **predators**. The animals that they eat are prey. If a predator kills all the prey it will die. In stable communities, the numbers of predators and prey stay in balance.

1 **Explain why humans are primary and secondary consumers.**

2 **Describe what happens to the predator population when:**

   a prey numbers are high

   b prey numbers are low.

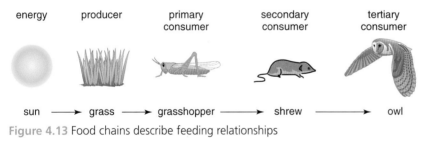

| energy | producer | primary consumer | secondary consumer | tertiary consumer |

sun ⟶ grass ⟶ grasshopper ⟶ shrew ⟶ owl

Figure 4.13 Food chains describe feeding relationships

Looking at more relationships

Mutualism is when two organisms live together. Each benefits from the relationship. Examples of mutualism are:

- Cleaner fish eat dead skin and parasites off large fish. They get food and avoid being eaten by larger fish.
- Leguminous plants, for example clover and peas, have colonies of nitrogen-fixing bacteria in nodules on their roots. The plants get nitrates from the bacteria. The bacteria get sugars for respiration from the plants.

Figure 4.14 What is special about the golden jellyfish?

- Zooxanthellae, live in the golden jellyfish tissues. They have a safe place to live and give the jellyfish some of the energy they need (from photosynthesis).

In **parasitism** one organism benefits but the other is harmed by the relationship. If parasites kill their host, they die too.

Examples of parasitism are:

- Tapeworms attach themselves to the intestinal wall of their human host and absorb nutrients. The person suffers from malnutrition.
- Holly leaf miners are flies. The larvae burrow into holly tree leaves to feed and leave pale trail marks on the leaf.

3 Explain the relationship between tapeworms and humans:

4 Explain what parasitism is.

Explaining population cycles

In predator–prey relationships the size of each population is dependent on the other. The Canadian lynx was the only predator in Canada. It eats mainly snowshoe hares. Data from a study between 1845 and 1937 were used to produce the graph showing their relationship (Figure 4.15). The snowshoe hare population rises and falls in a 10-year **cycle**. Because the lynx population is dependent on the snowshoe hare it also rises and falls, but it is out of phase (or lags behind) that of the hare population cycle by about 2 years. There is a clear pattern between the populations of the two animals, as shown in the graph.

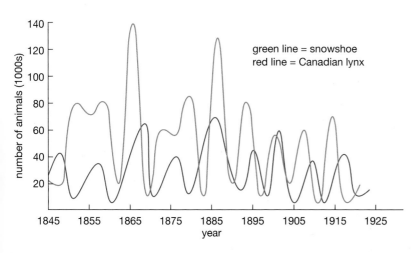

green line = snowshoe
red line = Canadian lynx

Figure 4.15 The size of the predator population follows the size of the prey population

> **REMEMBER!**
>
> The population cycle of the predator is out of phase with the cycle of the prey.

> **DID YOU KNOW?**
>
> Scientists study predator–prey cycles to decide if controlling predator populations can help to protect endangered species.

5 Explain how a large and a small predator population will each affect the number of prey.

6 Explain why the predator cycles and the prey cycles are out of phase with each other.

Competing for resources

Learning objectives:

- describe how competition impacts on populations
- explain why animals in the same habitat are in competition
- explain interspecific and intraspecific competition.

KEY WORDS

intraspecific competition
interspecific competition

If plants and animals are to survive, they need certain resources from their habitat. How do living things get what they need?

Why do organisms compete?

Organisms only survive if they have sufficient resources for their needs. They compete for the available resources in their habitat. Plants in a community may compete for:

- light
- space
- water
- mineral ions.

Animals often compete for:

- food and water
- mates
- territory.

Figure 4.16 What are these organisms competing for?

Animals and plants that get more of the resources are more successful than those that get less. Successful organisms are more likely to survive and reproduce so the size of their population is more likely to increase. For example, dolphins feed on several foods and are more likely to survive than dugongs that feed on just seagrass. Animals will travel to where food is available.

1 **How does competition affect the distribution and number of organisms?**

2 **Describe how organisms are competing in Figure 4.16.**

Competition

When species compete, if they are not perfectly matched one will eventually become more successful than the other. A less successful species may:

- do nothing and become extinct
- stay in its habitat but adopt new survival strategies
- move to another area looking for resources.

Humans are very successful organisms. We compete with animals and plants all over the world.

3 What happens when two organisms compete?

4 Explain why organisms in the same habitat are in competition.

Types of competition

There are two types of competition:

- **Interspecific competition** is competition between different species.
- **Intraspecific competition** is competition within one species. This may result in territorial behavior.

Intraspecific competition is often more significant than interspecific competition. For example, competition between grey squirrels is likely to affect the population of grey squirrels more than competition with red squirrels. Animals try to avoid competition with other species if they can.

When different species compete with one another for the same resources, it will affect the size and distribution of their populations.

Figure 4.17 How does a farmer compete with other organisms on their farmland?

COMMON MISCONCEPTION

Learn the difference between interspecific and intraspecific competition.

Figure 4.18 What types of competition are these?

5 Describe examples of interspecific and intraspecific competition.

6 Why is intraspecific competition often greater than interspecific competition?

DID YOU KNOW?

Competition for mates is intense, with many males putting a lot of effort into attracting females, by fighting or by having 'displays'.

MATHS SKILLS

Using graphs to show relationships

Learning objectives:

- to recognise direct proportionality in a graph
- to calculate reaction rates in linear graphs
- to use the gradient of a graph to calculate the rate.

KEY WORDS

directly
proportional
gradient
intercept
linear
rate

It is sometimes useful to see how one variable relates to another, such as how much we exercise affects how fit we are. A graph is a good way of displaying the relationship.

Types of graph

When we plot the results from investigations we sometimes get graphs in which the points are approximately in a straight line, so we can draw a straight line of best fit. Even if the line does not go through the origin (0,0), it has a strong correlation that approximates a linear relationship.

If this straight line passes through the origin (0,0), the relationship is **directly proportional**. This means that if one variable doubles in size, the other variable does too. The point where the line crosses the y-axis is called the **intercept**.

1. Where does the line intercept the *y*-axis in the linear graph in Figure 4.19?

2. Where is the *y*-intercept for any line showing direct proportionality?

Using a graph to work out the rate at which something is happening

Sometimes when we use data to plot a graph, one variable is a measurement of time. This is common in biology as we are often interested in the **rate** at which something is happening.

Look at this graph showing how puppies gain weight over the first couple of years. They all gain weight more quickly when they are young and the weight gain levels off when they become adults. The rate is shown by the **gradient**. The gradient is the steepness of the line. In this case, the steeper the gradient the more weight the dogs are gaining each month. The graph also shows that the rate is greater for larger breeds. Knowing the gradient is useful.

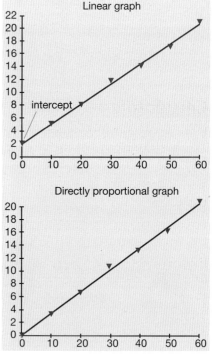

Figure 4.19 What is the difference between these two graphs?

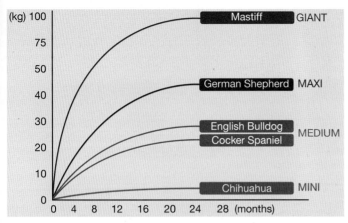

Figure 4.20 Rate of growth of different dog breeds

3 **a** How much weight will a German shepherd puppy put on in the first 4 months?
b On average, what would this be every month? (Your answer will be in kg/month – this is the rate)
c How much weight will the same dog add in the second 4 months?
d What is the average rate during this period?

4 Why might dog breeders find a graph like this useful?

5 Why might people choosing a breed of dog find this graph useful?

DID YOU KNOW?

The independent variable always goes on the x-axis, so that's where time goes, as we can't control how quickly it passes.

Calculating gradients

Linear relationships, as we've seen, have straight lines. The gradient is constant. It means the rate of increase (or decrease) isn't changing over time.

The gradient is the change in the y-values divided by the change in the x-values.

For example, if we heat water, the longer we heat it for, the hotter it gets, up to 100 °C.

In this experiment, from the end of the first minute to the end of the third minute the temperature went from 60 °C to 80 °C.

The change in y-values (the temperature) was 80 − 60 = 20 and the change in x-values (the time) was 3 − 1 = 2. The gradient of the graph can be dividing 20 by 2, which is 10, indicating that the rate at which the water is heated is 10 °C per minute i.e. for every minute on the graph, the temperature rises by 10 °C.

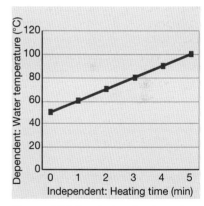

Figure 4.21 Graph showing how the temperature of water changes as it is heated

6 Look at the graph from the end of the third minute to the end of the fifth minute:
a What is the change in y-values?
b What is the change in x-values?
c What is the rate?

7 Why would this trend not continue after the fifth minute?

KEY INFORMATION

Straight-line graphs show a linear relationship. If the line goes through the origin, (0,0), it is also directly proportional.

Check your progress

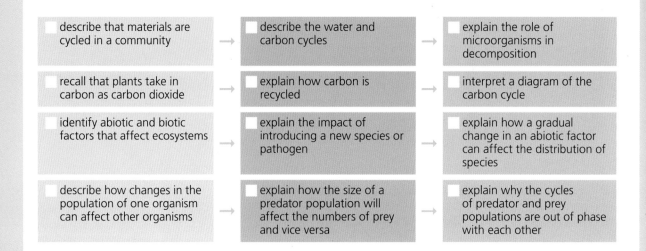

describe that materials are cycled in a community → describe the water and carbon cycles → explain the role of microorganisms in decomposition

recall that plants take in carbon as carbon dioxide → explain how carbon is recycled → interpret a diagram of the carbon cycle

identify abiotic and biotic factors that affect ecosystems → explain the impact of introducing a new species or pathogen → explain how a gradual change in an abiotic factor can affect the distribution of species

describe how changes in the population of one organism can affect other organisms → explain how the size of a predator population will affect the numbers of prey and vice versa → explain why the cycles of predator and prey populations are out of phase with each other

Worked example

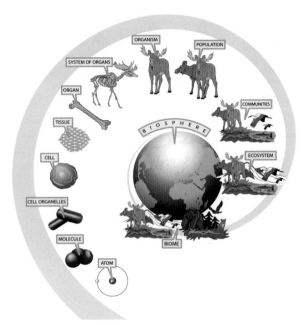

The diagram shows levels of organisation found within an ecosystem.

1 **What is meant by the term 'population'?**

It means how many organisms there are in an area.

This answer is correct but it could be improved by stating that a population is the total number of one species in an ecosystem.

2 **Name two abiotic factors that would affect the distribution of organisms in the ecosystem shown in the figure.**

Light and food

Light is correct but availability of food is a biotic (living) factor so would not get a mark. Other abiotic factors that would gain a mark are oxygen levels in the water and temperature.

3 **Use the diagram and your own knowledge to explain the difference between a community and an ecosystem.**

A community refers to all the plants and animals living within an ecosystem whereas an ecosystem is all the plants and animals and the physical environment around them

This is a correct answer and would gain two marks.

End of chapter questions

Getting started

1 What group of organisms break down dead organisms? `1 Mark`

2 Why can badgers be primary and secondary consumers? `2 Mark`

3 Give two factors that speed up decay. `2 Marks`

4 Explain why bluebells grow before the trees in a wood are in leaf. `2 Marks`

5 In what stage of the water cycle can water be:

   a a gas? `1 Mark`

   b a solid? `1 Mark`

6 What is an apex predator? `1 Mark`

Going further

7 What is a stable community? `1 Mark`

8 What is interdependence? `1 Mark`

9 The graph shows the relative population sizes of foxes and rabbits over several breeding seasons.

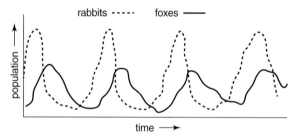

Describe the pattern in the data and explain how it affects the populations of foxes and rabbits. `2 Marks`

10 List three abiotic factors that might affect the distribution of species in a pond. `2 Marks`

11 For an ecosystem to be stable and self-supporting, it must have an external source of energy which is usually the Sun or an artificial light source.

Explain why this is. `4 Marks`

More challenging

12 Describe what is meant by the term 'producer'. `1 Mark`

13 Name a process that releases carbon dioxide into the air. `1 Mark`

14 Explain why the water cycle is important to living organisms. `2 Marks`

15 Why do decomposers need moist conditions to feed? `2 Marks`

16 Draw a labelled diagram to show how carbon is recycled in nature. `4 Marks`

Most demanding

17 Choose one abiotic and one biotic factor. Explain how a lack of each factor would affect a plant and an animal. `2 Marks`

18 Use the graph to explain why bluebells flower in April and May.

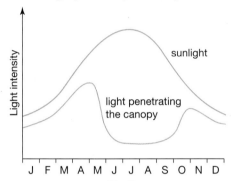

`4 Marks`

19 Explain the two different types of competition using named examples in your description for each type. `4 Marks`

`Total: 40 Marks`

GENES, INHERITANCE AND SELECTION

OUR CHARACTERISTICS ARE INHERITED AND PASSED ON

- Passing on genetic information is called heredity.
- Sexual reproduction in humans leads to similarities and variation between individuals.

THERE ARE DIFFERENCES BETWEEN AND WITHIN SPECIES

- Variation between individuals is continuous or discontinuous.
- Variation can be measured and the data represented graphically.
- Hereditary material is passed from one generation to the next through the genetic material, DNA.

VARIATION BETWEEN SPECIES CAN DRIVE NATURAL SELECTION

- Variation between individuals of the same species means that some organisms compete more successfully than others.
- When an animal or plant is more successful it passes more of its genes to the next generation. Less successful organisms will not pass on as many genes. This is natural selection.
- Genetics allows us to understand the inheritance of certain characteristics in humans and many other organisms.

CHANGES IN THE ENVIRONMENT CAN LEAD TO EXTINCTION

- Some individuals within a species, and some species, are less well adapted than others.
- Changes in the environment can lead to the extinction of those individuals that are less well adapted.
- Gene banks can be used to preserve hereditary material.

IN THIS CHAPTER YOU WILL FIND OUT ABOUT:

PRODUCTION OF SEX CELLS FOR REPRODUCTION

- During sexual reproduction, a cell divides by meiosis to produce four gametes, each with half the number of chromosomes.
- Meiosis ensures that we keep our chromosome number constant – 46 or 23 pairs – in each generation.
- Meiosis also produces gametes that are genetically unique, leading to variation between individuals.

CHARACTERISTICS ARE INHERITED FROM ONE GENERATION TO THE NEXT

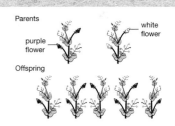

- Genetics allows us to understand the inheritance of certain characteristics in humans and in many other organisms.
- We can use genetic terms and predict the outcome of crosses.

VARIATION AND NATURAL SELECTION LEAD TO THE EVOLUTION OF NEW SPECIES

- Variation has genetic and environmental causes.
- Mutation, sexual reproduction and meiosis are processes that lead to variation.
- Variation results in differences in phenotypes and genotypes in a population.
- In any population, there is a struggle for existence.
- Because of variation, some individuals are better suited to the environment, so they reproduce and pass on their genes to the next generation, a process called natural selection.
- Natural selection acts on populations, and if the environment changes a new species may result, by the processes of evolution and speciation.
- The evidence for natural selection and evolution comes from observations of current organisms, the fossil record and biochemistry, including DNA.
- During the 100 years that followed the theory, many scientists pieced together the connection between inheritance, genetics, evolution, genes and the genetic code.
- Fossils are used to create evolutionary trees to help understand the relationships between groups of organisms.

THE CAUSES OF EXTINCTIONS

- Extinction arises from changes in the environment, diseases and the introduction of new species that are predators or out-compete existing species.
- The five mass extinctions to date are thought to have been caused by climate change, or a catastrophic event such as a volcanic eruption or a collision with an asteroid.

Genetics

Learning objectives:

- understand and be able to use genetics terms, such as gamete, chromosome, gene, dominant, recessive, genotype, phenotype, homozygous and heterozygous
- know that some human conditions are caused by a recessive allele.

Jenny has cystic fibrosis. She needs physiotherapy to keep her lungs working. Fifty years ago, children with cystic fibrosis rarely lived beyond the age of 5. Today, life expectancy is over 40.

Figure 5.1 Researchers are working with gene and stem-cell therapies to find a possible cure for cystic fibrosis

Cystic fibrosis is a gene disorder

Cystic fibrosis is an example of an inherited disorder. Sufferers produce mucus that is thicker and stickier than normal, making it difficult to breathe.

Cystic fibrosis is linked to a gene on chromosome 7. It codes for a protein called CFTR. The protein controls the movement of water and ions in and out of certain cells, including those of the tissue that lines the lungs.

Each gene can have more than one form, called **alleles**. Alleles are genetic variants. Cystic fibrosis occurs when alleles of the *CFTR* gene are defective.

A *CFTR* allele is present on each of the chromosomes of chromosome pair 7.

If a person has one normal and one defective allele, the presence of the normal allele means that they still produce CFTR protein. They do *not* have cystic fibrosis. But they are a carrier; they could pass on the allele to their children. A person with two defective alleles has cystic fibrosis.

1. What are different forms of a gene called?

2. In Figure 5.2, explain why a person with each combination that is shown has, or does not have, cystic fibrosis.

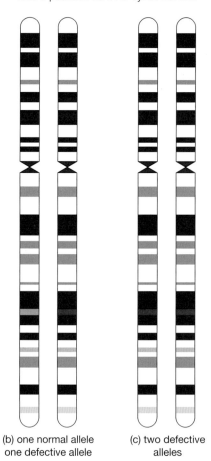

(a) two normal alleles
(b) one normal allele one defective allele
(c) two defective alleles

Figure 5.2 Three combinations of alleles of the *CFTR* gene are possible

An organism's genetics

Many characteristics are controlled by a single gene. Examples are red-green colour blindness in humans and fur colour in mice. Each gene has different forms called alleles. Alleles can be **dominant** or **recessive**. In Figure 5.2b, the person does not have cystic fibrosis. Both alleles are present in the gene pair; the dominant allele is expressed. The recessive characteristic is only shown if there are two recessive alleles.

When describing the genetics of an organism, we give the alleles letters. A dominant allele is given a capital letter; a recessive allele is written in lower case. If we use the letter 'C' for the *CFTR* gene, the combinations of alleles in Figure 5.2 are CC, Cc and cc.

The alleles present for a particular gene make up the organism's **genotype**. How the gene is expressed (the appearance or characteristics of an organism) is the **phenotype**.

When an organism has two alleles of the same type – either dominant or recessive – they are said to be **homozygous** for that characteristic. If the alleles are different, they are described as **heterozygous**.

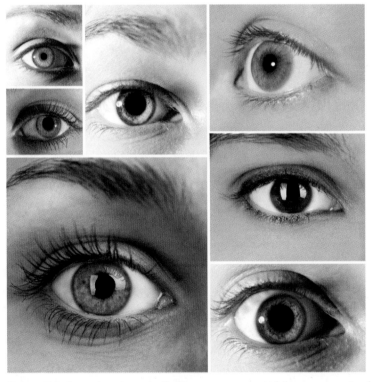

Figure 5.3 Eye colour is controlled by many genes. While we can write down the phenotype, it's not possible to write a genotype

REMEMBER!

It is important that you know, understand and can use the genetics terms on these pages.

DID YOU KNOW?

Height and skin colour are polygenic – they are controlled by several genes. These characteristics show a continuous gradation across populations.

③ **What is meant by a dominant allele?**

④ **Explain the difference between an organism's genotype and phenotype.**

⑤ **'A dominant trait is most likely to be found in the population.' Discuss this statement. Do you agree with it? Justify your answer.**

DNA and genes

Learning objectives:

- describe the genome as the entire genetic material of an organism
- describe a gene as a small section of DNA that codes for a protein.

DNA, deoxyribonucleic acid, the molecule that carries our inheritance, was first isolated by the Swiss scientist, Friedrich Miescher, from white blood cells in 1869. He called it nuclein, as it was from the cells' nuclei.

The genome of an organism

The **genome** of an organism is the entire genetic material of that organism.

The genetic information is carried by a chemical called deoxyribonucleic acid (DNA). DNA is a polymer of nucleotides made up of two strands that form a double helix. The DNA is found within structures called **chromosomes**.

A **gene** is a short section of DNA that contains the instructions for one characteristic of an organism. Genes control all our inherited characteristics. These characteristics range from things like our blood group, hair colour and eye colour, down to the minutest detail of our cells.

Genes work by providing the code for the production of a particular protein.

Figure 5.4 An illustration of DNA. The molecule consists of two strands and is like a ladder that has been gently twisted

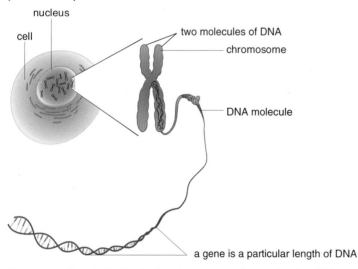

Figure 5.5 Each half of a double chromosome is a molecule of DNA

1. Describe the shape of a molecule of DNA.

2. What is a gene?

Genes

Our genes are distributed across our chromosomes.

The chromosomes in a chromosome pair have the same types of genes, in the same order, along their length.

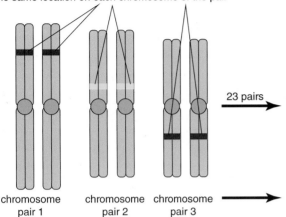

the genes controlling a certain characteristic are at the same location on each chromosome of the pair

23 pairs

chromosome pair 1   chromosome pair 2   chromosome pair 3

Figure 5.6 The chromosomes of an organism contain our genes. One gene pair per chromosome is shown here. In reality, there are thousands on each chromosome

Every person has two copies of each gene – one inherited from each parent.

3 Where are genes located on a chromosome pair?

4 How many copies of a gene does an organism have?

Figure 5.7 The female jumper ant has just one pair of chromosomes; the male just one chromosome. One species of fern has over a thousand

DNA, genes and chromosomes

Human cells have 46 chromosomes. This number varies from one organism to another. It's the chromosomes contained within a cell and their genetic make-up that determine the type of organism.

The DNA has proteins associated with it that help it to condense into chromosomes.

Certain other parts of the cell also contain DNA – for example, mitochondria.

The plasmids of bacteria are made from DNA. They're not part of the chromosome, so do not contribute to the running of the cell, but they have genes that help the survival of the organism, for instance, in antibiotic resistance.

5 Name two structures of human cells that contain DNA.

6 Give an advantage to a bacterium of having one or more plasmids.

7 Why do plasmids not contribute to the species of the bacterium?

8 What is the difference between a gene, DNA and a chromosome?

COMMON MISCONCEPTIONS

Don't think that the amount of DNA or number of genes in a cell is linked with complexity of an organism.

DID YOU KNOW?

The marbled lungfish has more than 40 times the amount of DNA per cell as humans. And the number of protein-coding genes of a chicken is similar to that of a human.

Meiosis

Learning objectives:

- explain how meiosis halves the number of chromosomes for gamete production
- explain how fertilisation restores the chromosome number
- understand that the four gametes produced by meiosis are genetically different
- describe sex determination in humans, using a genetic cross.

You already know that each cell in the human body has 46 chromosomes. How is this number kept at 46 during sex-cell production and fertilisation?

Meiosis is a reduction division

Mitosis is the type of cell division used during growth, or when old or damaged cells need replacing.

But another form of cell division takes place when sex cells are produced in the ovaries and testes in animals, and in the carpels and stamens of plants.

During meiotic cell division:

- four **gametes** are produced from one parent cell
- each gamete has half the number of chromosomes of the parent cell (in humans, that's 23 chromosomes instead of 23 pairs).

1 How many gametes are produced from one cell during meiosis?

2 How many chromosomes does a gamete have?

What happens during meiosis?

In meiosis, the DNA of each chromosome is copied, just as in mitosis. But it then divides *twice*, so the chromosome number is *halved*.

So, in mitosis, there is one replication of DNA and one division, but in meiosis, there is one replication of DNA and two divisions.

DID YOU KNOW?

In mammals, Y-chromosomes house the gene that controls gender. Both the X- and Y-chromosomes arose from autosomes around 200 million years ago. During evolution, the Y-chromosome has lost most of its genes.

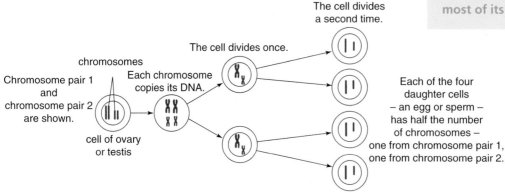

Figure 5.8 An overview of meiosis

When the gametes fuse at fertilisation, the normal number of chromosomes is restored. The zygote then divides by mitosis and the number of cells increases. As the embryo develops cells begin to differentiate.

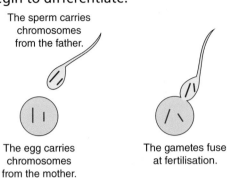

The sperm carries chromosomes from the father.

The egg carries chromosomes from the mother.

The gametes fuse at fertilisation.

In the zygote, the chromosome pairs are restored.

Chromosomes 1 and 2 are shown.

Figure 5.9 Fertilisation restores the chromosome number

Cells that have chromosome pairs are called **diploid**.

Those that have just a single chromosome from each pair are called **haploid**.

Haploid gametes are produced by meiosis. Fertilisation restores the diploid state. One of each chromosome pair is inherited from our mother; the other from our father. But for each chromosome pair, it's a completely random event as to which of these goes into the egg or sperm.

3 How many replications of DNA occur in meiosis?

4 How many divisions occur in meiosis?

All gametes are genetically different Another thing that makes each gamete unique is that there's some exchange of genetic material during meiosis. This contributes to **genetic variation**. When an egg or sperm is produced, it doesn't *just* receive *unchanged* chromosomes from the parent.

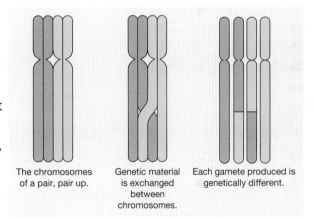

The chromosomes of a pair, pair up.

Genetic material is exchanged between chromosomes.

Each gamete produced is genetically different.

Figure 5.10 The set of chromosomes in a gamete is unique

What determines our sex?

Each gamete also contains one of the two sex chromosomes from pair 23. These carry the genes for **sex determination**. Female humans have two X-shaped chromosomes (XX). Males have an X- and a Y-shaped chromosome (XY).

All the eggs produced by the mother contain **X-chromosomes**. Half of the father's sperm contain the X-chromosome; half the **Y-chromosome**.

5 Explain how meiosis leads to genetic variation.

6 In the UK, the proportion of live births was in the proportion of 1.05 males : 1.00 females. Suggest why it isn't exactly 1 : 1.

		Mother (XX) gametes	
		X	X
Father (XY) gametes	X	XX female	XX female
	Y	XY male	XY male

Figure 5.11 In theory, 50% of live-born children are female; 50% male

Genetic crosses

KEY WORD

Punnett square

Learning objectives:

* use the terms dominant, recessive, genotype, phenotype, homozygous and heterozygous
* know that some human conditions, such as cystic fibrosis, are caused by a recessive allele
* complete or construct a Punnett square to predict the outcome of a genetic cross.

Cystic fibrosis has been recorded since the sixteenth century. One symptom is production of sweat with an increased salt content.

In the 1980s, the gene for cystic fibrosis was mapped to chromosome 7. We can now diagnose cystic fibrosis quickly and predict its inheritance.

Genetic crosses

Let's take an example where a mother with cystic fibrosis has children with a normal father.

The mother's genotype must be cc, as she has the condition. The father could be CC or Cc. Let's start by assuming he's CC.

All the sperm produced by the father will be C. The eggs produced by the mother will be c. So at fertilisation, *all* the children will be Cc. Their phenotypes will be normal.

① **What is the genotype of a person who is homozygous dominant for a gene, B?**

② **What types of gametes will the person produce?**

Genetic diagrams

Let's now assume the father is Cc – he's normal but a carrier. This time, the cross is a little more complicated. It's best to display the cross in a diagram called a **Punnett square** to show the possible outcomes. See Figure 5.13.

Figure 5.17 shows the possibilities when a couple are *both* carriers of the cystic fibrosis allele. We know that as carriers, they both have Cc genotypes. They will produce both C- and c-carrying gametes.

The ratio of normal children to children with cystic fibrosis would be 3:1. The ratio gives an *overall* probability, but of course which allele is in the sperm and which allele is in the egg will be completely random.

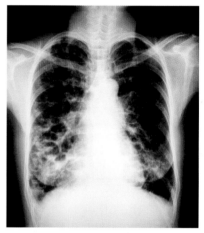

Figure 5.12 This X-ray shows a there is a widening of the airways and a build-up of mucus in the lungs

		Mother (cc) gametes	
		c	c
Father (Cc) gametes	C	Cc normal (but a carrier)	Cc normal (but a carrier)
	c	cc cystic fibrosis	cc cystic fibrosis

Figure 5.13 There is a 50%, or 1 in 2, chance that a child will be born with cystic fibrosis

3 The ability to taste a chemical called PTC is controlled by a single gene that codes for a taste receptor on the tongue. A man who is heterozygous for gene T has children with a woman who is homozygous recessive for the gene. Draw a Punnett square, showing the possible genotypes of the children.

4 For an eye colour gene in parrots, the brown allele is dominant to red.
Draw a Punnett square the genotypes and phenotypes of a mating between two heterozygous parrots.

		Mother (cc) gametes	
		C	c
Father (Cc) gametes	C	CC normal	Cc normal (but a carrier)
	c	Cc normal (but a carrier)	cc cystic fibrosis

Figure 5.14 The probability of the couple having a child with cystic fibrosis is 1 in 4

Family-tree diagrams

In genetics, we can use a genetic **family tree** to show how a condition is passed down through a family.

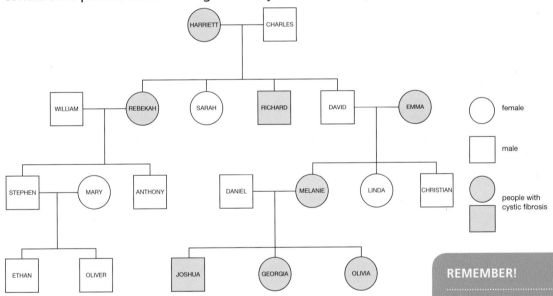

○ female

□ male

⬤ people with cystic fibrosis (grey circle)

▪ (grey square)

Figure 5.15 An example of the inheritance of cystic fibrosis in a family

Some of the genotypes of the family in Figure 5.15 can be worked out.

We know that Harriett, and the other members of the family affected by cystic fibrosis, *must* be cc. Anyone unaffected will either CC or Cc. Charles *must* be Cc, because both Rebekah and Richard have cystic fibrosis. If Charles were CC, none of his children could possibly have the condition.

5 What can we say about William's genotype?

6 Identify the people in the family tree who are certain to be carriers.

REMEMBER!

You need to be able to interpret Punnett square diagrams, and to construct them if working at a higher level. For most of the questions you'll encounter, you'll find a 1:1 ratio, a 3:1 ratio, or – if crossing a homozygous dominant individual with a homozygous recessive – the offspring will all have the dominant phenotype.

KEY CONCEPT

Genetics is simple – or is it?

Learning objectives:

- explain how certain characteristics are controlled by a single gene
- understand many characteristics are the result of multiple genes interacting
- describe the search for genes that are linked to disease.

KEY WORDS

complex diseases
Mendelian
 inheritance

Gene disorders caused by dominant alleles

Most, but not all, inherited conditions are caused by recessive alleles. Some are the result of a defective dominant allele.

In these instances, the presence of one allele will cause the characteristic to be seen in the phenotype.

Figure 5.16 A genetic counsellor can advise on the risks of passing on a genetic disorder

1 Write down the three possible genotypes and phenotypes for the polydactyly gene.

2 Draw a Punnett cross between a father who is heterozygous for polydactyly and homozygous recessive mother.

Genomics and inherited disease

Observations of populations, and more recently, investigations using genomics have confirmed that most of our characteristics are controlled by not just one gene, but usually by many.

The same is true of genetic diseases. Single-gene disorders, such as cystic fibrosis, follow what is known as **Mendelian inheritance**. But these single-gene disorders are rare.

Most diseases are referred to as **complex diseases**. These include heart disease, diabetes and obesity. They result from the interaction of many genes, non-coding regions of the genome and environmental factors.

Complex diseases do cluster in families but they have no clear pattern of inheritance, because multiple genes are involved.

3 Give two examples of a single-gene disorder.

4 Give two examples of a disease linked to multiple genes.

Studying pathogen genomes

Scientists are also analysing the genomes of human pathogens, to help us understand and control infectious disease. We now have complete genomes of many, including MRSA.

Figure 5.17 Research doesn't just focus on the *human* genome; 84% of the genes known to cause human disease have a zebrafish equivalent

One day, it will be possible to analyse the genomes of pathogens and quickly select the best treatment, according to genomics of the strain of bacterium.

Figure 5.18 A nurse with an MRSA patient

5 Describe how MRSA has arisen.

6 How could analysis of the MRSA genome help in the control of an outbreak?

7 Write a scientific argument to say why it is important for our government to invest money into researching pathogen genomes.

MATHS SKILLS

Fractions, ratio, proportion and probability

Learning objectives:

- understand and use fractions and percentages
- understand and use ratio and proportion
- understand and use probability when predicting the outcomes of genetic crosses.

KEY WORDS

fraction
percentage
probability
proportion
ratio

Predicting the outcome of genetic crosses quantitatively matters in understanding the inheritance of human characteristics, or of genetic diseases.

Fractions and percentages

In topics 5.4 and 5.5, you looked at the inheritance of cystic fibrosis.

$$\text{The fraction of affected children} = \frac{\text{the number of affected children}}{\text{the total number of children shown}} = \frac{1}{4}$$

			mother	
			Cc	
			C	c
father	Cc	C	CC normal	Cc carrier
		c	Cc carrier	cc cystic fibrosis

Figure 5.19 Punnett square showing the cross between two carriers of cystic fibrosis.

A quarter are born with cystic fibrosis.

When comparing fractions with different denominators it is helpful to convert them to a **percentage**.

$$\text{The percentage of affected children} = \frac{1}{4} \times 100 = 25\%$$

If we know the total number in a population, we can calculate the number in a fraction (or percentage) of that population.

In the UK, 48%, or 48/100 people, in a 2014 survey, had blue eyes. So, in the UK population of 63 500 000 in 2014:

$$\text{The number of people in the UK with blue eyes} = \frac{48}{100} \times 63\,500\,000 = 30\,480\,000$$

1 **In a cross between a heterozygous and a homozygous recessive individual for a recessive disorder, what fraction of the offspring would be expected to have the condition?**

2 **Three alleles of the MC1R gene are involved in the inheritance of red hair. One of them, R160W, is found in 9% of the UK population. What number of people in the UK have this allele?**

DID YOU KNOW?

In the early 1900s, a mathematical law for calculating the frequency of a genotype in a population of organisms was developed by Godfrey H. Hardy.

REMEMBER!

Geneticists can only work with probabilities and not certainties.

Ratio and proportion

In the Punnett square in Figure 5.21, there are three normal children to every one child with cystic fibrosis: a **ratio** of 3:1.

In other words: For every 4 people, 1 will probably have cystic fibrosis and 3 will not. These are often described as the **proportions** of a given population.

If we have a ratio of 3:1 in a population, we would *expect* that as the number of normal children increases, so will number of those with cystic fibrosis.

In genetics crosses, expected numbers will follow a certain multiplication factor, known as 'the constant of proportionality', so are said to be directly proportional.

3 The allele for Huntington's disease is dominant to the allele for normal. What ratio of offspring would you expect if a heterozygous couple had a family?

4 In a town with a population of 100 000, 40 people are affected with cystic fibrosis. Assuming direct proportionality, how many affected people would you expect in a population of a city with 1½ million people?

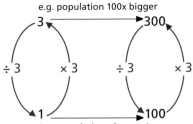

e.g. population 100x bigger

Figure 5.20 Numbers of normal children, and those with cystic fibrosis, increase by a multiplication factor of three.

Probability

A couple with a history of cystic fibrosis in the family visit a genetic counsellor to assess the probability – or likelihood – of their children being born with cystic fibrosis.

Probabilities can be expressed as a fraction, percentage, ratio or on a scale of 0 to 1, where 1 represents certainty. If an event happens once for every four trials, then the probability of this happening is ¼ or 25% or 0.25. In biology, we often work with the decimal representation and ratio.

The genetic counsellor draws up a Punnett square.

The *probability* of producing a child with cystic fibrosis will *never change* for this couple – It is always $\frac{1}{4}$.

In reality, probability will not be exact because fertilisation is random.

5 The first child of a couple who are carriers of cystic fibrosis does not have the condition. They think the chances of having an affected child will be increased next time. Explain to them why it isn't.

6 Suggest why, when working with plants, the ratio of the outcomes were very close to those expected, while those in a family might not be.

		mother	
		Cc	
		C	c
father Cc	C	CC child ①	Cc child ②
	c	Cc child ③	cc child ④

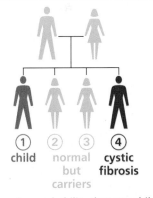

① child ② normal but carriers ④ cystic fibrosis

There is a probability that one child with cystic fibrosis will be born in every four children.
Two in every four will be carriers.
That is the case in this family.

Figure 5.21 Predicting the probability of children from two carriers of cystic fibrosis.

Variation

Learning objectives:

- recall that differences in the characteristics of individuals in a population is called variation
- describe examples of continuous and discontinuous variation
- understand the genetic and environmental differences leading to variation.

KEY WORDS

environmental variation
continuous variation
discontinuous variation
evolution
genetic variation

Harriett and Imogen are sisters. Their differences in appearance are the result of genetic and environmental variation.

Genetic and environmental variation

The sisters inherited genes from their parents. They are similar to, but not identical to, their parents. They also resemble each other.

Individuals of every organism that have been produced by sexual reproduction are different. With the exception of identical twins, we all have different genomes. Our genome gives us a unique set of characteristics.

Some of the sisters' features have nothing to do with genetics. Harriett wears spectacles and has braided hair. Differences that arise during development are part of **environmental variation**. Some environmental causes of variation are under our control, but others are not.

Figure 5.22 The two sisters have features in common, but they also have differences

Some human characteristics – the person's phenotype – are the result of the interaction of the genome with the environment.

Some characteristics in humans affected by:

Our genetics	The environment	A combination of both
blood group	hair colour and length	height
eye colour	language	skin colour
natural colour of hair	scars	weight
shape of earlobe	tattoos	sporting achievements

Some genetic variation, such as eye colour of hair, height and weight, shows a **continuous variation** through the population. Other variation, such as what blood group we belong to, is an either/or situation. We're either blood group O, A, B or AB. There are no intermediates. This is called **discontinuous variation**.

1 Give two characteristics in humans that result from:

   a genetic variation
   b environmental variation.

2 Give two characteristics in humans that result from a *combination* of genetic and environmental influences.

Variation and survival

Variation is essential to survival. There's usually a large amount of genetic variation within a population. This is essential to survival. Scientists studying populations of organisms can see how variation has led to changes. Variation is crucial to **evolution**. Each species in a stable environment is there because it has adapted to survive in that habitat.

Figure 5.23 Brown bears are adapted to life in the forest; polar bears to life on Arctic ice. Polar bears evolved from brown bears more than 350 000 years ago

3 How is an organism able to live in a specific habitat?

4 Suggest two characteristics that enable polar bears to live on the Arctic ice.

The mechanism of genetic variation

Genetic variation is the product of three processes that lead to differences in genomes: mutations, sexual reproduction and meiosis.

Mutations occur continuously. They happen spontaneously, by accident. Most mutations have no effect on an organism's phenotype. Often, mutations influence an organism's phenotype, though rarely do they determine it. Rarely, mutations give rise to new phenotypes where the new characteristics are advantageous. When this occurs, the change in an organism can be quite rapid – over generations, rather than millions of years. Examples include the peppered moth and antibiotic resistance in bacteria.

Figure 5.24 A series of mutations in rats and mice have made some populations resistant to warfarin poison.

5 List three processes leading to genetic variation.

6 Give an example of where a mutation has been beneficial to an organism.

> **REMEMBER!**
>
> The three processes that lead to genetic variation: mutations, sexual reproduction and meiosis. Also, some mutations are not expressed in an organism, but where they are, most are harmful.

> **DID YOU KNOW?**
>
> Warfarin disrupts the blood-clotting mechanism. It is used as a drug to help control strokes and heart attacks. When used as a rat poison, the animals bleed to death. As a result of mutations, and the fact that rats reproduce rapidly, many rat populations are now resistant to the poison.

The theory of evolution

Learning objectives:

- recall that all species of living things have evolved from simple life forms
- explain how evolution occurs through natural selection.

Figure 5.25 Insect species outnumber all others.

Around 1¾ million species of eukaryote have been named and described. But the real number of species alive today may be more like 9 million.

The theory of *evolution* states that the species alive today have descended from simpler organisms.

An early theory of evolution

An early theory was put forward by French scientist Jean-Baptiste Lamarck in 1809.

Lamarck believed that organisms survived by adapting to their environment. He suggested that body parts developed during an organism's life were passed to the next generation.

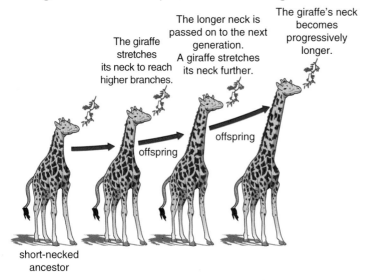

Figure 5.26 Lamarck's view of evolution

Lamarck also thought that one organism simply developed into another, rather than becoming extinct.

1. **Describe how Lamarck thought living organisms develop.**
2. **Why was Lamarck's theory wrong?**

How does evolution happen?

The environment does influence the phenotype, of course. But not in the way Lamarck thought. And these changes are *not* passed to the next generation. A body builder's muscles, for instance, are not passed on to their children.

Differences in phenotype are because individuals of a species show extensive *variation*.

In a population, differences will give some individuals, in that particular environment, advantages compared with others.

In animals, these advantages might make an organism better able to catch food, resist disease or attract a mate.

Organisms best suited to the conditions would survive and breed. If the desirable characteristics were genetic, they would be passed on to their offspring. These inherited characteristics are the result of genes and alleles.

This is called **natural selection**. Nature is, effectively, selecting the organism with the most useful genes. Evolution happens through natural selection.

3 Suggest characteristics that might help plants to survive.

4 What is natural selection?

Environmental change

Environmental change accelerates the rate of evolution. This could be a change in the climate. Or it could be through geographical isolation. Organisms can become isolated by a mountain range, valley or water. Each population will develop differently, dependent upon the demands of the unique habitat.

The animals – or plants – with the characteristics that are most suited to the new environment will survive to produce offspring.

Over time, organisms will develop that are quite different from the original population. Different species will evolve in the different locations. These can no longer breed with the original population to produce fertile offspring.

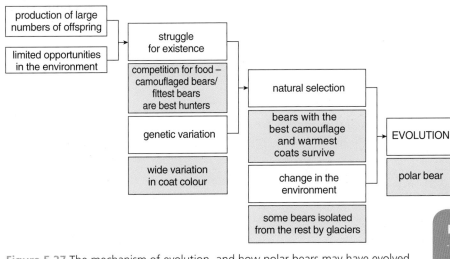

Figure 5.27 The mechanism of evolution, and how polar bears may have evolved from brown bears that were isolated by ice

5 What changes in an organism's environment might lead to different selective pressures?

6 At what point has a new species been produced?

KEY INFORMATION

Evolution explains the diversity of life on Earth and how organisms evolved from their ancestors.

The tree of life

Learning objectives:

- describe how living things have been classified into groups using a system devised by Linnaeus
- describe how new models of classification have developed.

In 2015, scientists discovered a new species of snake in a remote region of Western Australia. When a new species is discovered, scientists try to classify it.

Classifying organisms

Early attempts at classification – called **artificial classification** – had used levels that did not reflect relationships between organisms. Many, for instance, classified organisms according to their habitat.

With the invention of the microscope, and studies on the structure, reproduction and development of organisms, scientists began to recognise true relationships between them. They began to group organisms based on **natural classification**.

Today, all species are classified using the system developed by Swedish scientist Carl Linnaeus. Linnaeus divided all organisms into large groups called kingdoms. These were sub-divided into smaller groups, and these groups into smaller groups still: kingdom, phylum, class, order, family, genus, species. The smallest group is the species.

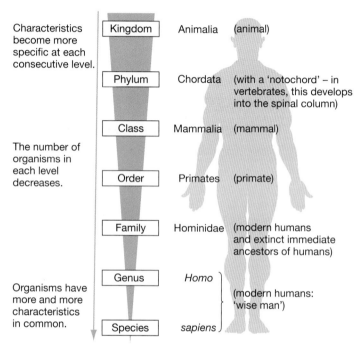

Figure 5.28 The classification of humans. Our scientific name is *Homo sapiens*. There are at least ten animals in our genus, but all are extinct except for humans

Linnaeus named species using the binomial system. Each organism has two names – a generic name and species name.

1. Who devised the classification system that we use today?

2. What system do we use to name an individual type of organism?

Evolutionary trees

An **evolutionary tree** shows how scientists think organisms evolved as they diverged from common ancestors.

There have been many versions of evolutionary trees, and new models continue to be developed. These developments have occurred because:

- Scientific examination has improved as microscopes have developed and our understanding of the physical characteristics (external and internal structures) of organisms has grown.
- Our understanding of biochemistry and biochemical processes has improved.

The study of the relationships between species, and groups of organisms, and how they are related through their evolutionary history, is called **phylogenetics**.

3 How have new models of classification developed?

4 Name the three domains that have been proposed.

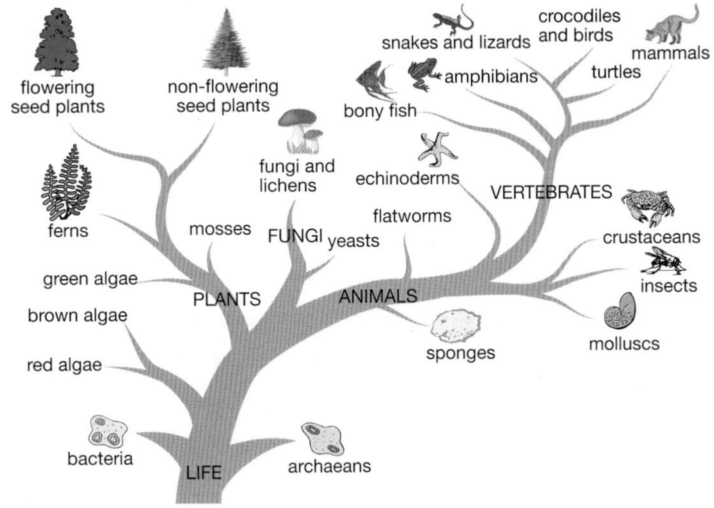

Modern evolutionary trees

The information for modern evolutionary trees comes from organisms that are alive today and from the fossil record. But now we also look at base sequences of portions of DNA, or the structures of other chemicals such as proteins.

Figure 5.29 One version of an evolutionary tree. Some scientists have now added an extra branch to produce three domains

Scientists look at areas of DNA that show large variations between species. As organisms evolve, differences in their DNA accumulate. So the degree of genetic difference – the number of changes in the base sequences of a group of related organisms – can give us an estimate of the relative times at which these branches occurred.

```
-GTTGCGATTCTGACCTTAGA-      Sequence 1
-GTAGCCATACTGACCTTAGA-      Sequence 2
-GTAGCGATACCGACCTTACA-      Sequence 3
-GTTGCGATTCCGACCTTACA-      Sequence 4
```

The distance value between sequences 1 and 2 = $\dfrac{\text{number of changes}}{\text{length}} = \dfrac{3}{20} = 0.15$

The distance value between sequences 3 and 4 = $\dfrac{\text{number of changes}}{\text{length}} = \dfrac{2}{20} = 0.10$

Figure 5.30 How similar are DNA sequences in different organisms? Calculations can show scientists that Sequences 3 and 4 are more closely related than sequences 1 and 2

Computer programs can generate comparisons between the sequences of equivalent lengths of DNA. New evolutionary trees can be built.

DNA evolutionary trees can help to clear up uncertainties in trees that are based on anatomical features. But we cannot be certain of these evolutionary relationships. And obtaining DNA from extinct species is difficult.

5 Explain how modern evolutionary trees are constructed.

6 Using the information in Figure 5.30, calculate the distance values between the other DNA sequences.

DID YOU KNOW?

The 'Barcode of Life' is an international initiative devoted to developing a 'DNA barcode' database of living species, which can be used in identification.

REMEMBER!

You type a scientific name in *italics*, or if it's handwritten, underline it. The genus name has a capital letter but the species name does not. Avoid thinking of some organisms on an evolutionary tree as 'higher' than others. We cannot rank organisms.

Evidence of natural selection and evolution?

Learning objectives:

* understand how scientific theories develop over time
* plan experiments to test hypotheses.

KEY WORDS

lichen
melanism
mutation

In some animals, a *gene mutation* occasionally causes a dark, or melanic form, to appear.

The peppered moth is white, 'peppered' with black spots. In 1848, in Manchester, the first mutant black, or melanic, peppered moth was recorded. By 1898, 95% of the moths were melanic.

Mutations are changes to our DNA

Mutations, changes to our DNA, occur continuously in our bodies. These changes can be the result of chemicals or radiation, but they also just happen. They are errors that are made when a cell divides, or when the instructions to produce a protein are being copied.

Sometimes, they can affect the way an animal or plant functions, leading to the death of the organism. If a mutation occurs in a body cell, cancer may result. If a mutation occurs in cells that produce eggs and sperm, it may lead to a genetic disorder in the offspring.

Sometimes, mutations lead to extra or reduced numbers of whole chromosomes. More commonly, a change in one or two bases of a gene happens.

Back in the nineteenth century, James W. Tutt suggested an explanation for the appearance of the melanic form of the moth. Polluted city air was laden with sulfur dioxide, and soot covered trees, killing **lichens** and blackening the bark. Dark moths were well camouflaged on tree trunks and less likely to be eaten by birds. In the countryside, the opposite would have been true: pale-coloured moths were camouflaged, but melanic forms were quickly seen and eaten.

In the heavily polluted Britain of the 1950s, the melanic moths appeared to have a selective advantage over the pale form.

1. What caused the dark form of the moth to be produced?

2. What was Tutt's hypothesis?

Figure 5.31 In Victorian times urban areas like Manchester became heavily polluted

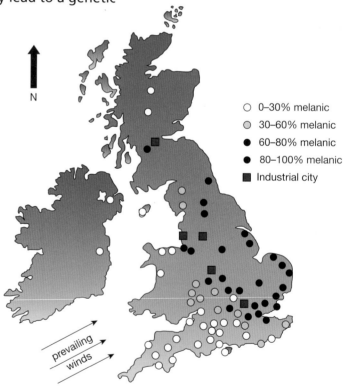

N

○ 0–30% melanic
◔ 30–60% melanic
● 60–80% melanic
● 80–100% melanic
■ Industrial city

prevailing winds

Figure 5.32 In the 1950s, the melanic form was spreading, in particular downwind from industrial areas

Testing Tutt's hypothesis

Bernard Kettlewell carried out a series of experiments to test Tutt's hypothesis.

His first experiment was in heavily industrialised woodland near Birmingham, with around 90% melanic moths.

Kettlewell released a large number of peppered moths, marking the underside of the wings with a spot of paint. He then caught 770 peppered moths. Recaptured moths from the first part of the experiment were identified by the spot of paint. Others were wild.

	Number of melanic moths	Number of pale moths
No. of moths released initially	447	137
No. of marked moths recaptured	149	20

In 1955, Kettlewell carried out a similar study in unpolluted woodland in Dorset. Here, none of the local moths were melanic.

	Number of melanic moths	Number of pale moths
No. of moths released initially	473	496
No. of marked moths recaptured	30	62

Kettlewell demonstrated that the distribution of peppered moths was correlated with the level of pollution.

3 **Suggest how Kettlewell might have improved the way he controlled variables.**

4 **Discuss possible difficulties that Kettlewell might have had with carrying out this experiment.**

Support of Kettlewell's study

In the meantime, anti-pollution measures of the 1950s and 1960s have taken effect. The dark form has decreased in abundance, just as predicted by the hypothesis. **Melanism** has also been observed in other species, such as ladybirds.

Although there has been some criticism of Kettlewell's work in the past 15 years, Professor Mike Majerus concluded in one of the most recent studies that the moth is "the proof of evolution".

5 **Why did air quality improve in the UK in the 1950s and 1960s?**

6 **What other evidence supported Kettlewell's findings?**

Figure 5.33 Kettlewell's photographs of peppered moths, on a lichen-covered tree and a green leaf

COMMON MISCONCEPTION

Do not think that pollution affects the moths. Melanic moths arise anyway, by random mutations, and they survive if they have a selective advantage.

DID YOU KNOW?

Scientists have used molecular genetics to show that one mutation of a single gene leads to moths becoming melanic.

Fossil evidence

Learning objectives:

- understand how, and the situations in which, fossils are formed
- understand how fossils are used as evidence for evolution of species from simpler life forms.

KEY WORD

fossil

Darwin's work in geology was important. He formulated a theory on how volcanic islands had formed.

Fossils are the remains of organisms that lived millions, or hundreds of thousands, of years ago.

How are fossils formed?

If an organism dies in water, or is washed into water, conditions may be right for it to be fossilised.

Most fossils are formed as a dead animal or plant becomes buried in mud, silt or sand. Oxygen must be excluded. Otherwise, microorganisms would feed on the body and it would quickly decay.

During the process of fossilisation, the hard parts of an animal (bones, shell or teeth) or hard woody parts of a plant become replaced by minerals.

Figure 5.34 Fossils were well known in Darwin's time. *Ichthyosaurus* – featured here in a commemorative stamp – was found in 1811 by fossil hunter Mary Anning

An organism dies.
It sinks to the bottom of the water.

The organism becomes covered in sediment.
The soft parts of the body decay.
The sediment begins to turn to rock.

More sediments settle. Other organisms die. If conditions are right, they begin to fossilise.
The sediments are compressed as further layers are added.
An exchange of minerals occurs between the skeleton and the water
The skeleton is turned to rock – it has become a fossil.

The rock layers become lifted up.
They are eroded by wind and rain.

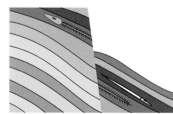

Faults in rocks and erosion expose the fossils.

Figure 5.35 How organisms become fossilised. Fossils may later become exposed by erosion and earth movements

1. **Describe how mineralised fossils are formed.**
2. **Which parts of an animal or plant are usually fossilised?**

Other remains of organisms

As well as mineralised remains, fossils can be formed in other ways.

Sometimes traces of organisms are left, such as footprints, burrows or spaces left by plant roots. Occasionally, whole organisms are found. Whole insects or plant parts have been found trapped in amber, a hardened form of tree sap. Occasionally, trunks of trees have been found after being buried in mud containing volcanic ash.

The conditions must be just right for fossil formation. It is actually a very rare occurrence.

3 What fossil traces of fossil organisms have been found.

4 Where have whole fossilised organisms been found?

Evidence from the fossil record

As layer upon layer of rock is added, each must be younger than the one beneath it. We can tell the relative ages of the rock layers. Nowadays, with radiometric dating, it is also possible to find the absolute age of rocks.

The fossil record shows us how organisms that lived in the past differ from those around today. It also shows how long a species existed for, by when it enters and leaves the fossil record. It shows us extinction, and the slow and successive appearance of new species.

> **COMMON MISCONCEPTION**
>
> Remember that fossils are not usually the remains of the organisms themselves. The remains have usually been replaced by minerals.

> **DID YOU KNOW?**
>
> Palaeontologists have been collecting fossils along the 'Jurassic Coast' in Dorset, for 200 years. Tilting of the rock layers has meant that rocks range from 250 million years old – the Triassic Period – at Lyme Regis in the west, to 65 million years – the end of the Cretaceous Period – and younger at Studland in the east.

younger fossils and rocks

older fossils and rocks

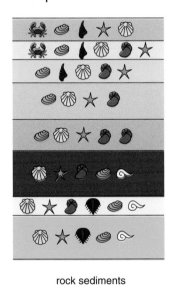

rock sediments

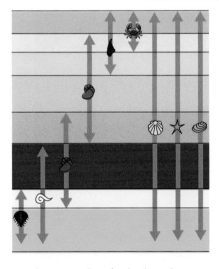

the succession of animal species through geological time

Figure 5.36 Palaeontologists record the fossils found in rock sediments. Rocks are dated and a picture is built up of the organisms that we know were present at the time

5 How are the relative ages of fossil species worked out?

6 How can scientists find the actual age of fossils?

How much have organisms changed?

KEY WORD

....

fossil record

Learning objectives:

- understand why the fossil record is incomplete
- use the fossil record to understand how much, or how little, organisms have changed as life developed on Earth.

About 250 000 fossil species have been discovered, but one estimate suggests that this represents less than 1 in 20 000 of the species that ever lived. There must, of course, also be large numbers that remain undiscovered.

Fossils *are missing from the record*

The **fossil record** is incomplete. Conditions must be just right for fossil formation. The chances of this are small. In addition, geological activity over many years will have destroyed most fossils. And the older a fossil is, the more likely it is to have been lost.

Many early life forms were microorganisms or they were soft bodied. So fewer traces of them exist. Sometimes, however, conditions have enabled soft-bodied animals to be found.

Figure 5.37 Palaeontologists, working with scientists using medical techniques, created these three-dimensional models of an early type of green alga.

And some of the Archaea and Bacteria have left traces of the unique chemicals that they have produced. There is now clear evidence of life going back 3.5 billion years.

Nevertheless, the fossil record is very incomplete. And Darwin appreciated that if life evolved, then there must be intermediate forms, or 'missing links', between different organisms, as they evolved.

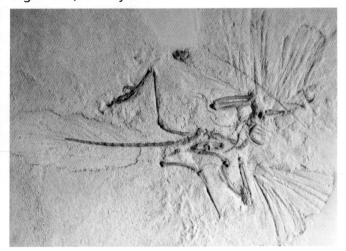

Figure 5.38 Darwin was delighted when an *Archaeopteryx* was found in Bavaria in 1861. It was reptile-like but had feathers. It was a critical piece of evidence showing that birds have evolved from reptiles

1. **Why do we have few fossils of early life forms?**

2. **Which early organisms have left traces?**

Fossil horses

Often, we can learn from the fossil record how much, or how little, life on Earth has changed.

When you look at the horse, for example, there is an extensive fossil record of horse-like animals. And new ones are still being found. We can trace the evolution of the modern horse, *Equus*, from an animal the size of a small dog, called *Hyracotherium*, which had toes. These toes have been lost during evolution and hooves developed.

3. **Which animal are horses thought to have evolved from?**

4. **Describe the trends in the evolution of the horse.**

Some life has changed very little

In contrast, other organisms, such as certain bacteria, have changed little in billions of years. It can also be easy to distinguish fossil archaeans from fossil bacteria because of traces of the unique chemicals in their cell membranes.

5. **Give an example of a type of organism that has changed very little in billions of years.**

6. **Explain how we know this.**

> **DID YOU KNOW?**
>
> Modern analysis of fossils has revealed features of the animals that lived. Analyses of *Archaeopteryx* fossils suggest that it had white feathers with black edges and tips.

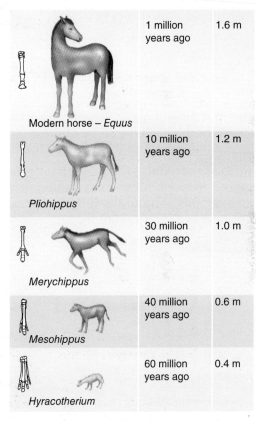

Modern horse – *Equus*	1 million years ago	1.6 m
Pliohippus	10 million years ago	1.2 m
Merychippus	30 million years ago	1.0 m
Mesohippus	40 million years ago	0.6 m
Hyracotherium	60 million years ago	0.4 m

Figure 5.39 The evolution of the modern horse. We now know that this evolution is not a simple straight line – their evolutionary tree branches and has offshoots – with some intermediate stages actually being smaller

> **REMEMBER!**
>
> Fossils are rare, so any 'missing links' will be even rarer.

Antimicrobial resistance

KEY WORDS

antimicrobial
resistance

Learning objectives:

- recall that bacteria develop that are resistant to antibiotics, which is evidence of evolution
- understand the mechanism by which antibiotic resistance develops
- understand the effects of the development of antibiotic resistance on the treatment of disease.

Antibiotics saved countless lives during the Second World War and after. In 1947, however, within 4 years of the first antibiotic – a type of penicillin – being introduced, the resistance of some bacteria to the antibiotic was observed.

Developing resistance

Bacteria and other microorganisms are becoming resistant to the drugs that have been designed to kill them.

The mutation of genes in pathogenic bacteria produces new strains of the bacteria. Some of these strains may be resistant to an antibiotic used on a patient. So the bacteria will not be killed.

As they reproduce, the genes that give the bacteria resistance spread throughout the population. Antibiotic resistance is an example of natural selection. Bacteria can evolve quickly because of their rapid reproductive rate.

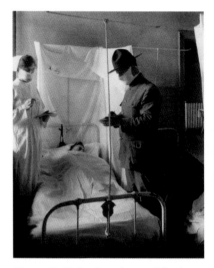

Figure 5.40 An American soldier is given a dose of penicillin. Penicillin significantly reduced the deaths of soldiers from infection

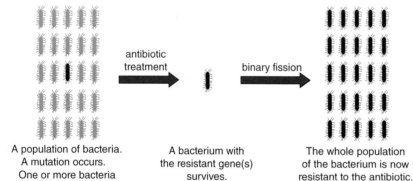

antibiotic treatment | binary fission

A population of bacteria. A mutation occurs. One or more bacteria in the population are resistant to the antibiotic.

A bacterium with the resistant gene(s) survives.

The whole population of the bacterium is now resistant to the antibiotic.

Figure 5.41 A simplified diagram of how resistance to antibiotics spreads throughout a population of bacteria. In reality, more than one mutation is required

Certain bacteria, such as *Staphylococcus aureus*, are building up resistance to antibiotics very quickly. *Staphylococcus* that are resistant to a broad range of antibiotics, including methicillin, are called MRSA.

1. Describe how antibiotic resistance develops.

2. Explain how this resistance is evidence for Darwin's theory of evolution.

Antimicrobial resistance

An antibiotic will not work against a resistant bacterium. An alternative antibiotic must be used. Gradually, bacteria become resistant to more and more antibiotics.

For serious infections, certain antibiotics are kept in reserve, the so-called 'last-resort' antibiotics.

Many scientists consider antibiotic resistance – or, more correctly, **antimicrobial resistance** (AMR), because resistance is also developing against antivirals, antiprotozoals and antifungals – to be the worst public health problem facing us today.

Dame Sally Davies, the UK's Chief Medical Officer, says Britain faces 'returning to a nineteenth century world where the smallest infection or operation could kill' us. Major advances in organ transplants and cancer treatment would be wiped out.

KEY INFORMATION

Remember that antibiotic resistance would occur anyway. It is just our misuse of antibiotics that is speeding the process up.

3 How do we currently treat bacteria that are resistant to common antibiotics?

4 Why is it suggested that we are returning to a medical world of the nineteenth century?

DID YOU KNOW?

MRSA is the term used for strains of the bacterium that are resistant to the antibiotic methicillin and, nowadays, to other commonly used antibiotics.

Growing resistance

AMR would occur anyway, but it is happening at a quicker rate than it should because of the over-prescription of antibiotics.

Antibiotics are often prescribed, inappropriately, for minor viral infections such as colds or respiratory infections. Doctors are also often persuaded by patients to prescribe them.

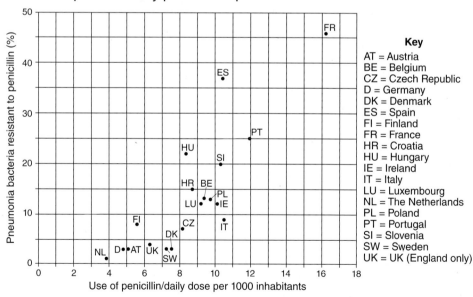

Figure 5.42 Antibiotic use and penicillin-resistant bacteria across Europe. In some countries antibiotics are available 'over the counter' without a prescription

5 What is the cause of growing resistance to antibiotics?

6 Describe trends in resistance of pneumonia bacteria to penicillin in the European countries.

Extinction ... or survival?

Learning objectives:

- list the causes of extinction
- explain how new predators, competitors and diseases can lead to extinctions.

KEY WORDS

seedbanks
extinction

The Svalbard Global Seed Vault – the 'Doomsday Vault' – is buried deep in the Norwegian permafrost. It was built to safeguard seed varieties from across the world from loss of genetic diversity or famine. *Seedbanks* are used to store the biodiversity of crop and other plants.

Mass extinctions

Extinctions occur when changes in the environment leave organisms unable to tolerate new conditions, or to compete or reproduce.

The fossil record shows that there have been at least five mass **extinctions** over geological time.

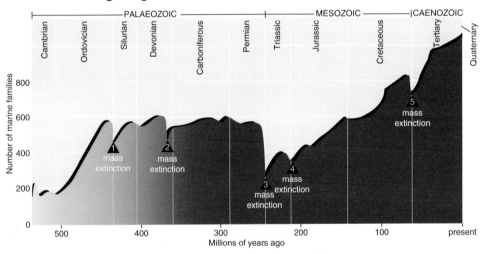

Figure 5.43 The five mass extinctions. The current rate of extinctions is comparable

Changes to the Earth's environment over geological time must have been a factor. The warming or cooling of the Earth, changes in seasons or ocean currents, and the changing position of the continents would have contributed.

Around 66 million years ago, however, it is thought that a massive asteroid impact killed three-quarters of life on Earth, including the dinosaurs. The dust thrown up would have blocked out sunlight. Plants would have declined, followed by herbivores, and then the carnivores that were dependent on the herbivores. Volcanic eruptions and sea-level change could also have contributed.

The Earth's environment is constantly changing. When the environment changes, organisms either adapt to these changes, or they become extinct. A species is considered to be extict when there are no remaining individuals of that species still living.

DID YOU KNOW?

According to one estimate in the scientific journal, *Nature*, humans have a century or perhaps two left. Can the sixth mass extinction be stopped?

1 Approximately when were the five mass extinctions?

2 Why can we only estimate the number of extinct species?

Invasive or alien species

Another important cause of extinctions is the introduction of a new species into a location. These may:

- be new predators
- compete with native organisms that are present for food
- introduce new diseases.

On the Galápagos Islands the animals had few natural predators. But then mammals were introduced, including rats, dogs and feral cats. Cats and dogs attacked birds and destroyed the nests of birds, tortoises and turtles. Projects are under way on the islands, or have already been carried out, to eradicate these predators.

In Britain, harlequin ladybirds are a new species. They eat other ladybirds and outcompete them for food. Scientists are worried that our native ladybirds might become extinct.

3 Why are scientists worried that some animals on the Galápagos Islands might become extinct?

4 Suggest one way of preventing these extinctions.

The verge of the sixth extinction?

Some scientists believe we are entering a sixth mass extinction, and that humans are the major contributing factor, through:

- transformation of the landscape
- overexploitation of species
- pollution
- introduction of alien species.

One serious concern in recent years has been the decline of bee populations. It is estimated that bees pollinate over 70% of the 100 crop species that provide 90% of global food supplies. If bees become extinct, the human race will follow soon after.

5 What may contribute to the sixth extinction?

6 How might bees contribute to human extinction?

7 'Humans are responsible for the extinction of species in modern times.' Do you agree with this statement? Justify your answer.

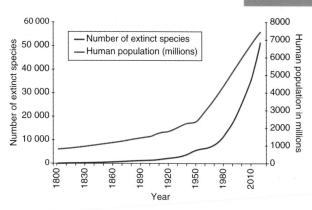

Figure 5.44 Humans are now the main cause of environmental change. This graph shows growth of the human population over time and the estimated numbers of extinctions

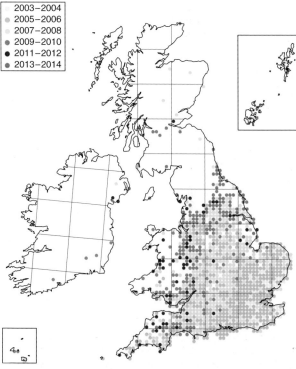

Figure 5.45 The spread of the harlequin ladybird, 2004–14

REMEMBER!

While humans have contributed to extinctions, we alone have the ability, although not always the inclination, to prevent many further extinctions.

MATHS SKILLS

Using charts and graphs to display data

Learning objectives:

- understand when and how to use bar charts
- understand how to show sub-groups on bar charts
- understand how to plot histograms.

KEY WORDS

grouped bar
  chart
stacked bar chart

The International Union for Conservation of Nature and Natural Resources (IUCN) monitors species in danger of extinction. It must make this huge amount of data understandable to the public.

Bar charts

Scientists use graphs and charts to display, summarise and analyse data. They can be used to simplify the presentation of complex data and highlight patterns and trends.

Bar charts are used to display data collected for distinct groups. If the data points in the groups can be counted then this data is known as discrete data.

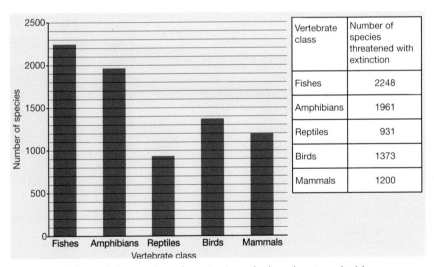

Vertebrate class	Number of species threatened with extinction
Fishes	2248
Amphibians	1961
Reptiles	931
Birds	1373
Mammals	1200

Figure 5.46 Data of the number of species in each class threatened with extinction are transferred from a table to a bar chart.

When drawing a bar chart:

- the *height* of the bars is proportional to the measured number or frequency
- the *width* of the bars should be consistent
- the bars do not touch each other; they represent distinct groups
- the bars can be placed in *any* convenient order. This shouldn't be haphazard.

① Draw a bar chart for the groups of organisms, shown below, found as fossils in a particular rock type.

Group of organism	Fossils found in %
Algae	14
Arthropods	33
Molluscs	3
Sponges	22
Worms	3

② What percentage of fossil organisms were unclassified?

DID YOU KNOW?

In his book of 1871, *The Descent of Man*, Darwin discussed the diversity of skull size and shape in different peoples.

More complex bar charts

Other types of bar chart could be used to provide further information about these endangered species.

From Figure 5.47, we don't know the number of species in each vertebrate class, so we don't have any indication of what proportion of each vertebrate class is endangered.

We can add this information to produce a dual bar chart. (also known as a **grouped bar chart**).

A similar type of bar chart is the **stacked bar chart**. We often see these in the media. Here, different sub-groups are stacked on top of each other to produce a single bar for each group included.
Note that bar charts can be constructed horizontally as well as vertically.

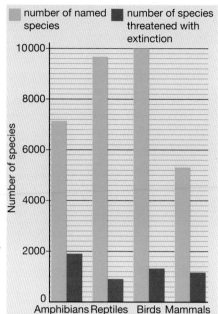

Figure 5.47 A dual bar chart for four of the vertebrate classes.

Histograms

A histogram is a statistical diagram, similar to a bar chart. In a histogram, the **area** of each bar is proportional to the frequency of the class interval. The data are continuous instead of being discrete. They're commonly used to show the variation of a characteristic, such as height. Remember:

- the variable on the x-axis is continuous, so there are no gaps between bars
- the size of the categories is represented by the area of the bars, although for many of the histograms you will plot the ranges on the x-axis have been chosen to be equal.

Histograms can be used to show the range of variation across groups of organisms. One characteristic determined for both living humans and extinct human ancestors is the cephalic index (CI).

$$\text{Cephalic index} = \frac{\text{Maximum head width}}{\text{Maximum head length}} \times 100$$

The CI varies between human populations of different demographic groups and over time.

Cephalic Index (C.I.)	Boys in %	Girls in %
72.0≤CI<75.0	7.3	4.8
75.0≤CI<80.0	28.4	32.8
80.0≤CI<85.0	30.0	42.6
85.0≤CI<90.0	34.3	19.6

3 Construct a bar chart to illustrate the proportion of endangered species of fish:

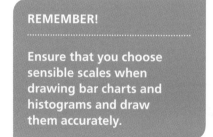

Number threatened with extinction	2248
Number of species	33100

4 Construct a stacked bar chart for the distribution of blood groups in England and Wales in 2014:
Your chart will have a single bar. The scale will be 0–100.

REMEMBER!

Ensure that you choose sensible scales when drawing bar charts and histograms and draw them accurately.

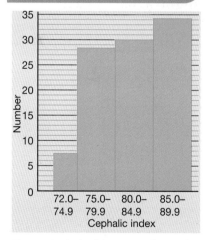

Figure 5.48 The histogram shows the range of the CI for the boys in a group of school children. Note that the bar for lowest category is narrower.

5 Plot a histogram for the range of CIs of girls in the group.

6 Plot a histogram for the range of heights in your biology group.

Check your progress

recall the definition of the genome	→ describe a gene as a section of DNA that controls a particular characteristic	→ describe DNA as a polymer that has a double helix shape
identify meiosis as the cell division used to produce gametes	→ explain the need for meiosis in producing gametes	→ explain that the gametes produced by meiosis are genetically unique
identify a mutation as a change in the DNA	→ describe how mutations can, on rare occasions, affect how an organism functions	→ explain how mutations can lead to changes in an organism's phenotype
recall that genes exist in different forms called alleles, and know key genetic terms	→ complete Punnett squares to show the inheritance of characteristics controlled by single genes	→ construct Punnett squares to predict the outcome of genetic crosses
distinguish between variation caused by genes and by the environment	→ describe how variation contributes to an organism's survival	→ understand the mechanism of genetic variation
recall early ideas about evolution	→ describe how natural selection leads to a struggle for existence	→ explain how environmental change operating with natural selection leads to the evolution of a new species
recall the evidence that led to the development of the theory of evolution	→ describe the evidence that led to the development of the theory of evolution	→ explain the evidence for the occurrence of evolution and natural selection
recall and use the classification system developed by Linnaeus	→ explain the features used to develop evolutionary trees	→ explain how microscopic examination, fossils and biochemistry have led to modern evolutionary trees
identify the causes of extinction	→ describe how new species, predators and competitors can lead to extinction	→ evaluate circumstances that may lead to another mass extinction

Worked example

A couple's second child was born with a condition called phenylketonuria (PKU). The condition is caused by a recessive allele.

The family tree shows that there is a history of PKU in the mother's (8) family. The father (7) was unaware of the condition in his family.

The couple would like another child. A genetic counsellor draws a family tree.

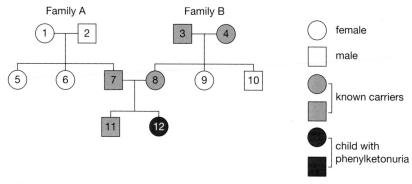

1. The genetic counsellor talks about the father's family's medical history.

   a What is the genotype of the father (7)?

      Pp

      The student has identified the genotype correctly.

   b What can be deduced about the genotype of the father's parents, 1 and 2? Explain your answer.

      One is a carrier.

      The answer would have been better with more explanation. One parent (or both) must be carriers. For 7 to be a carrier, he must have inherited one recessive allele. So, one parent must have passed on a recessive allele. The other parent would have passed on a dominant allele (otherwise 7 would have PKU). Their other allele *could* have been the recessive allele, which was not passed down to any of the three children.

   c Draw a genetic diagram to show how 12 came to have PKU.

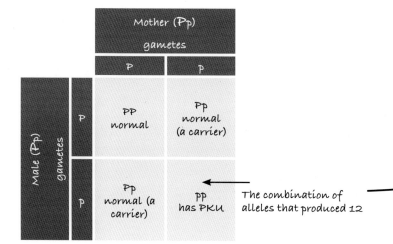

   The combination of alleles that produced 12

   This a very good answer. The student has included the parental genotypes, the gametes produced, the possible genotypes and phenotypes produced, and has highlighted the combination of alleles that must have produced 12.

End of chapter questions

Getting started

① Use the words provided to complete the sentences.

alleles	double helix	chromosomes	different positions
DNA	each chromosome	identical positions	one chromosome

Alleles for a particular characteristic are located at _____ on _____ of the chromosome pair. `1 Mark`

The structure of _____ is like a twisted ladder. This shape is described as a _____ . `1 Mark`

② People can either roll their tongue into a U-shape, or are unable to roll their tongue.

  a The diagram shows a pair of chromosomes.

    Is the allele for tongue-rolling dominant or recessive? Explain your answer. `2 Marks`

  b Give the other possible genotypes related to tongue rolling. `1 Mark`

  c Give the phenotypes for these genotypes. `1 Mark`

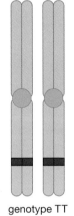

genotype TT
can roll tongue

③ **a** Draw a bar chart for the groups of organisms show below, found as fossils in a particular type. `2 Marks`

  b Calculate what percentage of fossil organisms were unclassified. `2 Marks`

Group of organism	Fossils found %
Algae	11
Arthropods	30
Molluscs	4
Sponges	23
Worms	2

Going further

4 What is meant by the term 'natural selection'? 1 Mark

5 Draw two lines to match the types of cell division with where they occur. 1 Mark

Cell division   Where it occurs

| Asexual reproduction in bacteria |

| Meiosis |

| Growth of a human embryo |

| Mitosis |

| Sperm production |

6 The diagram shows a process that is taking place when pollen grains are being produced.

What conclusion can you draw? Explain your answer.

2 Marks

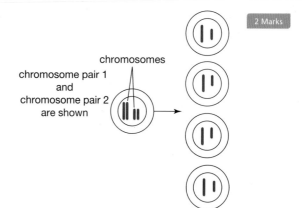

chromosome pair 1 and chromosome pair 2 are shown

chromosomes

daughter cells

7 The occurrence of a dark form of the two-spot ladybird was monitored by scientists between the 1960s and the 1980s.

Some of the scientists' results are shown below.

Year	Frequency of the dark form (%)
1960	47
1965	37
1970	27
1975	19
1980	12
1985	10

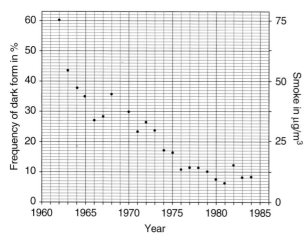

The scientists also recorded the yearly amounts of smoke in the air.
The readings for smoke concentration have already been plotted on the graph.

a Plot the frequency of the dark form of the ladybird from 1960 to 1985 on the graph above.

Draw a line of best fit.

`4 Marks`

b Suggest a reason for the change in frequency of the dark form of the ladybird. Predict what may have happened to the ladybird population after 1984.

`2 Marks`

More challenging

8 In a species of mouse, black coat colour is dominant to white.

Two black mice mate.

a Complete the Punnett square below to show the genotypes and phenotypes of the offspring.

`2 Marks`

b Calculate the probability of producing a white mouse. Express your answer as a fraction.

`1 Mark`

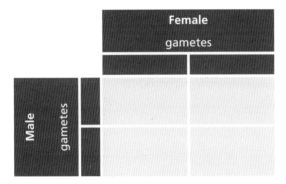

c The chromosome containing the genes for coat colour was found to have 220 million base pairs. Write this number in standard form.

`1 Mark`

9 A plant breeder crosses a pure-breeding plant with blue flowers with a pure-breeding plant with purple flowers.

`4 Marks`

All the offspring have purple flowers.

The plant breeder would like to find the genotype of *one* of the purple-flowered plants from the cross.

Describe how he could do this. Explain your answer using the appropriate genetics.

10 Some scientists believe we may be on the verge of entering a sixth mass extinction. What human actions are potential contributing factors?

`2 Marks`

Most demanding

11 Explain how meiosis leads to the production of gametes that are different genetically.

2 Marks

12 The inheritance of detached and attached earlobes was thought to be controlled by a single gene pair, with one allele dominant to the other.

Few studies had been carried out on this, however.

Then, in 1973, scientists in India published the following results.

Parents (D = detached A = attached)	Number of offspring with detached earlobes	Number of offspring with attached earlobes	Percentage of offspring with detached earlobes
D × D	13	1	93
D × A	7	7	50
A × A	5	29	15

Explain fully what can be concluded about the inheritance of attached and detached earlobes from the data.

4 Marks

13 MRSA is a bacterial infection.

The graph shows the number of cases of hospital patients with MRSA infections from 1993 to 2005.

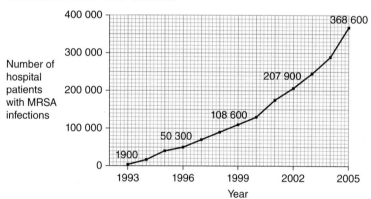

Explain the trend in the graph, even though the patients were treated with antibiotics.

4 Marks

Total: 40 Marks

GLOBAL CHALLENGES

HEALTH CAN BE AFFECTED BY DRUGS AND DISEASE

- Smoking is damaging to health because cigarette smoke contains harmful chemicals.
- Drugs can be medicines and may help people suffering from pain or disease.
- Lack of exercise and a poor diet can lead to a higher BMI.
- Alcohol affects our response time and behaviour.

BACTERIA ARE SINGLE-CELLED LIVING ORGANISMS

- Some bacteria can multiply by simple cell division every 20 minutes, if conditions are favourable.
- Temperatures greater than 25°C increase the likelihood that microbes will grow.
- Antiseptics can kill bacteria.
- A specific antibiotic can kill a specific bacteria.

ORGANS WORK TOGETHER IN SYSTEMS TO PERFORM CERTAIN FUNCTIONS

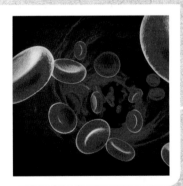

- Air enters the respiratory system through the nose.
- The trachea and bronchi are organs in the respiratory system.
- The stomach produces hydrochloric acid.
- The skin covers the outside of the body.
- Blood is the transport system in the body; red blood cells transport oxygen from the lungs to all cells.

GREEN PLANTS ALL HAVE ORGAN SYSTEMS THAT HAVE SPECIFIC FUNCTIONS

- Plants photosynthesise to increase biomass, which is tranferred to animals in higher trophic levels.
- Plants can be damaged by a range of ion deficiency conditions.

IN THIS CHAPTER YOU WILL FIND OUT ABOUT:

FACTORS THAT AFFECT OUR CHANCES OF CATCHING A NON-COMMUNICABLE DISEASE

- Factors in our environment can increase our risk of disease.
- Our lifestyle can increase the chance of us developing a non-communicable disease.
- Sometimes a number of risk factors of developing a disease interact.
- When cell division accelerates out of control, cancer develops.
- Lifestyle factors can increase the risk of a person developing cancer.
- Stem cells could be used to treat certain conditions and diseases that are currently untreatable.

HOW COMMUNICABLE DISEASES ARE SPREAD

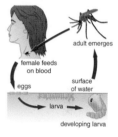

- Pathogens are microorganisms that cause disease in plants and animals.
- Bacteria, viruses, fungi and protists can cause disease.
- Toxins produced by bacteria make us feel ill.
- Understanding the lifecycles of some pathogens allows us to control the spread of disease.

HOW WE CONTROL THE SPREAD OF DISEASE

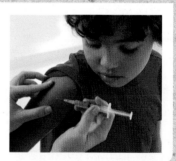

- The skin, nose, respiratory system and stomach all protect us from pathogens.
- The immune system is our major defence system against disease.
- White blood cells protect us from pathogens in a number of ways.
- Vaccination protects us from viral and bacterial pathogens.

HOW PLANTS ARE AFFECTED BY DISEASE AND PROTECTED FROM ATTACK

- Plant diseases can usually be detected by visible symptoms.
- Viral, bacterial and fungal pathogens cause plant diseases.

PRACTICAL

Sampling techniques

Learning objectives:

- describe how to use a range of sampling techniques to measure the abundance of organisms in a habitat
- explain the capture–recapture technique.

Scientists studying the environment count organisms to investigate how abiotic factors affect the distribution of organisms.

Sampling techniques

We cannot count every organism in a habitat. Samples are taken to estimate population size. Animals must be handled carefully and released back into their habitat after sampling.

> These pages are designed to help you think about aspects of the investigation rather than to guide you through it step by step.

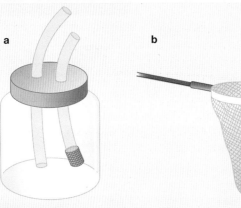
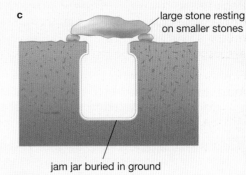

large stone resting on smaller stones

jam jar buried in ground

Pooter – a small re-sealable jar used for collecting insects. The lid contains two tubes. The end of one tube is covered with a line mesh, with the other end placed in the user's mouth. The second tube is placed over the insect, the user then sucks on the first tube drawing the insects into the jar.

Nets – commonly used to collect airborne insects. This is a form of active collection

Pitfall trap – a small jar is buried within the ground and lightly covered with leaves or stones. Small insects, amphibians and replies fall in and cannot escape. This is called passive collection

Figure 6.1 Sampling animals

Randomly thrown **quadrats** are used to sample plants. Species in or half way in the quadrat are counted. The same size quadrat is used to sample many areas. The mean number of organisms per m² is found and then scaled up to the actual size of the area. Quadrats are used to compare the distribution of one organism across a habitat or the variety of organisms in different habitats. **Keys** are used to identify the organisms found.

1 Describe how to use a quadrat and a pooter.

2 Why do scientists use sample populations?

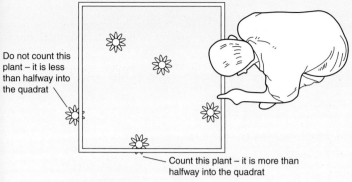

Do not count this plant – it is less than halfway into the quadrat

Count this plant – it is more than halfway into the quadrat

Figure 6.2 Using a quadrat

Techniques in detail

Estimating animal populations is difficult because they move. The **capture–recapture** method improves accuracy.

* animals are trapped, recorded and marked without harming them.
* Animals are released and traps reset a few days later. Animals with and without markings are recorded.

$$\text{population size} = \frac{\text{number in 1st sample} \times \text{number in 2nd sample}}{\text{number in 2nd sample previously marked}}$$

Percentage cover of different species can be found at different distances as abiotic factors change by placing a quadrat each metre along a straight line. This is a line transect. Kite diagrams are used to show the distribution and number of species found.

Finding the distribution range, mean, median and mode gives more information.

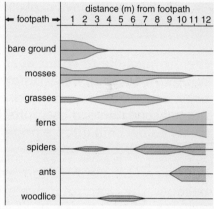

Figure 6.3 a kite diagram

3 **Explain the use of transect lines.**

4 **What does the data in the kite diagram show?**

Working accurately

Random quadrat samples ensure results are valid and reflect the true distribution of organisms.

Animal population sizes continually change because:

* animals are born or die
* animals move in and out of ecosystems.

Small errors in small samples cause a large error when multiplied to the actual area being investigated. To increase accuracy:

* the process is repeated
* sample sizes are as large as possible.

When capture–recapture is used, it is assumed that:

* there are no deaths, immigration or emigration
* identical sampling methods are used each time to allow comparisons
* marking animals does not affect their survival through damage or altering their camouflage.

DID YOU KNOW?

Scientists estimate population size and distribution of organisms to monitor the effect of changes to their ecosystem.

REMEMBER!

Make sure that you know what the mean, mode and median are.

5 **Explain why assumptions are made in the capture–recapture method.**

6 **Why are random samples important?**

PRACTICAL

Measure the population size of a common species in a habitat

Learning objectives:

- use scientific ideas to develop a hypothesis
- plan experiments to test a hypothesis
- explain the apparatus and techniques used to sample a population
- explain how a representative sample was taken
- develop a reasoned explanation for some data.

It is impossible to count every plant or animal in a habitat, but it can be estimated by taking samples of the organisms from the habitat. The larger the sample, the more accurate your estimate of the population size is likely to be This allows population sizes to be compared between different areas.

Plants can be sampled more easily than animals because they cannot move around.

Developing a hypothesis

It is summer time. Two students are going to investigate the population size of daisies in trampled and un-trampled areas of the school field. The centre of the school field is used to play cricket, tennis and train for athletic events. The students run, jump and lie on the grass. Not many students go on the parts of the field away from these areas.

Two students need to make a **hypothesis** before they do the investigation. They have made some observations on the field and now know that:

- trampling on soil compacts it
- trampling on plants can destroy the **meristems** as well as crush delicate leaves and flowers
- daisy leaves are not very delicate
- in well-trampled nearly bare ground, plants will have to tolerate large variations in temperature where there is no grass to protect them
- daisy plants have very long fibrous roots and thick leaf cuticles
- plants compete with each other for limited resources.

1 **How do you think compaction may affect**

   a **the soil?**

   b **the daisies growing in the soil?**

These pages are designed to help you think about aspects of the investigation rather than to guide you through it step by step.

Figure 6.4 A daisy population

Figure 6.5 Leaf, root and flower of a daisy

2 If meristems, leaves and flowers can be crushed by trampling how may this affect the daisies?

3 How can periods of very high temperatures affect the daisies?

4 Suggest a hypothesis for the fieldwork investigation that the students are going to do.

Planning an investigation

The teacher has given the students this equipment. They know that it is important to take random samples, make repeat observations and count whole daisy plants.

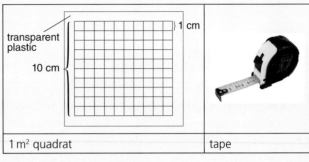

Figure 6.6 Quadrat and tape

5 Suggest how the students can use this equipment to collect representative data to test the hypothesis from Question 4.

6 Why is it important to count whole daisy plants and not just daisy flowers? How many daisies are in the **quadrat**?

7 How can the students calculate the mean number of daisy plants in each area?

8 Another student has asked the students for a copy of their results. Suggest why they asked for it.

Developing explanations

The students did their investigation. Look at their data.

Quadrat position on tape (m)	Un-trampled area	Trampled area
0	3	6
5	4	6
10	3	7
15	2	6
20	2	4
25	4	7
30	3	6

Figure 6.7 Quadrat placed over daisies

ADVICE

Sampling many small sections of an area gives a representative sample of the whole area.

Scientists always use evidence to explain the data they collect. The evidence can be from knowledge or observations. They also relate their data to their original hypothesis.

9 Suggest what the students can conclude from their data.

10 Explain the data using the information that the students knew before they started the investigation.

11 Was the hypothesis in Question 4 proved or disproved?

Learning about land use

Learning objectives:

- identify why land use has changed
- describe the effects of changing land use
- evaluate a change in land use.

KEY WORD

....

biodiversity

Scientists agree that human activity has changed environments and that we need to protect the Earth's biodiversity.

Human population growth

The world's population has increased rapidly, from 1 billion (1000 million) in 1880 to about 7 billion in 2012. People use increasing amounts of the Earth's resources, resulting in a decrease in the land available for other organisms.

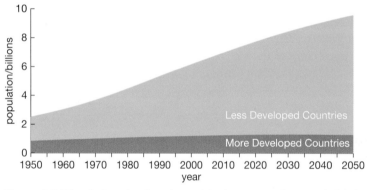

Figure 6.8 Why do less developed countries have a greater population increase?

Humans are using more land for:

- farming
- building
- quarrying
- dumping waste.

Sudden increases in the populations of animals and plants are usually controlled by predators, food availability, disease or toxic waste products. Humans have no predators, grow large amounts of food and have the ability to cure or prevent disease.

Figure 6.9 Intensive farming using fertilisers produces large crops

1 **How do humans change the use of land?**

2 **Why do farmers use fertilisers?**

Using the land

As our population increases, **biodiversity** decreases:

- More land is needed for homes, shops, factories and roads. Building sites destroy habitats. Roads divide habitats making it harder for organisms to find food and mates.
- New quarries are mined to provide stone, slate and metal ores for building materials. Habitats are destroyed.
- More farmland is needed and fertilisers are used. Many farms grow one crop over huge areas. This affects food availability for insect pollinators. There are fewer available nesting sites for birds.
- More waste is sent to landfill, and more sewage and industrial waste are produced. This can pollute the land.

Figure 6.10 An abandoned quarry

Human population is growing exponentially. This means that the increase in any year is greater than in the previous year because the birth rate is greater than the death rate.

3 **Suggest the impact if human populations keep rising.**

4 **Describe the impact of two land-use changes.**

Polluting water

Figure 6.11 Why are there no fish in this water?

If water contains a lot of fertilisers (caused by run-off from farmers' fields) or sewage, the nitrates and phosphates in the water increase and so then algal growth increases. Algae cover the water surface and prevent light from reaching water plants. The plants and algae die. Bacteria respire as they break down dead plants and use up oxygen in the water. The other living organisms in the water die. This is called eutrophication.

5 **Explain the impact of fertiliser run-off.**

6 **Evaluate a change in land use.**

7 **Why do we need to maintain local and global biodiversity?**

REMEMBER!

Humans reduce land availability for other organisms by building, farming, quarrying and dumping waste.

DID YOU KNOW?

When landfill sites are closed, the waste is left to degrade and stabilise. The land is re-used for parks, golf courses and even airports.

Changing the landscape

Learning objectives:

- identify the reasons for deforestation
- describe the impact of peat bog destruction and deforestation
- evaluate the destruction of peat bogs and forests.

KEY WORDS

deforestation
peatlands

Many species in tropical forests and peatlands are struggling to survive as their habitat is destroyed.

Why are landscapes changing?

Huge areas of tropical forest are being destroyed. This **deforestation** is happening to:

- provide land for cattle and rice fields
- grow crops, for example, oil palm and sugar cane to make biofuels. Biofuel crops are sometimes grown at the expense of food crops.

Cleared forests are often used to grow a monoculture (one crop) over huge areas.

Figure 6.12 Peat cut to be used for fuel

Peat bogs form over thousands of years in marshy areas. Decomposers cannot completely break down plant material in acidic conditions with little oxygen, so peat forms. Peat stores carbon.

Peat is used as a fuel and as cheap compost by gardeners. Compost improves soil quality to increase food production.

1 Why are forests cut down?

2 What is peat and how is it used?

The impact of changing landscapes

Forests are often destroyed by burning. Mass destruction of trees has:

- increased the release of carbon dioxide into the atmosphere (due to burning and the respiration of microorganisms that are decaying the remaining plant material)
- reduced the rate that carbon dioxide is removed from the atmosphere (by photosynthesis)
- reduced biodiversity; some of the lost plants and animals may have been useful in the future
- increased methane in the atmosphere because cleared land is used to grow rice in swamp-like fields.

> **REMEMBER!**
>
> Trees and plants in peatlands all use carbon dioxide to photosynthesise. Carbon is then stored in these plants.

Figure 6.13 How will forest fires affect the atmosphere?

Figure 6.14 Orangutans are losing their food sources

Insufficient trees are being replaced. Peat is being destroyed faster than it is being made. Peat and trees are both important carbon 'stores' that are being lost. The loss of peat bogs reduces the variety of different plants, animals and microorganisms that live there. Monocultures also reduce biodiversity.

3. **Describe and explain the impacts of deforestation.**
4. **How can woodland habitats be preserved?**

Balancing act

There is a massive conflict between:

- the need for deforestation to increase land available for food production
- the use of peat as cheap compost to increase food production
- the need to conserve forests and peatlands as habitats for biodiversity
- the need to reduce carbon dioxide emissions from using peat as a fuel and from burning forests.

5. **Evaluate the destruction of peatlands.**

> **DID YOU KNOW?**
>
> About 13 million hectares of forest have been cleared or lost through natural disasters. By 2030, there may only be 10% of our forests left.

Thinking about global warming

Learning objectives:

- recall what global warming is
- describe the causes of global warming
- explain how global warming impacts on biodiversity.

The future of the human species on Earth relies on us maintaining a good level of biodiversity, yet we are threatening it by our actions.

What is global warming?

The average global temperature of the Earth and its atmosphere is increasing. This is **global warming**. It is caused by increasing atmospheric levels of:

- carbon dioxide
- methane.

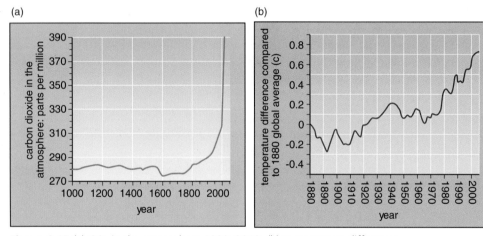

Figure 6.15 (a) CO_2 in the atmosphere 1880–2012; (b) temperature difference from 1880 global average temperature, 1880–2012. What do these graphs tell you?

These gases occur naturally in the atmosphere, but levels have increased over the last 150 years because:

- power plants burn fossil fuels
- petrol is used as fuel in vehicles
- rice crops and cattle farming are increasing
- deforestation and destruction of peatlands are increasing.

As the human population increases more pollution is produced from fossil fuels, particularly by relatively small populations in developed countries.

1. What is global warming?
2. What causes global warming?

Impact on ecosystems

Scientists think that global warming is changing the climate. The average world temperature rise is small (about 0.8 °C since 1880), but some species are sensitive to this, for example, coral reefs.

3 **How do human actions affect global warming?**

4 **Explain how global warming might affect biodiversity?**

Case studies

The white lemuroid possum is the first mammal in Australia to have become almost extinct due to global warming. There are just four known adults left. The white possum's habitat spans cooler areas of high-altitude rainforest. Possums are vulnerable to increases in environmental temperature because they cannot maintain their body temperature.

Little terns are vulnerable to high tides and storms. These are happening more often because of global warming. Little terns migrate to the UK each spring and make their colonies just above the high tide line. Their nests are vulnerable to flooding by stormy seas.

Coastal mangrove forests grow in equatorial regions. Increasing numbers of storms and typhoons are undermining the fine sediment that the mangroves grow in. Seedlings cannot root and essential nutrients for the mangrove ecosystems are washed away.

Figure 6.16 Penguins are losing their habitats. Where else can they survive?

REMEMBER!

Learn three ways that global warming affects biodiversity.

DID YOU KNOW?

If sea levels rose by 1 m, half of the world's important coastal wetlands would be threatened.

Figure 6.17 How does global warming affect little terns?

5 **Explain how global warming affects biodiversity.**

Looking at waste management

Learning objectives:

- describe how waste production is linked to human population growth
- describe the impact of waste on ecosystems
- explain how waste impacts on biodiversity.

KEY WORD

biodiversity

As our population keeps increasing, so our impact on the environment and biodiversity is also increasing.

Pollution

Human population growth and living standards are increasing, particularly in developed countries. We use more resources. As living standards increase, the demand for agriculture, manufacturing and industry increase, producing more waste.

Domestic and industrial waste must be handled correctly to avoid causing more pollution.

Waste substances include:

- sewage
- smoke and toxic gases
- herbicides, pesticides and fertilisers
- lead
- paper and cardboard
- plastic products.

Waste can kill plants and animals and reduce **biodiversity**.

Figure 6.18 Waste tips reduce biodiversity. They are home to decomposers and some birds

1 Why is the amount of waste we produce increasing?

2 Name three types of waste produced by people.

Waste and ecosystems

Causes of pollution include:

- Fertilisers. These can enter waterways, causing eutrophication.
- Toxic chemicals from household and industrial waste. If taken to landfill sites, they can spread into soil and enter waterways. Pesticides and herbicides are also washed into waterways. Toxins build up in food chains, kill organisms and affect feeding relationships.
- Sewage. If untreated, chemicals and parasites can enter waterways. Microorganisms that decompose sewage use dissolved oxygen, causing aquatic organisms to die.
- Smoke and gases. Soot in smoke covers and damages trees; organisms may find breathing difficult.

> **REMEMBER!**
>
> Learn how and where pollution is produced. Pollution reduces biodiversity.

3 How do human actions affect water quality?

4 Suggest how soot damages trees.

Acid rain

Acidic gases are produced when fossil fuels burn. They dissolve in water vapour to make acid (about pH 4). Acid rain:

- damages leaves and roots of plants
- washes mineral ions out of soil, causing mineral deficiencies in plants
- washes aluminium ions from soil into lakes, which affects gills in fish and they cannot survive
- acidifies waterways, so aquatic organisms cannot survive
- can travel in air; acid rain produced in the UK has affected trees and fjords in Norway.

Pollution reduces the available space for other organisms; some species cannot survive. We need to balance our development while sustaining the environment for future generations. Many countries (including the UK) have legislation that controls the use of toxic chemicals, use of landfill sites and treatment of sewage.

Figure 6.19 How does acid rain affect trees?

5 Explain how dangerous levels of toxic chemicals can build up through trophic levels.

> **DID YOU KNOW?**
>
> The Mbeubeuss waste tip in Senegal is one of the world's largest waste tips, receiving 475 000 tonnes of rubbish a year. It covers about 175 hectares (around 266 football pitches).

Investigating pollution

Learning objectives:

- identify pollution levels using indicator species
- explain how indicator species measure pollution
- compare different methods of measuring pollution.

Scientists monitor environmental change to understand how it affects living organisms.

What is an indicator species?

Living organisms are sensitive to different abiotic conditions. If conditions change – for example, pollution – the distribution of organisms can also change. Some organisms are used to measure environmental change. They are called **indicator species**.

 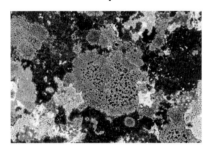

Figure 6.20 The cleaner the air, the leafier the lichens that grow. (a) Leafy lichen; (b) crusty lichen.

Lichens grow on trees, roofs and rocks. They are rarely found growing in cities because they cannot survive in polluted air. The sampling of numbers and types of lichens informs scientists about pollution levels.

Lichens are sensitive to sulfur dioxide concentrations in the air.

Very few types and numbers of lichens grow near power stations. The further away they are, the greater the number and different species that are found.

1. **How does pollution affect living organisms?**

2. **What is an indicator species?**

More indicators

Pollution also affects the distribution and numbers of animals. Aquatic invertebrates are used as indicators of pollution and dissolved oxygen in water, as shown in the following table.

- Sludge worms can live in polluted water. This is because they are adapted to cope with the low oxygen levels in polluted water.
- Mayfly larvae can live in slightly polluted water. There is sufficient oxygen for their needs.
- Alderfly larvae cannot live in polluted water. They cannot survive when oxygen levels are low.

Figure 6.21 Power stations produce sulfur dioxide

Animal	Sensitivity to pollution
stonefly larva	sensitive
water snipe fly larva	sensitive
alderfly larva	sensitive
mayfly larva	semi-sensitive
freshwater mussel	semi-sensitive
damselfly larva	semi-sensitive
bloodworm	tolerates pollution
rat-tailed maggot	tolerates pollution
sludgeworm	tolerates pollution

Pollution affects the distribution of aquatic invertebrates

Water containing lots of different species is a healthy environment.

Pollution levels are also measured directly using:

- probes attached to computers to measure precise conditions, for example, pH, temperature, oxygen and carbon dioxide
- special tests to indicate levels of different chemicals, for example, nitrates.

3 A water sample from a river contained sludgeworms but no stonefly larvae. Is the water polluted? Explain your answer.

4 Suggest two methods to measure the pH of a stream.

Using indicator species

The animals in three different aquatic habitats near a town were sampled and identified. Unfortunately, the names of the habitats came off the sample jars. The samples were taken from a polluted pond, a stagnant pool near a water outlet and a fast-running stream.

Sample	Animals found
A	stonefly larva, mayfly larva, damselfly larva, alderfly larva, water snipe fly larva
B	rat-tailed maggot, sludgeworm, bloodworm
C	sludgeworm, damselfly larva, freshwater mussel

5 Which sample came from which habitat?

6 Which sample contained the least dissolved oxygen? Explain your answer.

7 Suggest one advantage and one disadvantage of using chemical tests instead of indicator species to test for pollution.

DID YOU KNOW?

Coral reefs are water quality indicators because they only tolerate narrow ranges of temperature, salinity and water clarity.

REMEMBER!

Pollution alters the numbers and distribution of plant and animal species.

Maintaining biodiversity

Learning objectives:

- describe some conservation measures
- describe the impact of breeding programmes
- explain how habitats are regenerated.

KEY WORDS

conservation
regeneration
sustainable
ecotourism

Every species depends on others for food, shelter, pollination, etc. Because of interdependence, if one species is removed the whole community is affected.

Protecting ecosystems

Programmes have been developed to reduce negative effects on ecosystems and biodiversity, which are caused by our actions. These measures include:

- Introducing breeding programmes for endangered species.
- The protection and **regeneration** (restoring) of rare habitats.
- Re-introducing field margins and hedgerows on farmland where monocultures are grown. Hedgerows are a habitat for many wild species.

Figure 6.22 Why are hedgerows being replanted?

- Reducing deforestation and carbon dioxide emissions. **Sustainable** strategies include replanting trees.
- Recycling resources instead of dumping waste in landfill. Many materials are recycled in the UK.
- Cloning plant species. Cloning can be done quickly and economically using stem cells found in the meristems. This protects plant species from extinction.
- The development of **ecotourism** practices to reduce the impact of tourism on natural ecosystems, local plants, animals and communities.

Figure 6.23 Why must we recycle waste?

1. How are ecosystems and biodiversity protected?

2. How do hedgerows increase biodiversity?

Conservation

Conservation programmes are introduced:

- because we have a moral responsibility to protect endangered species
- so more plant species may be identified for medicines
- to minimise damage to food chains and webs
- to protect future food supplies.

Captive breeding programmes are planned to ensure genetic diversity is maintained, such as for the Arabian oryx and for giant pandas. Successful programmes allow species to be reintroduced to the wild. The wild Arabian oryx became extinct in the wild in the 1970s, but a successful breeding programme means the animal has now been reclassified as 'vulnerable'.

Many endangered species, for example rhinos, and tigers, are hunted and poached, despite legal protection. Seed banks store seeds carefully to protect plant species for the future.

Figure 6.24 Arabian oryx populations are growing

3 Why are conservation programmes introduced?

4 How do breeding programmes help endangered species?

> **REMEMBER!**
>
> Learn the different programmes for protecting ecosystems and biodiversity.

Protecting rare habitats

There are many difficulties and issues associated with organising conservation programmes. Some of these include:

- ensuring long-term funding
- having qualified scientists who understand the issues
- animals and plants do not recognise boundaries
- many organisations and governments may be involved, working locally, nationally and internationally. It is often difficult to get agreement from all parties for conservation schemes.
- lack of monitoring of protected areas because of difficulties of getting all parties to agree to how this should be carried out.

Mangrove forests are rich ecosystems that prevent coastal erosion and reduce carbon emissions. They are declining rapidly due to land development, and their use as a fuel and building material. In Abu Dhabi, however, mangroves are increasing due to massive planting programmes over the last two decades. The local environment agency works with land developers and the public to maintain healthy, litter-free sustainable forests. The forests protect seagrass beds, which are the sole food of the endangered manatee.

Figure 6.25 Many species depend on sustainable mangrove forests

5 What difficulties are involved in managing conservation programmes?

6 Explain how mangrove forests are protected and regenerated.

7 Explain why it is important to protect biodiversity'

> **DID YOU KNOW?**
>
> Siberian tigers are endangered because of deforestation, hunting and poaching.

Selective breeding

Learning objectives:

- describe the process of selective breeding
- recall how selective breeding enables humans to choose desirable characteristics in animals
- explain how selective breeding can lead to inbreeding.

KEY WORDS

breed
inbreeding
selective
  breeding

Humans have been domesticating animals and plants for thousands of years. DNA evidence suggests that dogs were the first animals to be domesticated, perhaps as early as 33 000 years ago.

Selective breeding

Among the first animals to be domesticated were goats, then sheep. They would have been kept and bred for their meat, milk and hides or skins, which were used for clothes and shelter.

Animals in a population show genetic variation. Humans would have selected those with the characteristics required – the ones that produced the most meat or milk, for instance – and allowed them to breed.

From the offspring of those animals, the humans would then have selected those animals producing the largest yields and bred those. This was repeated over many generations.

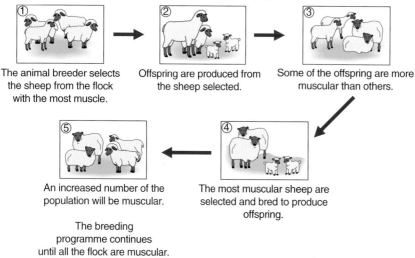

① The animal breeder selects the sheep from the flock with the most muscle.

② Offspring are produced from the sheep selected.

③ Some of the offspring are more muscular than others.

④ The most muscular sheep are selected and bred to produce offspring.

⑤ An increased number of the population will be muscular.

The breeding programme continues until all the flock are muscular.

Figure 6.26 Sheep are bred for their lean meat and how quickly the meat is produced

This is called **selective breeding**. Darwin referred to it as artificial selection, in contrast to natural selection.

The outcomes of different selective breeding programmes are different **breeds**. The breed produced will depend on the characteristics required.

Related characteristics are often selected together, such as quality *and* volume of milk produced in cattle.

Figure 6.27 The Belgian blue (top) has been bred for its meat, which is muscle. The Jersey (bottom) has been bred to produce rich, creamy milk

1 Suggest what other characteristics sheep may be bred for.

2 Describe the technique of selective breeding.

Domesticating dogs

Breeding dogs for hunting, or for their appearance and temperament, has involved selective breeding. The dog breeder selects dogs with characteristics of the breed.

Popular breeds of large dogs look different, but they are all the same species. They can still interbreed.

A person buying a dog looks for its 'pedigree'. This is a record of the animal's parentage, to show how true a dog is to the breed.

3 List some characteristics that dogs are bred for.

4 Explain why, even though they look very different, all dogs belong to the same species.

Problems with inbreeding

Pedigree dogs are bred with individuals of the same breed. This maintains their characteristics. They will have a limited gene pool, or range of genes in the population. They will become inbred. Usually, the incidence of rare disease alleles will increase in inbred animals.

Studies show that **inbreeding** puts dogs at risk of birth defects and genetically inherited health problems, and makes them prone to disease. Unnaturally small or large dogs are particularly prone to problems.

> **REMEMBER!**
>
> Make sure that you understand, and can describe, the principles of selective breeding.

> **DID YOU KNOW?**
>
> Analysis of mitochondrial DNA suggests that modern dogs are related to the first dogs – which would have been kept for hunting – which originated in Europe between 19 000 and 32 000 years ago.

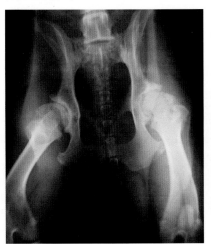

Hip dysplasia, where the hip joint is not correctly formed, and size are correlated in large dogs.

Many Dalmations are predisposed to deafness.

In bulldogs the large head and narrow hips mean that sometimes puppies have to be born by Caesarean section.

Figure 6.28 Some problems with inbreeding in certain dog breeds

5 Explain why breeding dogs with other dogs of the same breed causes problems?

6 List some of the problems with this process.

7 Evaluate whether the benefits of breeding pedigree dogs outweigh the health risks to the dog.

Producing new plant varieties

Learning objectives:

- describe the process of selective breeding
- recall how selective breeding enables humans to choose desirable characteristics in plants.

KEY WORDS

environmental change
genetic variation
mixed population

Lack of *genetic variation* in potatoes cultivated in Ireland in the 1850s was a factor that contributed to the potato famine. Many people died of starvation. Most of the potatoes grown were one variety: the Lumper.

Producing new plant varieties

In modern agriculture, new crop varieties are bred for disease resistance. Increased yields and improved quality of food crops are also the main goals of plant breeders. Other beneficial characteristics are that crops:

- grow and mature quickly
- have a distinctive taste, aroma or colour, for example, in strawberries
- have long shelf-life, store well or can be frozen.

Selective breeding enables crop growers to plant large areas with identical plants, giving maximum yields. But this does mean that many crops are genetically uniform. The whole crop could be lost if there is **environmental change**. Selective breeding has had a huge impact on the world's food production.

1 **Suggest three characteristics that crop plants could be bred for?**

2 **What could happen to a crop made up of just one variety if the environment changed?**

Figure 6.29 In a plant-breeding programme, plants of one variety or species are crossed with another

Traditional plant breeding

In traditional plant breeding, a plant with a desirable trait is crossed with another plant having the same or another desirable trait. The plants selected would be from a **mixed population**, or existing varieties. Pollen is transferred from the flowers of one plant to the other. The plant is prevented from self-fertilising or being cross-pollinated by another plant.

The process is repeated over several generations until the plants breed true for the required characteristics.

Plants in horticulture are developed, for instance, for the size and colour of their flowers and scent.

Clematis is a wild flower that grows in hedgerows and climbs trees. In the nineteenth century, plant breeders in Britain, France, Belgium and Germany raced to produce varieties with the largest, most colourful flowers.

REMEMBER!

You do not need to know about specific examples, but you do need to be able to explain the benefits of and risks of selective breeding.

Figure 6.30 Wild clematis (left) and flowers in two modern clematis varieties. Plant breeders still use wild clematis because it is tolerant of clematis wilt disease

3 How does the plant breeder control which pollen is transferred to which female flower?

4 Explain why it is still useful to use wild versions of a cultivated plant in breeding programmes.

Producing a new variety

It can be very difficult to combine several desirable characteristics in a plant, for example, yield, disease resistance and perhaps other characteristics. And it is expensive.

A traditional plant-breeding programme will commonly take 12–15 years. It will involve the selection and crossing of suitable individual plants, various selection processes and a series of trials.

DID YOU KNOW?

Many plant scientists are now using marker-assisted techniques in plant breeding. We can identify genetic markers in a plant's DNA linked to key important characteristics such as nutritional qualities, disease resistance, yield, etc.

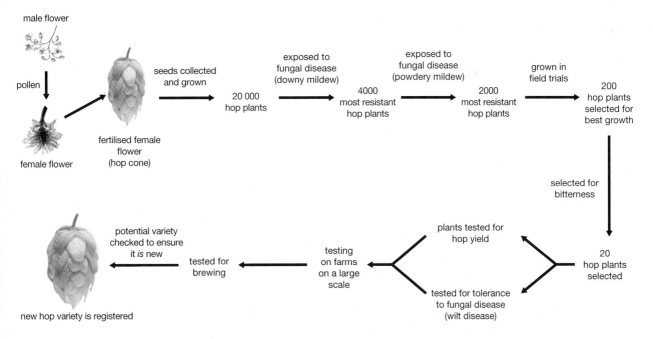

Figure 6.31 A hop-breeding programme uses traditional plant-breeding techniques

5 Explain why a plant-breeding programme can take up to 15 years.

6 What three characteristics are hops bred for?

Genetic engineering

Learning objectives:

- describe the process of genetic engineering
- give examples of how plant crops have been genetically engineered to improve products
- describe the main steps in the process of genetic engineering.

KEY WORDS

genetic
 engineering
GM crops
vector
restriction enzyme
sticky ends
ligase
host bacteria
antibiotic resistance
 markers

Genetic engineering **involves taking specific genes from one organism and introducing them into the genome of another. Scientists can now, more or less, transfer genes from any organism, including plants, animals, bacteria or viruses to introduce desirable characteristics.**

Genetically engineered plants

Genetic engineering has transformed crop production. Genes from many organisms, often not even plants, are cut out of their chromosomes and inserted into the cells of crop plants. Such crop plants and other organisms are called genetically modified, **GM crops** or GM organisms (GMOs).

GM crops can:

- be resistant to insect attack or to herbicides.
- produce increased yields because of the characteristics chosen, such as larger fruits, disease resistance or herbicide resistance.

GM crops could provide more food or more nutritious foods, for example, golden rice. Rice is a staple food for Asian communities. As a result, many people in Asia suffer from vitamin A deficiency. This can result in night blindness, where the eyes are unable to adjust to dim light but up 500 000 children go on to become *permanently* blind every year. Half of these die.

Golden rice has been developed using genes from maize and a common soil bacterium. The gene from maize produces the ß-carotene that our bodies use to make vitamin A. It's the same gene as in carrots – that's why it's called carotene.

Plants have been engineered to be resistant to disease, and to increase yields, such as producing bigger, better fruit. Several types of crop plant have been produced that are resistant to diseases caused by viruses.

In the wet summer of 2012, potato plants became exposed to the potato blight fungus. In 2014 British scientists produced a GM potato that is resistant to potato blight. Genes from two wild relatives of the potato were inserted into the Désirée potato variety.

KEY INFORMATION

If genes are transferred to plants, this needs to be at an early stage of their development. Older organisms have too many cells that would need to be modified.

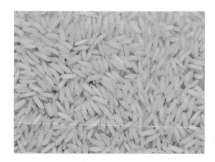

Figure 6.32 The more ß-carotene that golden rice contains the more yellow-orange it is. The first generation of Golden rice, which had only a fraction of the ß-carotene, was produced using a daffodil gene.

Figure 6.33 Pesticides are sprayed over crops to protect them from diseases. Disease resistant GM plants don't need the pesticides.

1 **Describe how golden rice might help to prevent night blindness.**

2 **Give two reasons for the genetic modification of plant crops.**

3 **What types of organism cause disease in plants?**

HIGHER TIER ONLY

The genetic engineering technique

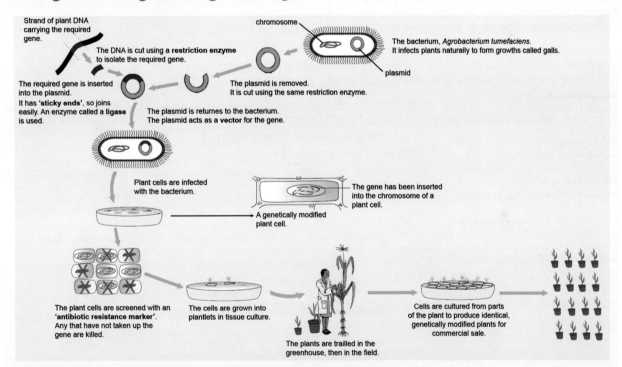

Figure 6.34 The genetic engineering engineering technique used to produce a crop plant

Enzymes are used to remove the required gene, or genes, from the organism that carries the gene(s).

The gene is transferred, using a **vector**, to the organism that is to be modified. The vector is often a plasmid. The gene is inserted and sealed into the plasmid DNA using another enzyme. Bacteria have plasmids, and so do some eukaryotes, such as yeast. Viruses may also be used as vectors, including tobacco mosaic virus(TMV). Viruses that have had other genes modified, so that they are not infective, have been used in vaccine production.

4 **How is the required gene removed from the donor organism?**

5 **How is the gene transferred to the organism that is to be genetically modified?**

Genetically modified crops: the science

Learning objectives:

- explain the benefits of, and concerns about, genetic modification
- explain the ethical concerns of genetic engineering.

Biotechnologists in Britain aim to increase wheat yields to 20 tonnes per hectare by 2035.

Herbicide- and insecticide-resistant crops

Weeds reduce crop-plant yields and encourage fungal disease. GM crops have had genes inserted that make them resistant to a particular herbicide. As the crop grows, the field is sprayed with herbicide. The crop is unaffected, but the weeds are killed.

Another key area is the development of GM crops that resist insect attack. *Bacillus thuringiensis* (Bt) is a soil bacterium that produces a natural insecticide. The gene for this has been inserted into crops.

Bt insecticide is a protein that kills the caterpillar, or larva, that eats the crop plant. It only works on some orders of insect, such as butterflies and moths, which are the most serious pests.

Figure 6.35 After a few bites of the leaves of this Bt peanut, the caterpillar died

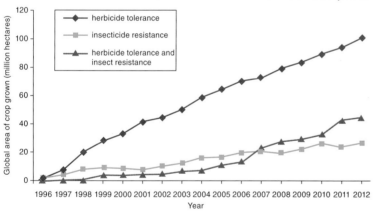

Figure 6.36 Global production of herbicide-tolerant and insect-resistant plants

1. Why are herbicide-tolerant genes inserted into crops?

2. The reproductive rate in insects is very fast. Suggest why some populations are becoming resistant to the *Bt* gene.

Ecological effects

GM crops growing in the wild have been reported in many countries. 'Escaped' populations usually die out. GM crops may also cross-pollinate a wild or cultivated relative of the crop. GM oilseed rape is genetically capable of cross-pollinating with eight wild relatives.

GM crops have been reported to be swapping genes with other GM crops. A study of 288 oilseed rape plants in America showed that two had 'man-made' genes for multiple pesticides.

Of concern is the *Bt* gene's effect on non-target organisms. Only insects that eat the crop should be affected. However, pollen of some GM crops is carried in the wind. The pollen could be toxic to other insects that are essential pollinators of crops and other plants.

The monarch butterfly

A monarch butterfly larva, feeding on milkweed

Figure 6.37 One study in 1999 showed that the growth of monarch butterfly caterpillars was affected when its foodplants were dusted with Bt pollen

Studies suggest, however, that the density of pollen in the wild would rarely come close to the levels needed to harm the caterpillars. The monarch butterfly is in decline, and research is ongoing to find out why.

3 **Explain the possible spread of GM plants.**

4 **What are the concerns about Bt plants?**

5 **Do you consider GM products to be safe? Justify your answer.**

> **REMEMBER!**
>
> Be careful what you read about genetic modification. Newspapers report scientific information second hand. Look for the original source of the information.

> **DID YOU KNOW?**
>
> Researchers aim to start growing a vitamin-enhanced 'super-banana' in Uganda. The bananas are genetically engineered to have increased levels of β-carotene, which is converted to vitamin A by the body. A deficiency in vitamin A can be fatal.

Is genetic modification safe?

KEY WORDS

antibiotic
 resistance
 marker

Learning objectives:

- explain the concerns that people have about genetic modification
- explain the possible safety issues of genetic engineering in agriculture and medicine.

GM food crops and production of hormones by GM have had beneficial effects. But are GM products safe?

Safety concerns of GMOs

Worldwide, GM microorganisms are being used to produce various foods, along with food additives. And some GM plants and seeds are being fed to animals that provide us with meat, milk and eggs.

Are these foods safe to eat? The bacterium *Escherichia coli* (*E.coli*), and the fungus, yeast, are microorganisms that are often genetically modified.

E. coli lives in our large intestines. Yeast, in the wild, lives on the surface of fruit. If they escaped from biotechnology production facilities might they be dangerous?

Genetic modification of viruses that are used to transfer genes causes real concern. Viruses can only reproduce in the cells of other organisms, so their genetic manipulation is worrying. The solution is to inactivate genes related to infection.

Figure 6.38 Some farmers use GM maize as animal feed.

1 **Why are people concerned about GMOs escaping from fermenters?**

2 **How are viruses used to transfer genes made safe?**

Antibiotic-resistance genes

When organisms or cells are modified, not all cells take up the foreign gene. The cells that have not need to be screened out. When the cells are modified, an **antibiotic resistance marker** is inserted into the organism's genome as well as the required gene. This marker gene is usually one giving antibiotic resistance. When the culture of cells is treated with antibiotic, any cells that have not taken up the required gene successfully will be killed. Resistance is created to the antibiotic kanamycin, which is rarely used today.

3 **Why is a genetic marker gene used when genetically modifying organisms?**

4 **Why has the gene for resistance to the antibiotic kanamycin been chosen as the antibiotic resistance marker.**

Assessing the safety of GM products

The EU's approach to GM crop development is the most stringent in the world.

One significant concern is whether a GM food might cause allergic reactions. No GM products to date have been found to produce new allergies, or are any more or less allergenic than their non-GM versions. GM foods, modified appropriately, could become the solution to, rather than the cause of, food allergies.

Most scientists have found no differences that are statistically significant between other health impacts of GM crops and non-GM versions.

Recent studies have suggested that some GM products may cause cancer. But these studies are controversial.

GM plants are commonly made resistant to a herbicide called glyphosate, or Roundup®. Some harmful effects could be caused by the herbicide, and not the genetic modification itself.

Glyphosate is described as harmless to humans and other animals, and is said to break down quickly in the environment. But now some scientists have identified correlations between glyphosate use and an increase in conditions ranging from autism to cancer.

Figure 6.39 A GM field of maize sprayed with glyphosate. Use of this herbicide has increased in the USA since the introduction of GM crops

Figure 6.40 Environmental activists protesting against Monsanto's GMO programs and demanding that foods be labelled

5 Discuss the evidence for GM crops being harmful.

6 Suggest why crop treatments, and not the crops themselves, might be harmful.

REMEMBER!

Be prepared to analyse and discuss negative and positive aspects of genetic modification from information that you are given.

DID YOU KNOW?

US scientists have engineered a bacterium that, to live, needs an amino acid that does not occur in nature. If any of the organisms escape the culture vessel, they cannot survive.

Ethically wrong, or essential?

Learning objectives:

- explain the benefits of, and concerns about, genetic modification
- explain the ethical issues of genetic engineering in agriculture and medicine.

The glowing GM fish in the photograph were created during attempts to produce a fish that would glow in polluted water. Unfortunately, these GM fish glowed all the time.

The ethics of genetic modification

Was the sale of the Glofish® ethical? Or its development in the first place?

Should we be inserting genes from one organism into another? Very often these species are not even closely related. And should we be inserting human genes into other organisms?

Figure 6.41 Glofish® didn't work as a pollution indicator, but quickly went on sale in pet shops and then on the Internet.

Some religious teachings suggest that it is wrong to change natural organisms that God has created. What right do we have to change the genome of another organism? Is it acceptable to do this for the benefit of the human race? Is genetic engineering *ever* justified?

1 Give one ethical reason in favour of genetic modification.

2 Give one ethical reason against genetic modification.

Producing and marketing GM foods

Farmers cannot collect and sow the seed from GM crops because they will not breed true. They have to buy more for the next growing season. The seed companies are perceived as exploiting poor farmers.

Food producers are required to label GM foods, making it clear when a food is genetically modified. Customers can decide whether or not to buy them.

GM food must be clearly defined. And food manufacturers must ensure that no other food is contaminated with GM ingredients. Unscrupulous food manufacturers might substitute cheaper GM ingredients for more expensive conventional ones.

3 Explain why farmers should not collect seed from a GM crop to sow the following year.

4 Why should GM foods be labelled?

5 How could GM contaminants be detected in food?

Embryo transplants

Cloning is also important in animals. It enables the animal breeder to produce many animals that have identical characteristics. This can be important commercially, perhaps related to producing high milk volumes or quality beef. Cloning in animals is done by **embryo transplants.**

A developing embryo is removed from a pregnant female early in the pregnancy, so the cells have not yet become specialised. The cells are separated, grown for a while in culture and then transplanted into host mothers.

In the future, it's possible that embryos for implantation may be genetically modified.

6 What is the purpose of embryo transplants?

7 Describe the technique of embryo transplantation.

> **REMEMBER!**
>
> You should understand the potential of cloning techniques in agriculture, but you do not need to know details of the techniques themselves.

GM or traditional methods?

Many scientists believe that genetic engineering, while it has great potential, hasn't lived up to its promise. And while it may have revolutionised the production of pharmaceuticals, for instance the hormone, insulin, it may have made the ecological impact of crop production worse. There are also questions about the ethics of GM animals.

What is important is that further research is carried out. Many argue that this research should be done by scientific institutions rather than agricultural companies. They also suggest that we should not abandon traditional breeding programmes, which are slower, but have a proven success rate and safety record.

> **DID YOU KNOW?**
>
> Scientists genetically modify plant cells in one of two ways: using plasmids inserted into the soil bacterium *Agrobacterium tumefaciens,* or using a gene gun, which shoots DNA into plant cells.

Learning about health

Learning objectives:

- describe the relationship between health and disease
- describe communicable and non-communicable diseases
- describe the interactions between different types of disease.

KEY WORDS

communicable
immune system
mental health
tuberculosis
HPV
non-communicable

The word 'health' can mean many different things, depending on the people involved and their situation.

Health and disease

Good health is complete physical and mental well-being. It is about feeling good and having a positive frame of mind. **Mental health** is as important as physical health.

The major causes of physical and mental ill health include:

- disease
- diet
- stress
- life situations.

Diseases are disorders that affect part or all of an organism. They can be **communicable**, like measles and HIV, or **non-communicable**, such as cancer and cardiovascular disease.

Different types of disease may interact; for example, viruses living in cells can cause cancers. Cervical cancer is linked to infection with human papilloma virus (HPV), which causes genital warts.

Being overweight is strongly related to having high blood pressure. Having high blood pressure damages the body's arteries in the long term, making the walls thick and stiff, rather than flexible and elastic.

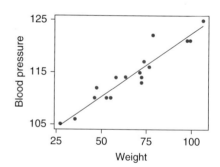

Figure 6.42 What do these data show?

1. Describe what we mean by 'health'.
2. Name the major causes of ill health.
3. Name one communicable and one non-communicable disease.

Diet, life situations and stress

Poor nutrition can contribute to the risk of developing some diseases:

- high fat or sugar-rich diets can cause high blood pressure, depression, heart disease and strokes, eating disorders and Type 2 diabetes.
- low-calcium diets cause osteoporosis.
- red meat and processed meat increase the risk of bowel cancer.

Stress develops when life situations occur, for example, moving home, death in the family or divorce.

When you are stressed, hormones are released, blood vessels constrict and blood pressure rises. Stress often causes depression. It increases the risk of obesity, heart disease, Alzheimer's disease and diabetes; it can also trigger asthma in people who already have it.

Different diseases can interact:

- **immune system** diseases, such as AIDS/HIV, can cause an increased risk of contracting infectious diseases, for example, **tuberculosis**.
- immune reactions initially caused by a pathogen can cause allergies, such as skin rashes. Severe viral respiratory infections in early childhood can trigger asthma as children grow.
- severe physical ill health, for example obesity or cancer, can cause depression and other mental illnesses.

Figure 6.43 Name a cause of asthma

4 **Explain how lifestyle factors affect mental health.**

5 **Explain one example of how different diseases interact.**

HPV and cervical cancer

HPV is found in most cervical cancers. People with weak immune systems are less able to resist HPV. Not everyone who gets HPV develops cancer. Worldwide, cervical cancer is the second most common female cancer. It often takes many years to develop after having HPV and does not usually show symptoms until it is quite advanced. It is hard to treat.

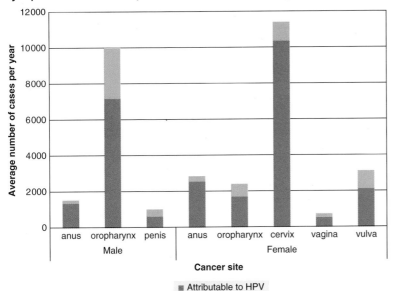

Figure 6.44 What do these data show?

6 **Explain the graph in Figure 6.44.**

7 **Discuss the human and financial cost of cancer on individuals, families and nations.**

> **DID YOU KNOW?**
>
> Around 80 000 children aged between 5 and 16 years suffer from severe depression.

> **KEY INFORMATION**
>
> Don't forget that ill health can lead to poor mental health.

Studying pathogens

Learning objectives:

- explain how communicable diseases are spread
- explain how communicable diseases can be controlled
- distinguish between epidemics and pandemics.

KEY WORDS

antigen
epidemic
pandemic
pathogen
protist

Ebola haemorrhagic fever (EHF) first appeared in 1976 in two outbreaks. One was in Sudan, and the other was in a village near the Ebola River in the Democratic Republic of Congo.

What are pathogens?

Pathogens are microorganisms that cause infectious diseases. They depend on their hosts to provide the conditions and nutrients they need to grow and reproduce. Pathogens can be

- viruses, for example, measles
- bacteria, such as *Salmonella* which causes food poisoning
- **protists**, a protist causes malaria
- fungi, like rose black spot.

Pathogens can infect plants or animals. They are spread by direct contact, by water or through the air.

The spread of diseases caused by pathogens can be prevented or reduced by:

- testing the patient's DNA
- detecting the antigen (toxin) that is causing the disease
- visual identification of the disease by a plant pathologist (someone who studies plant diseases).

Figure 6.45 What type of pathogen causes rose black spot?

1. **Give four examples of pathogens.**
2. **Describe how pathogens spread.**

Pathogens in detail

Bacteria and viruses can reproduce rapidly in the body.

- Bacteria produce toxins that damage tissues and make us feel ill.
- Viruses live and reproduce inside cells, damaging them.

Pathogens replicate quickly. In each generation, the number of bacteria double. This happens about every twenty minutes. Viruses replicate many times inside each infected cell and then the host cells burst to release the many new viruses.

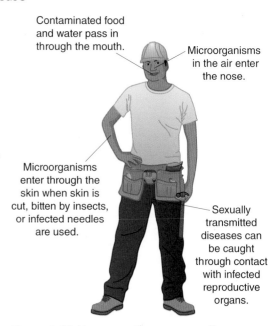

Contaminated food and water pass in through the mouth.

Microorganisms in the air enter the nose.

Microorganisms enter through the skin when skin is cut, bitten by insects, or infected needles are used.

Sexually transmitted diseases can be caught through contact with infected reproductive organs.

Figure 6.46 How are pathogens spread?

The toxins released by pathogens cause the symptoms of infection. These include high temperatures, nausea, headaches and rashes. People get a communicable disease because they receive the pathogen from someone who has it. Measures to prevent or reduce the spread of diseases include:

- simple hygiene, such as covering your mouth when coughing, using a handkerchief when sneezing and washing your hands after using the toilet
- isolation of infected individuals
- destroying vectors, for example mosquitoes are the malaria vector
- vaccination.

3 **Why do pathogens make us feel ill?**

4 **Explain how the spread of diseases can be reduced or prevented.**

Figure 6.47 Why do doctors and nurses wear protective clothing?

A case study

Ebola haemorrhagic fever (EHF) is a deadly virus: 50–90% of people infected with EHF die. The last outbreak of EHF began in December 2013, in Guinea, and spread to Nigeria, Sierra Leone and Liberia.

Fruit bats carry EHF and may infect animals and humans. The disease is caught by direct contact with body fluids (blood and saliva) of an infected individual. Symptoms include fever, headache, diarrhoea, nausea and rashes. Currently, there is no cure for EHF but two vaccines are under development.

Prevention measures include:

- reducing the risk of contact with infected animals
- wearing protective clothing
- washing hands frequently
- isolation of infected people and safe burials of the dead
- travel restrictions.

An **epidemic** is when disease spreads rapidly to many people. EHF in 2013–14 was an epidemic. If EHF had spread globally, it would have been a **pandemic**.

5 **Evaluate the control measures for EHF.**

6 **Explain the difference between an epidemic and a pandemic.**

Figure 6.48 Fruit bat meat is a delicacy in West Africa

DID YOU KNOW?

In 1918, Spanish influenza killed 40–50 million people.

KEY INFORMATION

Pathogens come in many different forms, and that each one causes a different disease.

Analysing and evaluating data

KEY WORDS

bias
correlation
trend

Learning objectives:

- translate information between graphical and numerical forms
- use scatter diagrams to identify correlations
- evaluate the strength of evidence.

Analysing and evaluating data is a key skill for all scientists, but it is vitally important in medical research.

Looking for patterns

Scientists try to identify links between variables. Sometimes there is no link. When interpreting graphs:

- identify patterns or **trends**
- use axis labels and units when describing the graph; for example, 'as vaccination uptake increases, cases of measles fall'
- look for particular features of the graph, such as maximum and minimum values, the range, outliers and patterns that do not fit trends
- quote numbers to clarify descriptions.

Useful words to describe graphs are: increased, decreased, faster, slower, constant, plateau, maximum, minimum.

1. What do the data in Figure 6.49(a) show?

2. Describe the trends in the data shown in Figure 6.49(b). Are the two trends linked?

Exploring links in data

A **correlation** is an association between two sets of random data. A correlation does not prove that A affects B, or that B affects A. Both A and B could be caused by another variable. In medical research, scientists have to determine links between treatments and cures, or risk factors and disease. This is difficult if:

- the proposed cause only sometimes results in the disease
- the disease has many possible causes
- there is a long delay between proposed cause and effect.

If one variable increases as the other increases, this is a positive correlation. If one variable increases as the other decreases, it is a negative correlation. To prove a causal mechanism, an investigation needs to be carried out.

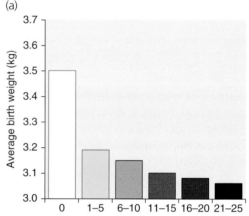

(a)

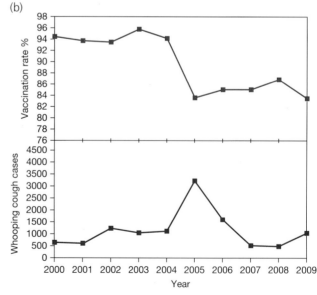

(b)

Figure 6.49 (a) Smoking in pregnancy and birthweight (b) Whooping cough incidence and vaccination uptake

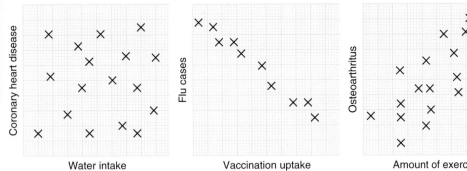

Figure 6.50 Do these graphs show correlation or not?

3 Explain the data in Figure 6.51.

4 Why is it often difficult to determine links between variables?

Evaluating data

When evaluating data think about these questions:

- are the data reliable? Was there an appropriate control group?
- are the data valid?
- was the sample size sufficient?
- how could better data be collected? (Think about length of study, sample selection etc.)
- how could more accurate data be collected? Do the data answer the question?
- are there any anomalies in the data? Can these be explained?
- how confident are you that the evidence supports the conclusion? Has a causal relationship been proved? Could anyone use the same data to support a different conclusion?
- are the data biased? Who completed the research? Do they have a personal interest in the data?

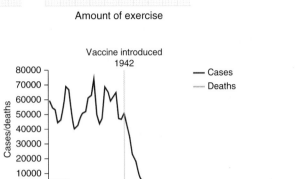

Figure 6.51 Diphtheria cases in the UK

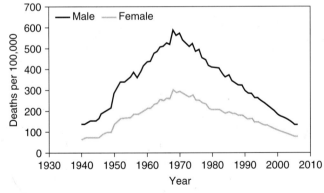

Figure 6.52 Deaths due to coronary heart disease in Australia

5 Describe the male trend in Figure 6.52. Compare both trends.

6 Evaluate the data in Figure 6.52.

Learning about malaria

Learning objectives:

- recall that malaria is a protist disease
- explain how malaria is spread
- evaluate control methods for the spread of malaria.

KEY WORDS

protist
vector

Malaria is the most prolific parasitic disease of humans in the World. More children die from malaria than any other communicable disease.

What is malaria?

The pathogens that cause malaria are called **protists**. Protists are single-celled organisms. The protist that causes malaria is called *Plasmodium*. For part of its lifecycle, it lives in human blood.

The protist is spread by female mosquitoes, which feed on blood. They suck infected blood from someone with malaria and then pass the protists on when they feed on a new person.

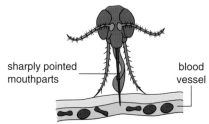

sharply pointed
mouthparts

blood
vessel

Figure 6.53 How do you catch malaria?

Organisms that spread disease, rather than causing it themselves, are called **vectors**. The mosquito is the vector for malaria.

Symptoms of malaria appear from 7–18 days to over a year after infection and include:

- recurrent episodes of fever
- sweats and chills
- muscle pains
- headaches
- diarrhoea
- cough.

Malaria can be fatal if not treated.

1 **What causes malaria?**

2 **What are the symptoms of malaria?**

3 **What is a vector?**

Spreading malaria

The mosquito has a complicated lifecycle. Mosquitoes breed and lay eggs in still water. The eggs hatch and each larva develops into a pupa in the water. When an adult mosquito hatches, it rests on the water surface to let its body dry and harden so it can fly.

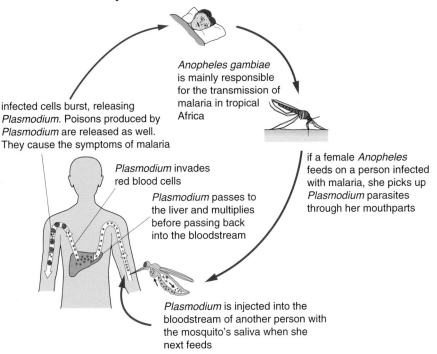

Anopheles gambiae is mainly responsible for the transmission of malaria in tropical Africa

infected cells burst, releasing *Plasmodium*. Poisons produced by *Plasmodium* are released as well. They cause the symptoms of malaria

Plasmodium invades red blood cells

Plasmodium passes to the liver and multiplies before passing back into the bloodstream

if a female *Anopheles* feeds on a person infected with malaria, she picks up *Plasmodium* parasites through her mouthparts

Plasmodium is injected into the bloodstream of another person with the mosquito's saliva when she next feeds

Figure 6.54 Mosquito lifecycle

Malaria is controlled by breaking the lifecycle of the vector or by avoiding contact with it. Control measures include:

- spraying pools of water with insecticide to kill the mosquitoes
- draining stagnant water pools
- spraying pools with oil to prevent the larvae from breathing
- using mosquito nets to avoid bites
- taking drugs to kill the protist in the blood.

Malaria can also be spread by using dirty needles for injections or can be passed from a pregnant woman to her baby.

4. **Explain how malaria is spread.**

5. **Describe the lifecycle of the malarial vector.**

DID YOU KNOW?

Malaria is not found in the UK, but about 1400 people were diagnosed with it after returning from holiday in 2012. Two people died.

KEY INFORMATION

Knowledge of the mosquito lifecycle helps us to control the spread of malaria.

Learning about viral diseases

Learning objectives:

- describe the symptoms of some viral diseases
- describe the transmission and control of some viral diseases including HIV
- explain how some viral diseases are spread.

KEY WORDS

HIV
TMV
vaccination

Communicable diseases are caused by pathogens that pass from one person to another.

Viral diseases

Viruses are very small pathogens. They are not living cells. They have a strand of genetic material inside a protein coat. The genetic material replicates inside host cells to make new viruses, which are then released.

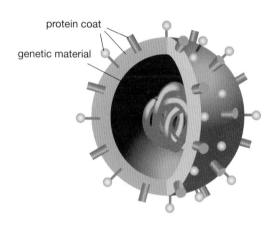

protein coat

genetic material

Figure 6.55 How are viruses different from living cells?

Examples of viral diseases are:

- measles, a serious illness. Symptoms include fever and a red rash over the skin. It can be fatal if there are complications.
- **HIV**, which initially causes a flu-like illness.
- tobacco mosaic virus (**TMV**), which this affects over 150 plant species including tomatoes. Leaves have discoloured 'mosaic' patterns. This reduces photosynthesis and affects plant growth, and the quality and number of fruits are affected.

1. How do viruses reproduce?

2. **Describe the symptoms of two viral diseases.**

Figure 6.56 Suggest how TMV got its name

Spread and control

Virus spread and are controlled in various ways.

Virus	Mechanism for spread	Control
Measles	**Droplet infection** Talking, coughing and sneezing all cause the expulsion of tiny droplets into the air. Inhaling droplets that carry viruses causes measles to spread.	Most young children have **vaccinations** to protect them against this possibly fatal disease.
HIV	**Direct contact** HIV is spread by sexual contact or exchange of body fluids such as blood. This can occur if drug users share needles.	Antiretroviral drugs are prescribed to stop the virus entering the lymph nodes.
TMV	**Enters plants via wounds** The virus gains access through a break in the skin or plant epidermis.	It is controlled by: removal of infected plant material, controlling pests, sterilising tools (using heat), washing hands after handling infected plants.

Figure 6.57 Suggest why these commuters are wearing masks

3 Describe how HIV is spread and suggest control measures.

4 Describe how TMV is spread and controlled.

Counting the cost

Viral diseases are harder to treat than bacterial diseases. Bacteria are living cells that survive outside body cells. They can be treated with prescribed drugs. Viruses are only found inside host cells, where they are protected from drugs. This is why we are vaccinated against some viral diseases.

HIV is very difficult to control. If it is not successfully controlled by antiretroviral drugs, the virus enters the lymph nodes and attacks the body's immune cells. Late-stage HIV, or AIDS, occurs when the body's immune system is no longer able to deal with other infections or cancers.

5 Explain how HIV leads to AIDS.

6 Why is it harder to treat viral diseases than bacterial diseases?

7 Compare the mechanism for spread for measles and HIV. Explain which disease is most infectious.

DID YOU KNOW?

Each type of virus attacks a specific cell. For example, the measles virus attacks skin and sensory nerve cells.

KEY INFORMATION

Viruses are not living things. They have many different shapes (just one of which is shown in Figure 6.55).

Studying bacterial diseases

Learning objectives:

- describe the symptoms of some bacterial diseases
- explain how some bacterial diseases are spread
- explain how some bacterial diseases can be controlled.

Some pathogens are bacterial. Bacteria can reproduce very quickly in our bodies.

Bacterial diseases

Many bacteria are not harmful and some are actually very useful. We use them to make cheese and yoghurt, to break down our waste and make medicines. Some bacteria, however, are pathogens and cause diseases, infecting both plants and animals.

Examples of bacterial diseases are:

- *Salmonella*, which causes food poisoning. A build-up of toxic bacterial waste products causes symptoms that include:
  - › fever
  - › abdominal cramps
  - › vomiting
  - › diarrhoea.
- **Gonorrhoea**, a sexually transmitted disease. The toxic bacterial products cause symptoms that include:
  - › a thick yellow or green discharge from the vagina or penis
  - › pain when urinating.

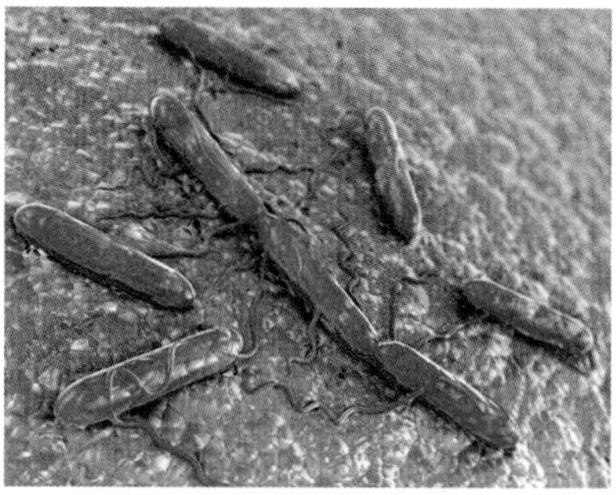

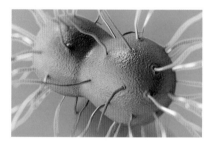

Figure 6.58 *Salmonella* bacteria cause food poisoning

1 Name some bacterial diseases.

2 Describe the symptoms of *Salmonella* and gonorrhoea.

Figure 6.59 How are these gonorrhoea bacteria different from *Salmonella* bacteria?

Spread and control

Bacteria are spread and controlled in various ways.

Salmonella is spread by:

- ingesting (eating) food that is contaminated with *Salmonella* bacteria
- preparing food in unhygienic conditions; for example, using contaminated knives or chopping boards.

In the UK, the spread of *Salmonella* is controlled by vaccinating poultry against the bacterium. Food should be prepared in hygienic conditions and cooked thoroughly. Washing hands before and after food preparation and after using the bathroom also help.

Figure 6.60 Why must food be cooked thoroughly?

Gonorrhoea is spread by sexual contact. The spread can be controlled by:

- treatment with antibiotics. In the past, the disease was easily treated with the antibiotic penicillin, but in recent years many resistant strains of the bacteria have appeared
- use of a barrier method of contraception, such as a condom, to prevent contact.

3 **Describe how *Salmonella* is spread.**

4 **Explain how gonorrhoea can be controlled.**

Symptom delay

People with communicable infections do not develop symptoms as soon as they are infected with the pathogen. There are distinct stages of infection:

- the pathogen enters an organism.
- the pathogen reproduces rapidly in ideal conditions to increase numbers. This is the incubation period.
- pathogens make harmful toxins, which build up. The more bacteria that are present, the quicker the toxins build up.
- symptoms develop, for example, fever and a headache.

The graph shows *Salmonella* cases over a period of 12 months.

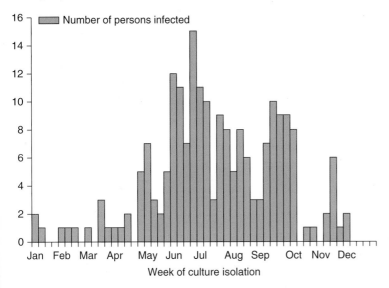

Figure 6.61 *Salmonella* cases over 1 year

DID YOU KNOW?

In 2015 there was an outbreak of a highly drug-resistant strain of gonorrhoea bacteria in the UK.

KEY INFORMATION

Bacteria are living things, unlike viruses. Bacterial diseases can be treated with antibiotics, unlike viral diseases.

5 **Describe the pattern of *Salmonella* cases shown in the bar chart and suggest explanations for it.**

6 **Explain how knowledge of the spread of bacterial diseases can lead to their control.**

7 **Compare and contrast bacterial and viral diseases.**

Looking at fungal diseases

Learning objectives:

- recall the name and symptoms of a fungal disease
- describe the transmission and treatment of barley powdery mildew
- explain how barley powdery mildew affects the growth of the plant.

KEY WORDS

spores
fungicide
mycelium

Barley powdery mildew is one of the most destructive diseases of barley across the world. It is caused by a fungus.

What is barley powdery mildew?

Erysiphe graminis is a fungus that causes powdery mildew on barley. It causes most damage in cool, wet conditions where it grows and spreads quickly.

The fungus produces small greyish patches of fluffy, string like growth on the upper surface of lower leaves and on the ears of barley. The spots look like small patches of white powder. The leaves often turn pale green to yellow on the leaf surface around the spots as the fungus uses up nutrients. If the spores are washed off by rain, old infections can be seen as brown patches on the leaves. The leaves eventually turn yellow, die and drop off.

Powdery mildew can be treated using fungicide but it is best to grow varieties that are disease resistant.

Figure 6.62 Lower leaves are more susceptible to powdery mildew

Figure 6.63 Severe infections affect the heads of grain

1. What are the symptoms of barley powdery mildew?

2. What conditions does the fungus need to grow?

Transmission and risk factors

The fungus produces spores (similar to seeds). The spores are released in wet, humid conditions, for example, when it rains. Wind helps spores to disperse and is the main source of infection for barley crops. In favourable conditions the complete life cycle of the fungus (spore germination, infection of barley and spore production) can be completed in as little as six days.

Disease risk factors include:

- planting barley varieties known to be vulnerable to powdery mildew
- planting in areas of previous season infections
- heavy rainfall, high humidity and temperatures of 5–20°C. The fungus cannot survive in temperatures greater than 25°C.
- heavy crop canopies that keep conditions wet.

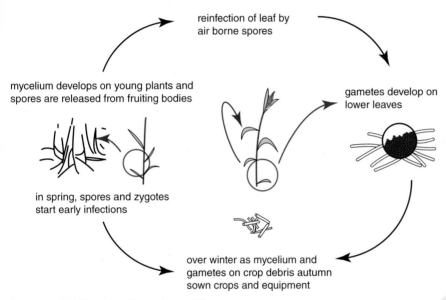

Figure 6.64 Life cycle of powdery mildew

3 Describe how powdery mildew is transmitted.

4 Explain three risk factors of powdery mildew.

How does the pathogen affect growth?

Barley growth is greatly reduced because affected leaves are unable to photosynthesise efficiently. Individual powdery pustules (spots) of fungal mycelium merge together when conditions are favourable to cover most of the leaf and stem surfaces. The cells can then no longer absorb all the light energy they need to photosynthesise efficiently to make sufficient food the plant needs to grow and store in the grain.

5 Explain how the powdery mildew affects yield in barley crops.

DID YOU KNOW?

Athlete's foot and ringworm are both caused by a fungal pathogen.

REMEMBER!

Learn the symptoms, spread and treatment for powdery mildew.

Looking at plant diseases

Learning objectives:

- recall the causes and symptoms of plant diseases
- describe how some plant diseases are spread and controlled
- describe how plant diseases can be detected and identified, both in the lab and in the field.

KEY WORD

TMV
crown gall
 disease
barley powdery
 mildew

Plants are affected by viral, bacterial and fungal pathogens, as well as by pests such as insects.

Plant pests and diseases

Plant diseases are important because:

- plants are the main producers in food chains
- they destroy crops and are hard to control.

The first plant virus to be identified was tobacco mosaic virus **(TMV)**. TMV affects many plants including tomatoes. Symptoms are:

- mottling or discoloured leaves
- curled leaves
- stunted growth
- yellow streaks or spots on leaves.

Aphids (greenfly) are destructive small insects that reproduce quickly. Symptoms of aphid infestation include decreased growth rate, mottled or yellow leaves, wilting, low yields and death.

Crown gall is a bacterial disease caused by *Agrobacterium tumefaciens*. Bacteria enter plants through root or stem wounds. They cause plant tissues to grow in a disorganised way, to form swollen galls.

Barley powdery mildew (*Erysiphe graminis*) is a fungal disease. It causes fluffy white growths on the surface of the leaf.

Just like us, plants need mineral ions to be healthy. Plants with mineral deficiencies have poor growth.

- Nitrate is needed to make amino acids, which are used in protein synthesis for growth. Plants that are deficient in nitrate have stunted growth.
- Magnesium is needed to make chlorophyll. Lack of magnesium results in **chlorosis** (yellow leaves).

1 **What are the causes of plant disease?**

2 **Why are magnesium and nitrate ions needed by plants?**

Figure 6.65 Plant diseases reduce biomass in food chains

Action and control

TMV destroys chloroplasts and slows down photosynthesis. Control measures include:

- removal of weeds (they may have TMV)
- removal of infected plants
- disinfection of all tools.

Identification of TMV is difficult. Symptoms are similar to other plant diseases.

Aphids damage plants and act as disease vectors, carrying pathogens from plant to plant. Aphids pierce phloem tubes using specially adapted mouthparts. They feed on sap, lowering turgor pressure and causing wilting. Viruses are transferred to the phloem by saliva during feeding.

Aphid infestations are easily spotted. They are controlled by natural predators (such as ladybirds) and insecticides.

3 **Describe the symptoms and identification of TMV.**

Figure 6.66 Ladybird larva feeding on aphids

HIGHER TIER ONLY

Identifying plant diseases

Plant diseases can be indicated by:

- stunted growth
- spots on leaves
- areas of decay (rot)
- growths
- malformed stems or leaves
- discolouration
- the presence of pests.

Identification of diseases can be made by:

- diagnosing the disease in the 'field' by careful observation using the naked eye and microscopy.
- taking infected plants to a laboratory for visual identification of the disease by a plant pathologist.
- laboratory detection of the DNA or antigen (toxin) from the disease causing organism.

4 **Pick one plant disease and describe how you would identify it.**

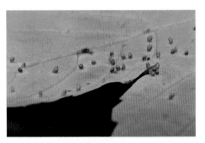

Figure 6.67 Galls (growths) are formed by insects or mites feeding or laying eggs

DID YOU KNOW?

Adult female aphids produce daughters without mating, so the population grows quickly.

REMEMBER!

Plant diseases are caused by fungi, viruses, insects and mineral deficiencies.

Protecting the body

Learning objectives:

- describe non-specific defence mechanisms of the human body against pathogens
- explain how the skin acts as a defence mechanism.

KEY WORDS

cilia
goblet cells
platelets

The body has defence mechanisms for each way that pathogens are transmitted.

How does the body defend itself?

Millions of pathogens are around us each day, but your body protects you from being infected. Non specific defence systems are not specialised for a specific pathogen. Some non-specific defence systems are:

- your skin acts as a barrier and produces antimicrobial secretions via glands in the skin.

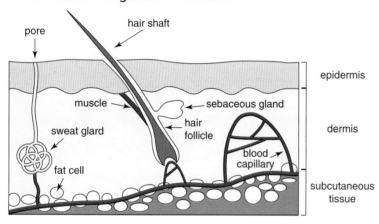

Figure 6.68 Structure of the skin

- the nose traps particles that may contain pathogens.
- your trachea and bronchi secrete mucus, which traps pathogens.
- the stomach produces acid, which kills the majority of pathogens that enter via the mouth.
- **platelets** (cell fragments in your blood) start the clotting process at wound sites. Clots dry to form scabs which seal the wound.

1 How does the body protect itself from pathogens?

2 Which of these defence mechanisms will protect you against pathogens in water and in food?

Hygiene and wounds

When you cough or sneeze, thousands of tiny drops of liquid are sprayed into the air. If you have a disease, the droplets may contain pathogens. This is why you should use a paper tissue and then put it in the bin. Coughing up phlegm and then spitting it out can also spread infections to those around you. Children playing may fall on it and any pathogens can enter the body through wounds in the skin.

When the skin is cut, platelets in the blood are exposed to the air at the wound site. They make protein fibres (fibrin) that form a mesh over the wound. Platelets have a sticky surface and can stick together. The platelets and red blood cells get caught in the mesh. When they dry, it pulls the wound together and seals it with a clot.

3 Explain how coughing and sneezing spread pathogens.

4 How do clots form over wounds? Explain how the formation of a scab helps to protect the body.

Defence mechanisms in detail

Skin protects the body from physical damage, infection and dehydration. The outer layer of skin cells is dry and dead. Pathogens cannot easily penetrate these dead cells. Sebaceous glands in the skin produce antimicrobial oils.

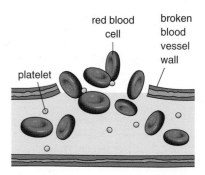

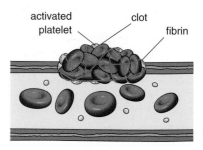

Figure 6.69 Platelets form clots at wound sites

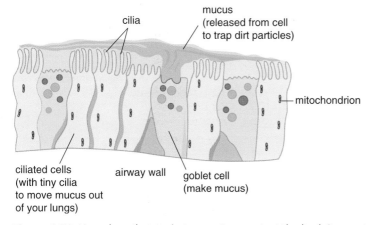

Figure 6.70 How does the respiratory system protect the body?

Every time you breathe, you take in many microbes. Hairs in the nose trap larger microbes and dust particles. The trachea and bronchi have a ciliated epithelium. **Cilia** are tiny hair-like structures. **Goblet cells** in the epithelium produce mucus; mucus traps smaller dust particles and microbes. Cilia beat together to waft mucus to the back of the throat, where it is swallowed. Ciliated cells have many mitochondria to supply the energy needed to do this.

5 How does skin act as a defence against pathogens?

6 Explain the adaptations of the respiratory system to protect us against pathogens.

7 Smoking can damage and paralyse the cilia. Explain why smokers are more susceptible to respiratory infections.

DID YOU KNOW?

It has been estimated that a sneeze expels mucus at 160 km/h.

REMEMBER!

Cilia are like hairs; they are not cells and cannot be killed.

Exploring white blood cells

Learning objectives:

- describe phagocytosis
- explain how antibody production can lead to immunity
- explain how white blood cells are adapted to their funtion
- explain the specificity of immune system responses.

KEY WORDS

antibody
antitoxin
immunity
lymphocyte
phagocyte

Although the body's defence mechanisms prevent many microbes from entering the body, some will succeed. The immune system is our major defence system against disease.

White blood cells

The immune system recognises and destroys pathogens that enter the body. White blood cells are an important part of the immune system.

They attack invading pathogens. If a pathogen enters the body, white blood cells defend it by:

- ingesting pathogens (phagocytosis)
- producing antibodies
- producing antitoxins.

There are two main groups of white blood cell: **phagocytes** and **lymphocytes**. Phagocytes can leave the blood by squeezing through capillaries to enter tissues that are being attacked. They move towards pathogens or toxins and ingest them. This is called phagocytosis. Phagocytes are also a non-specific defence system.

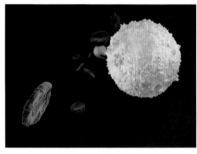

Figure 6.71 White blood cell adaptations include:

- irregular shape so they can squeeze out of capillaries to reach infection sites
- flowing cytoplasm so they can surround and engulf bacteria
- they can increase in numbers to fight disease.

1 Aphagocyte moves towards a bacterium
2 The phagocyte pushes a sleeve of cytoplasm outwards to surround the bacterium
3 The bacterium is now enclosed in a vacuole inside the cell. It is then killed and digested by enzymes

Figure 6.72 Phagocytes ingest pathogens during phagocytosis

1. **How do white blood cells protect the body?**
2. **What happens to a pathogen during phagocytosis?**

Antitoxins and antibodies

Pathogens make us feel ill because they release toxins into our body. White blood cells, called lymphocytes, produce **antitoxins** to neutralise toxins made by the pathogen. Antitoxins combine with the toxin to make a safe chemical. Antitoxins are specific to a particular toxin. Lymphocytes are a specific defence system.

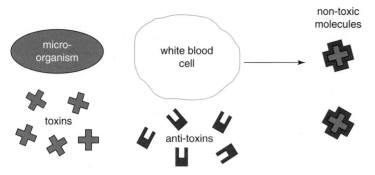

Figure 6.73 Antitoxins neutralise toxins made by pathogens

Lymphocytes also produce chemicals called **antibodies** that destroy pathogens. Lymphocytes recognise when pathogens are present. They quickly reproduce to make lots of antibodies that:

- cause cell lysis (the pathogens burst)
- bind to the pathogens and destroy them
- cover the pathogens, sticking them together. Phagocytes then ingest them.

If the same type of pathogen enters the body again, lymphocyte cells recognise it and immediately make lots of antibodies. This is **immunity**: the person is immune to that disease.

3 How do antitoxins work?

4 Explain how antibody production leads to immunity.

5 Explain how phagocytosis and antitoxin production protect the body.

Producing antibodies

Each lymphocyte has a specific antibody to attack a specific pathogen. Pathogens carry chemicals called antigens on their surface. The appropriate antibodies lock onto the matching antigens, sticking the pathogens together to destroy them.

HIV damages white blood cells, meaning that they cannot make antibodies or kill other infected cells. When HIV has destroyed sufficient white blood cells, the body cannot make appropriate immune responses. Then the person has AIDS. They have fewer or no lymphocytes to recognise simple infections and release antibodies. This means that they can die from simple infections that healthy people can overcome.

6 Explain the specificity of antibodies.

7 Why can a person with AIDS die from a simple infection?

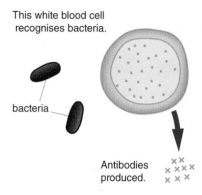

This white blood cell recognises bacteria.

bacteria

Antibodies produced.

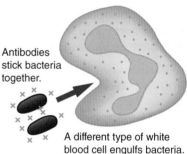

Antibodies stick bacteria together.

A different type of white blood cell engulfs bacteria.

Figure 6.74 How do these white blood cells work?

DID YOU KNOW?

Only 1% of all the cells in blood are white blood cells. There are 5000–10000 of them in a microlitre of blood.

COMMON MISCONCEPTION

Remember, white blood cells do not *eat* pathogens; they *ingest* them.

Building immunity

Learning objectives:

- recall how vaccinations prevent infection
- explain how mass vaccination programmes reduce the spread of a disease
- evaluate the global use of vaccination.

KEY WORDS

immunity
vaccination
vaccine

One in three people who caught smallpox in the 1600s died from it. Smallpox is now almost eradicated globally.

What is vaccination?

A **vaccination** introduces a small quantity of an inactive or dead form of a pathogen into the body to protect us from disease. Lymphocytes produce antibodies to fight the 'infection' but we don't actually become ill. When live pathogens of the same type infect you, your immune system starts to protect you immediately.

Different **vaccines** are needed for specific pathogens. For example, polio, whooping cough, flu and HPV (human papilloma virus) all have a different vaccine. MMR vaccinations contain three vaccines (for measles, mumps and rubella).

Vaccinations are usually given to children and people who are going to travel to countries where there is a risk of serious disease. Vaccines are given by injection, orally or nasal sprays.

1. What is a vaccination?
2. What do vaccinations do?

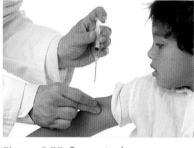

Figure 6.75 Suggest why vaccinations are given to children

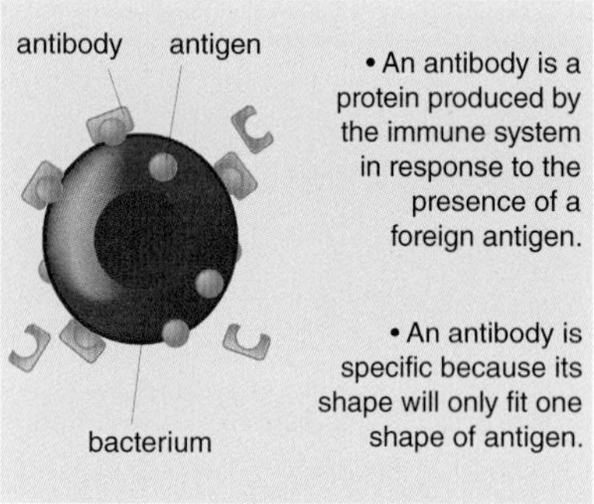

antibody   antigen

- An antibody is a protein produced by the immune system in response to the presence of a foreign antigen.

- An antibody is specific because its shape will only fit one shape of antigen.

bacterium

Figure 6.76 Antibodies are specific to a particular antigen on a pathogen

How do vaccines work?

After the vaccination:

- lymphocytes detect antigens on the dead or inactive pathogen; they produce a specific antibody for these antigens
- antibodies lock onto the antigens
- lymphocytes 'remember' the shape of the antigens
- when there is a real infection due to a live pathogen entering the body, lymphocytes instantly recognise the pathogen because it has the same antigens as the vaccine
- lymphocytes quickly make many specific antibodies
- antibodies lock onto the pathogens and kill them before they have a chance to make you feel ill. This is **immunity**.

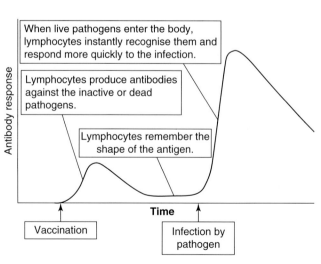

When live pathogens enter the body, lymphocytes instantly recognise them and respond more quickly to the infection.

Lymphocytes produce antibodies against the inactive or dead pathogens.

Lymphocytes remember the shape of the antigen.

Antibody response

Time

Vaccination

Infection by pathogen

Figure 6.77 The immune response

Mass vaccination programmes increase the number of people who are immune to a pathogen, making it difficult for the pathogen to pass to people who are not immunised. If a large proportion of the population is immune to a pathogen, its spread is very much reduced. Global vaccination programmes have eradicated polio, except in Pakistan and Afghanistan. Nigeria did not have any new polio infections in 2015.

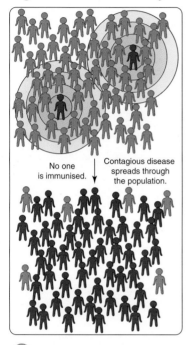

No one is immunised.

Contagious disease spreads through the population.

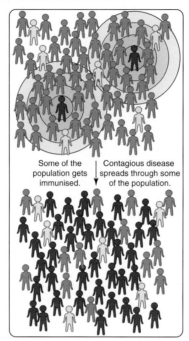

Some of the population gets immunised.

Contagious disease spreads through some of the population.

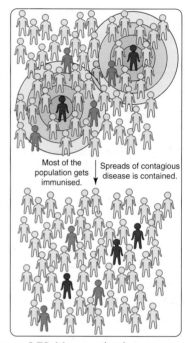

Most of the population gets immunised.

Spreads of contagious disease is contained.

Figure 6.78 Mass vaccination programmes reduce the spread of disease

= not immunised but still healthy

= immunised and still healthy

= not immunised, sick and contagious

3 Look at Figure 6.77.

   a Why were antibodies produced more quickly after the second infection?

   b Will the person be ill after the second infection?

4 How do mass vaccination programmes reduce the spread of disease?

Vaccination and populations

Some viruses frequently mutate into new strains. This means that lymphocytes do not recognise the new strains. As a result, new vaccines are made regularly for some diseases, such as flu.

Some antibodies give lifelong protection, such as those that are active against measles. Sometimes antibodies fall below the critical level needed for immunity, as happens in the case of tetanus. Booster doses are needed to increase the antibodies again.

5 Explain why new flu vaccines are made each year.

6 People now travel widely across the world. Evaluate the global use of vaccination.

DID YOU KNOW?

Flu vaccine is stored in eggs because it needs to be in a living organism to survive.

REMEMBER!

Lymphocytes make *antibodies*. Pathogens have anti**gens**.

Using antibiotics and antivirals

Learning objectives:

- describe the uses of antibiotics and antivirals
- explain how antibiotics and antivirals can be used to treat diseases
- explain the limitations of antibiotics and antivirals.

You can take medicines to make you feel better when you have an infectious disease.

Useful drugs

A drug is any chemical that alters how the body works. Medicines contain useful drugs. Many medicines only relieve the symptoms caused by an infection, for example, painkillers and cough medicines. Other medicines work inside the body to kill bacterial pathogens.

Antibiotics work by interfering with the pathogen's metabolism; for example, with processes that make bacterial cell walls. Antibiotics do not affect human cells and they do not kill viral, protist or fungal pathogens. They only kill bacterial pathogens.

Antivirals are drugs that treat viral infections. They prevent viruses reproducing.

1 **What is a medicine?**

2 **How are antibiotics and antivirals similar and different?**

How do medicines work?

There are many different antibiotics. Some antibiotics work against one type of bacterial infection. Others are used to treat many different bacterial infections. It is important to use the correct antibiotic for a specific bacterium.

If a bacterium cannot be killed by an antibiotic, it is resistant to that antibiotic. A prescribed course of antibiotics has the correct amount to kill the bacterial pathogen completely. This is why you must always take the complete antibiotic course.

The use of antibiotics has greatly reduced deaths from infectious bacterial diseases. But, misuse of antibiotics has led to the emergence of strains of bacteria that are antibiotic resistant.

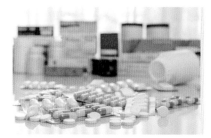

Figure 6.79 Antibiotics and painkillers are medicinal drugs

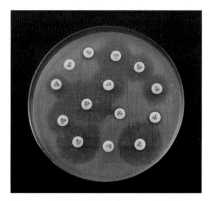

Figure 6.80 Antibiotic test: the size of the clear area around the antibiotic disc indicates the effectiveness of the antibiotic against the bacteria growing on the agar plate

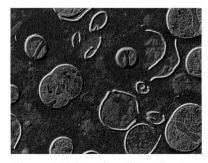

Figure 6.81 How has the antibiotic affected these bacteria?

3 What are resistant bacteria?

4 Why are there many types of antibiotics?

Antiviral drugs

Antibiotics cannot be used to kill viral pathogens. Antiviral drugs are used to treat viral infections. Antivirals are specific to a particular virus. While antibiotics can kill bacteria, antiviral drugs only slow down viral development. It is difficult to develop drugs which kill viruses without also damaging the body's tissues.

5 Explain the limitations of antibiotics and antivirals.

6 The graph shows the bacteria present during an infection.

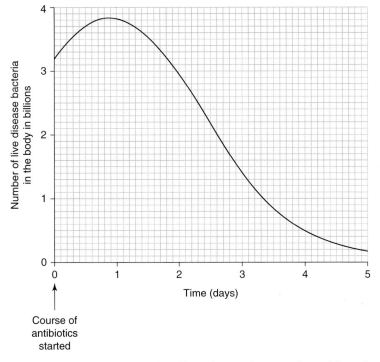

DID YOU KNOW?

Alexander Fleming discovered penicillin, the first antibiotic, in 1928.

Figure 6.82 Graph showing the effect of an antibiotic on bacterial numbers

KEY INFORMATION

Antibiotics kill bacteria. Antivirals treat viral infections.

a Explain why the numbers increase after antibiotics were taken.

b Explain why the full course of antibiotics needs to be taken.

PRACTICAL

Investigating disinfectants

Learning objectives:

- carry out experiments with due regard to health and safety
- present and process data, identifying anomalous results
- evaluate methods and suggest further investigations.

KEY WORDS

antiseptic
incubation

For use in a hospital, choosing the right disinfectant or **antiseptic** to achieve the appropriate hygiene levels is essential. The correct dilution is also important: a concentration high enough to work, but not so high as to be wasteful.

These pages are designed to help you think about aspects of the investigation rather than to guide you through it step by step.

Setting up a disc-diffusion investigation

Scientists need a number of different skills to carry out this investigation. This topic looks at some of those skills.

The method used to test the effectiveness of a disinfectant (or an antiseptic or antibiotic) is the disc-diffusion technique.

In this experiment, different concentrations of the disinfectant sodium hypochlorite are investigated.

1 In the investigation, which is the independent variable and which is the dependent variable?

2 Suggest the other possible variables that need to be controlled.

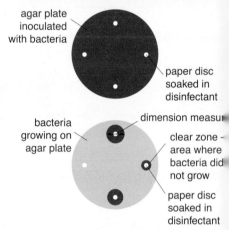

Figure 6.83 Disc-diffusion technique

Health and safety

Before scientists can begin a disc-diffusion investigation, they must carry out a Risk Assessment.

Hazard	Type of hazard	Risk	Safety precautions
Ethanol			
Sodium hypochlorite			
Bacteria			
Agar plate			
Add more rows to include the activities involved, e.g. flaming an inoculating loop.			

3 Complete the Risk Assessment table.

4 Suggest why:
- scientists would use Mueller–Hinton blood agar; in the school lab, you would use nutrient agar
- you would incubate the plate at 25°C; the scientists at 37°C.

Presenting and processing data

The agar plates are **incubated**, and the zones of inhibition (clear zones) measured. Scientists need to analyse the data they have collected:

Concentration of sodium hypochlorite (g/dm³)	Area of clear zone around disc (mm²)			Mean area of clear zone around disc (mm²)
	Test 1	Test 2	Test 3	
0.0	0	0	0	0
0.5	0	0	0	0
1.0	32	31	34	32
1.5	91	89	91	90
2.0	470	381	379	380
2.5	499	505	497	
3.0	546	552	551	
3.5	575	568	567	
4.0	578	582	580	
4.5	580	580	580	
5.0	579	578	583	

5. How is the area of a clear zone calculated? Hint: you need to recall a formula.

6. Complete the table by calculating the mean area of the clear zones.

7. Identify the anomalous result. How did you recognise it?

8. Which set of results has the highest degree of repeatability?

9. Plot a graph of area of clear zone against concentration.

Evaluating the investigation

The experiment's aim was to find out the concentration of disinfectant that would be best for a hospital to use against the bacterium *Staphylococcus aureus*.

10. Do you have all the information needed to draw a full conclusion, or should the scientists collect more information? Use your graph to help you make your recommendation.

11. We know that in the clear zone, bacteria do not grow. But we do not know if they have been killed, or just prevented from growing. Suggest a follow-up investigation.

> **REMEMBER!**
>
> The area of a circle can be calculated using the formula:
> area = πr^2
> where r is the radius, the distance from the centre to the edge of the circle.

> **KEY SKILLS**
>
> In a Risk Assessment, you should group hazards into categories: organisms, chemicals, physical hazards and practical activities. Use the correct terminology for the type of hazard (for example, biohazard, irritant, oxidising). Think about the concentration of chemicals used. Don't forget the hazards and risks before and after the experiment, for example, the agar plate after incubation.

Making new drugs

Learning objectives:

- recall some traditional drugs and their origins
- describe how new drugs are developed
- explain why 'double-blind' trials are conducted.

Doctors, politicians, drug companies and scientists all have roles in deciding the development of new drugs.

Making new drugs from old

Researchers sometimes use traditional medicines to start developing new drugs. Traditionally, drugs were extracted from plants and microorganisms, for example:

- the heart drug digitalis comes from foxgloves
- the painkiller aspirin comes from willow trees
- penicillin was discovered by Alexander Fleming in *Penicillium* mould.

Chemists working for pharmaceutical companies formulate most new drugs. The starting point is often chemicals that are extracted from plants.

New drugs are tested and trialled before being prescribed to ensure they are:

- effective – able to prevent or cure a disease, or make you feel better; this is the drug's **efficacy**
- safe –not too toxic or with any undesirable side effects
- stable – it must be possible to store any new drug for a period of time.

1 Name three traditional drugs and state the source of each.

2 Why do new medicinal drugs need to tested and trialled?

Developing new drugs

Stages in drug development are:

- **preclinical testing** in laboratories (using cells, tissues and live animals) to find out side effects and efficacy
- **clinical trials**, which use healthy volunteers and other patients. Low **doses** of the drug are given at the start. Then, if the drug is deemed safe, further trials are performed to find the optimum dose. Clinical trials are split into phases, as shown in Figure 6.85.

Figure 6.84 Suggest why research may start with traditional medicines

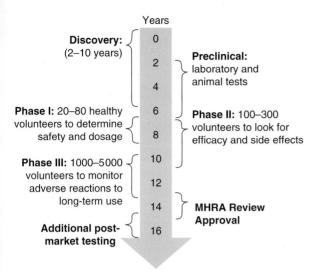

Figure 6.85 Developing new drugs

Trial results are peer reviewed by medical professionals and, only then, are they published.

Clinical trials involve some risk because unexpected side effects can occur.

3 Describe the stages in the development of a drug.

4 Why are potential drugs tested on human cells, animals and healthy human volunteers before being tested on patients?

Double-blind trials

Double-blind trials are when patients are allocated randomly to groups, so that doctors and patients do not know, until the trial is complete, if they are taking:

- the new drug (this is the test group)
- a **placebo** (a treatment that does not contain the drug). This is the control group.

Clinical trials must not be influenced by the people involved in them, whether patients, doctors or employees of pharmaceutical companies. Sometimes, people feel better just because they think they will if they take a medicine. This is the 'placebo effect'.

5 Why are double-blind trials conducted?

6 What is the placebo effect?

7 In a blind trial patients don't know which drug they are receiving but the doctors do. Results from such trials are not always reliable. Suggest why this might be the case.

REMEMBER!

A placebo is a treatment that does not contain the drug.

KEY CONCEPT

Looking at risk factors

Learning objectives:

- recall the causes of some non-communicable diseases
- describe the impact of lifestyle on non-communicable diseases
- explain the impact of lifestyle on non-communicable diseases.

KEY WORDS

causal
  mechanism
risk factor

In developed countries, non-communicable disease is
the largest cause of death.

Risk factors

Risk factors increase the chance of having a disease. Risk
factors can be aspects of a person's lifestyle, and substances
in the person's body or environment. They include diet,
exercise, type of workplace, sexual habits, smoking, drinking
and drug-taking.

Non-communicable diseases may be caused by the
interaction of a number of factors:

- factors involved in cardiovascular disease may be diet/
  obesity, age, genetics and exercise.
- lung disease (bronchitis) factors are smoking and
  cleanliness of the environment.
- alcohol, diet/obesity, genetics, drugs and viral infection
  may be involved in liver disease (cirrhosis).
- genetics, diet/obesity and exercise may affect Type 2
  diabetes.

Figure 6.86 Why is this person at
risk of cardiovascular disease?

We cannot control some risk factors, such as genes and
age, but we can control lifestyle factors, like drinking and
smoking, to reduce the risk of contracting some diseases.

1 **What factors increase the risk of Type 2 diabetes?**

2 **How could the risk of liver disease be reduced?**

Causal mechanisms

A **causal mechanism** is
one risk factor that may
be partly responsible for
a disease. Research has
shown a causal mechanism
for some risk factors.

Disease/condition	Risk factor with causal mechanism
cardiovascular disease	poor diet, smoking and lack of exercise
type-2 diabetes	obesity
liver and brain damage	alcohol
lung disease, cancer	smoking
low birth weight and premature birth	smoking
abnormal foetal brain development	alcohol
cancer	carcinogens (including ionising radiation)

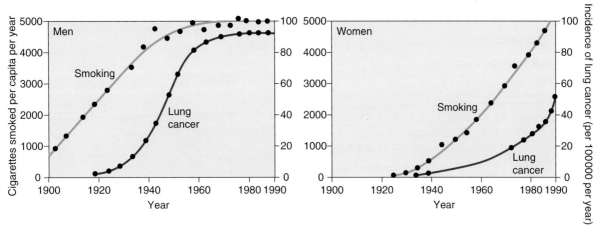

Figure 6.87 Smoking and lung cancer

3 Use the data in Figure 6.87 to describe the smoking habits of men from 1900 to 1990. Describe what happened to the incidence of lung cancer during this time.

4 What conclusion can you draw from the data shown in figure 6.106?

Time lag

There is a long time lag between when people start to smoke and the development of cancer. So, it took a long time to compile evidence to prove smoking was the causal mechanism for lung cancer.

Human and financial costs of smoking include:

* serious health problems, possible death, damage to unborn children, dangers of passive smoking
* cost of cigarettes, loss of family income and a depleted workforce
* financial burden of healthcare costs on local, national and global economies.

An isolated case of disease does not provide evidence for or against a risk factor. Large sample groups need to be monitored. Groups are randomly selected, or matched in terms of age and gender.

5 Explain the impact of lifestyle on non-communicable diseases.

6 Suggest why there is a time lapse between the rise in cigarette consumption and the rise in lung cancer deaths.

7 The data on the graph proves that smoking causes lung cancer'. Do you agree with this statement? Justify your answer.

Figure 6.88 Smoking does not cause lung cancer immediately

DID YOU KNOW?

Research shows that teenagers who eat fast food at least once a week are more likely to develop insulin resistance, a risk factor for type-2 diabetes.

KEY INFORMATION

Smoking is a causal mechanism for lung cancer but cancer is caused by the chemicals in cigarettes.

Treating cardiovascular disease

KEY WORDS

artificial
 pacemaker
coronary heart
 disease
statin
stent

Learning objectives:

- describe the causes and symptoms of coronary heart disease
- describe medical and surgical treatments for cardiovascular disease
- evaluate different treatments for cardiovascular disease.

Heart disease is one of the main causes of death in the UK. Cholesterol is made in the liver and transported in the blood. High levels of cholesterol are linked to heart disease.

Heart problems

In **coronary heart disease**, fatty material builds up inside the coronary arteries. Blood flow is reduced and less glucose and oxygen reach the heart for respiration. Less energy is available for the heart to contract. If cells are starved of nutrients, they can die and a heart attack may happen. Factors that contribute to coronary heart disease include genetic factors, gender, age, diet and if they smoke or not.

Heart valves prevent the backflow of blood. They can become faulty due to heart attack, infection or old age. Faulty valves may not open fully or can leak, causing oxygenated and deoxygenated blood to mix. Symptoms of leaky valves include:

- tiredness and lack of energy
- breathlessness.

1 Describe the symptoms of coronary heart disease.

2 What causes coronary heart disease?

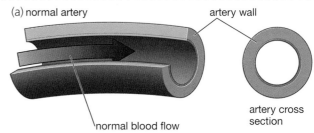

(a) normal artery

artery wall

normal blood flow

artery cross section

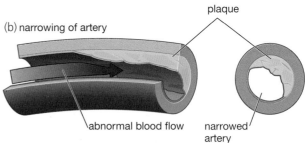

(b) narrowing of artery

plaque

abnormal blood flow

narrowed artery

Figure 6.89 How does coronary heart disease affect blood flow?

Treatments for heart problems

- Some people cannot control their heart rate. **Artificial pacemakers** can be fitted under the skin. A wire is passed from a vein to the right atrium. This sends electrical impulses to the heart to control heartbeat.
- Faulty heart valves can be replaced using biological (from humans or other mammals) or mechanical valves.
- High cholesterol levels are treated with drugs called **statins** which stop the liver producing as much cholesterol. Patients can also change their diet to help reduce cholseterol.
- **Stents** are used to treat narrow coronary arteries. If the coronary artery is too damaged, bypass surgery is used. A vein is transplanted from the leg to bypass the blockage.

1. Stent pushed through catheter into position using X-rays.

2. Balloon inflated, expanding stent.

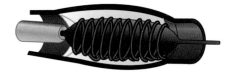

3. Catheter taken out, leaving stent to open up artery.

Figure 6.90 Inserting a stent

When heart failure occurs, the only effective treatment is a donor heart transplant. An artificial heart can be used in the short term, while the patient is waiting for a heart transplant, or to allow the heart to rest to help recovery.

3 How is coronary heart disease treated?

4 What are artifical valves and what do they do?

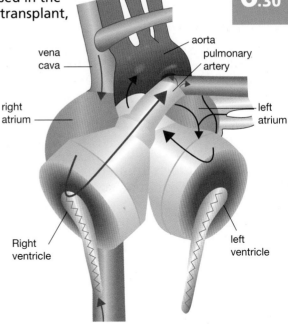

Figure 6.91 An artificial heart

Evaluating heart treatments

All treatments help keep patients alive.

Treatment	Advantage	Disadvantage
artificial valves	no rejection	can damage red blood cells patient needs anti-clotting drugs
biological valves	red blood cells not damaged	valves can harden and need replacing
stents	little risk	fatty deposits can rebuild
bypass surgery	no rejection	major surgery
statins	reduce cholesterol	possible side effects, e.g. liver damage
artificial pacemakers	major surgery not required	immune system can reject the pacemaker may need replacing
heart transplant	better quality of life	major surgery anti-rejection drugs needed (leading to greater infection risk) shortage of donors

5 Evaluate the use of artificial pacemakers or artificial heart valves over heart transplants.

6 Why are doctors increasingly prescribing statins for their patients?

KEY INFORMATION

The coronary artery takes oxygen and glucose to heart muscles for respiration.

DID YOU KNOW?

Over 300 000 people in the UK have a heart attack every year.

Cancer

Learning objectives:

- describe cancer as a condition resulting from changes in cells that lead to their uncontrolled growth, division and spread
- explain the differences between different types of tumour.

KEY WORDS

benign tumour
malignant
  tumour
secondary tumour

Every year, over 300 000 people in the UK are diagnosed with cancer. It is estimated, however, that four in ten cases of cancer could be prevented by lifestyle changes.

What is cancer?

Normally, cells grow and divide by mitosis when the body needs new cells to replace old or damaged cells. When a cell becomes cancerous, it begins to divide uncontrollably. New cells are produced even though the body does not need them.

The extra cells produced form growths called tumours. Most tumours are solid, but cancers of the blood, for instance leukaemia, are an exception.

1. What is cancer?
2. Name one type of cancer that does not form a solid tumour.

Types of tumour

Benign tumours divide slowly, do not spread and are harmless. Warts are benign tumours. They can be removed by simple surgery or a squirt of liquid nitrogen.

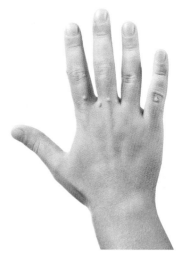

Figure 6.92 Warts are benign tumours

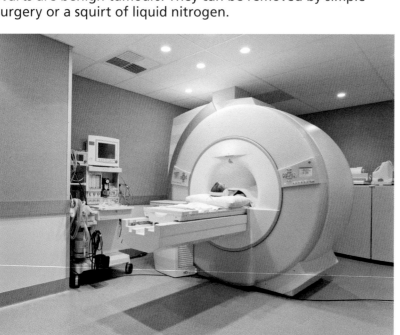

Figure 6.93 A CT scanner, used to detect cancer

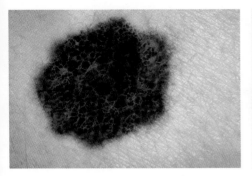
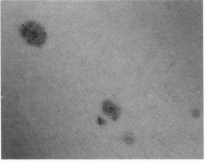

Figure 6.94 How are benign and malignant moles different?

Malignant tumours divide very quickly. They can invade tissues around them and spread via the blood to different parts of the body, where they form secondary tumours. Malignant tumour cells are cancers.

3 Name two types of tumour.

4 Explain why a tumour needs a blood supply.

5 What is the name of the type of tumour formed when a cancer spreads?

Type of tumour	Characteristics
Benign	• slow growing • often have a capsule around them, so can be removed easily • not cancerous and rarely spread to other parts of the body • they can press on other body organs and look unsightly.
Malignant	• grow faster • can spread throughout other body tissues • as the tumour grows, cancer cells detach and can form **secondary tumours** in other parts of the body.

Malignant cells develop.

The malignant cells divide and can invade normal tissues.

Malignant cells can detach from the tumour and spread to other parts of the body.

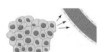

The tumour secretes hormone-like chemicals.

Blood vessels are stimulated to grow around the tumour; the blood vessels supply the tumour with food and oxygen.

Malignant cells detach from the tumour and are transported away in the blood.

The malignant cell squeezes through the capillary wall.

The cell divides to produce a secondary tumour.

Figure 6.95 The growth and spread of a tumour

KEY INFORMATION

Malignant tumours cause cancer, whereas benign ones do not.

Cancer is a non-communicable disease

Learning objectives:

- recall that non-communicable diseases are caused by the interaction of a number of different factors
- explain the impact of non-communicable diseases.

In the UK, over 33% of people will develop a form of cancer during their life. It is estimated, however, that four in ten cases of cancer could be prevented by lifestyle choices.

Cancer facts

Cancer is a non-communicable disease. It is not passed from person to person. A number of factors can trigger cancer. These often interact with each other.

1. **What is a non-communicable disease?**

2. **How can cancer be triggered?**

What triggers cancer?

Chemicals and other agents that cause cancer are called **carcinogens**.

Carcinogens cause cancer by damaging DNA. A change in the DNA of a cell is called a **mutation**. Mutations can also occur by chance as a cell is dividing.

There are natural checks for such errors during the cell cycle. Some of our genes suppress developing tumours.

Several mutations, not just one, are necessary to trigger cancer. This is why we are more likely to develop cancer as we get older.

Mutations that lead to cancer can be caused by several agents:

- viruses (e.g. HPV; see topic 6.15).
- chemicals in the home, industry or environment
- ionising radiation
- ultraviolet radiation
- lifestyle choices, such as alcohol intake or diet (see Figure 6.96).

There are also genetic links to certain cancers. The Human Genome Project is helping us to understand these.

DID YOU KNOW?

Many treatments for cancer come from plants, such as the Pacific yew and the Madagascan periwinkle. These drugs work by interfering with mitosis.

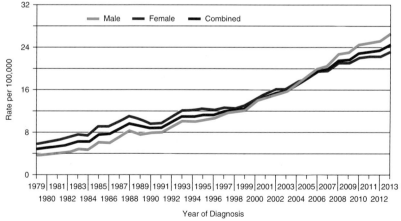

Figure 6.96 Cases of a skin cancer called malignant melanoma in the UK, 1975–2010. The cause is usually ultraviolet radiation – either from the Sun or from industrial use

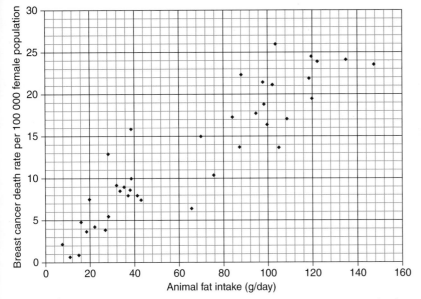

Figure 6.97 Scattergraph showing the correlation between breast cancer deaths and animal fat intake. Each data point represents a different country

6.32

DID YOU KNOW?

Breast, lung, prostate and bowel cancers are the most common in the UK. They account for 50% of diagnosed cancers.

3. List five causes of cancer.

4. Describe the pattern shown by the scattergraph and draw a conclusion.

Smoking and cancer

Smoking is the biggest preventable cause of cancer worldwide. The link between smoking and cancer was known for many years before being widely accepted. Lung cancer symptoms include a cough, chest pains, shortness of breath, poor appetite and weight loss, and coughing up blood. Each person with lung cancer costs the NHS over £9000 every year. The total workforce is reduced and the economy is weakened.

REMEMBER!

Be prepared to interpret data on the correlation between type of cancer and external factors such as diet.

Figure 6.98 Over 25% of UK cancer deaths are caused by smoking

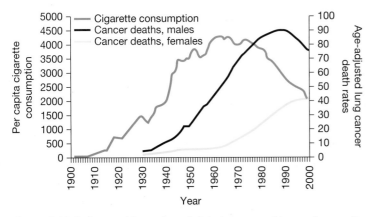

Figure 6.99 Is there evidence for a link between smoking and cancer?

5. Describe and explain the graph in Figure 6.99.

6. Explain the impact of cancer on individuals, families and nations.

Stem cells in medicine

Learning objectives:

- discuss potential benefits and risks associated with the use of stem cells in medicine.

Scientists predict that, in the future, vast banks of stored stem cells will be available to treat many medical conditions.

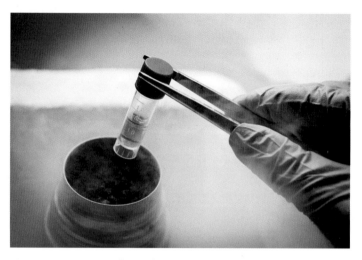

Figure 6.100 Stem cells can be stored in liquid nitrogen

Rejection of stem cell transplants

The stem cells from a bank originate from many different people. Rejection of stem cell transplants by a patient's immune system is, therefore, a problem.

One current solution is to find as close a match as possible between **donor** and patient cells. Another is to give the patient drugs to suppress their immune system. Scientists are looking for other ways to avoid **transplant rejection**.

One possible source of stem cells is blood left in the **umbilical cord** and placenta after a baby is born. Cord blood is easy to collect and store.

1 **Suggest sources of stem cells that would give the best match between donor and patient.**

2 **Suggest some possible advantages and disadvantages of having a baby's blood stored to treat possible disease or injury in later life.**

Stem cell research and therapy is controversial

Stem cell research is necessary to find out more about stem cell development, and the best types to use in treatments. The use of embryonic stem cells, which are removed from a living human embryo, is especially controversial. Until recently, the embryos providing the stem cells were usually those left over from fertility treatments involving *in-vitro* fertilisation (IVF). Spare embryos would be destroyed if they had not been donated by the IVF couples for research. British law now allows embryos to be created purely for scientific research. Some people object to this. Some religious beliefs argue that new life begins at the point of conception, so an embryo has rights. And who should decide when a human life ends?

These are moral and **ethical** questions. A moral question looks at whether something is right or wrong. An ethical question discusses the reasons why something might be right or wrong.

3 **Why do some people object to stem cell transplants?**

4 **Write down one ethical objection to stem cell research.**

Scientific and social questions

Many questions arise from stem cell therapy.

The first scientific question is how successful might these therapies be? Others consider safety: stem cells kept in culture can show similarities to cancer cells. After about 60 cell divisions, **mutations** have been observed. It is also possible for viruses to be transferred with stem cells, leading to infection.

There are also important social questions. What are the potential benefits from successful stem cell treatment and do these outweigh the objections? And should patients be given false hope based on a currently unproven treatment? Public education on this issue is important.

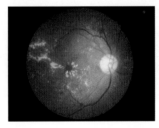

Figure 6.101 Blind patients have had their sight restored by stem cells. It has been possible to safely treat the part of the eye responsible for central vision

5 **What are the potential benefits and drawbacks of using stem cells in medicine?**

The Human Genome Project

Learning objectives:

- describe the Human Genome Project
- explain the importance for medicine of our increasing understanding of the human genome
- understand that a large proportion of the human genome regulates gene expression.

> **KEY WORDS**
>
> gene expression
> gene therapy
> genome
> genomics
> genome editing

The Human Genome Project (HGP) was a study to map all the genetic information on the chromosomes of a human being. The work began in 1990 and the research was published in 2003.

Work is continuing. Now a new science – *genomics* – has developed with the aim of increasing our understanding of human DNA.

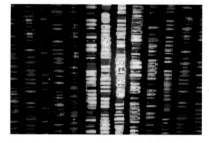

Figure 6.102 Sequencing of the human genome in the early days of the project

Increasing our understanding of genes

The HGP has helped scientists to understand more about human diseases, such as diabetes, cancer and heart disease. So far, around 4000 genes have been shown to be involved in human diseases.

The HGP has also helped scientists to understand more about inherited disorders. Some of these, such as cystic fibrosis, are linked with just a single gene. One way to develop effective treatments is to target and correct defective genes. **Gene therapy** and **genome editing** are techniques being developed to do this.

① **How might the HGP help in the way we deal with human diseases?**

② **Name one condition resulting from a defective single gene.**

Is personalised medicine possible?

Most conditions and diseases are associated, not with single genes, but with many genes that interact in complex ways. These genes also interact with the environment. Understanding these genes, and the regions of DNA that vary from person to person, is key to effective medicine.

In future, by understanding a person's **genome**, doctors may be able to:

- recommend better preventative medicine
- identify the targets of drugs more effectively
- tailor healthcare to the individual.

③ **How might an understanding of genes lead to personalised medicine?**

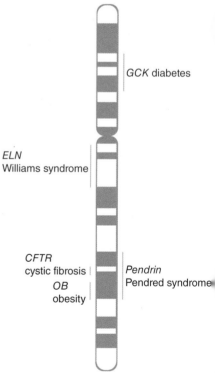

Figure 6.103 A simplified map of chromosome 7. Five genes that are linked with diseases are shown. Note that the chromosome actually has 1800 genes in total

Understanding more about the human genome

Late in the twentieth century, before the work of the HGP, it had been estimated that there were around 100 000 genes in the human genome. We now know that there are many fewer. The HGP and on-going research have revealed that there are 20 000–25 000 genes that code for proteins; this is only around 1.5% of the human genome.

Scientists used to think that the remainder of the DNA – the part that *didn't* code for proteins – was simply 'junk'. We now know that it's teeming with biological activity. Much of this DNA – we're not yet sure how much – is responsible for switching genes on and off. This is called **gene expression**.

Figure 6.104 DNA base sequence

> **DID YOU KNOW?**
>
> The 100 000 Genome Project has been set up by the Department of Health. It will analyse complete genomes of people suffering from rare diseases, cancer and infectious disease.

> **COMMON MISCONCEPTIONS**
>
> It's convenient to think that genes just code for production of proteins – that's what we used to think – but far more are involved in gene regulation.

4 What percentage of our genome is made up of genes that code for proteins?

5 What is the one function of the non-coding regions of our DNA?

6 How are genes expressed in a muscle cell, for example?

7 The Human Genome Project was estimated to have cost about 2.7 billion US dollars. Evaluate whether it was worth the money.

Gene technology in medicine

Learning objectives:

- describe the principles of gene technology
- explain some of the possible benefits of gene technology in medicine.

KEY WORDS

genome editing
gene therapy

In 2015, five-month-old Layla Richards developed incurable leukaemia. A pioneering gene technology – used before only on mice – was tested on Layla. Scientists used a technique to edit the genome of some donated human immune cells called T-cells. The cells were 'programmed' to seek out and destroy Layla's cancer cells. In November 2015, her leukaemia was in reverse.

Gene technologies are in the pioneering phase

We do not know, yet, whether Layla's cancer has been completely cured. It's too early to tell. And there may be complications later on. But gene technologies are developing quickly.

With our increasing understanding of how genes are linked with disease, it is clear that in the future, it will be a routine task to modify many defective genes.

Gene therapies are not new. But in the early days, there were many failures. In the late 1990s, a gene therapy was developed to treat patients with SCID, or 'bubble-boy' syndrome. In small trials, the children showed a dramatic improvement, but 3-6 years later, some developed leukaemia and died.

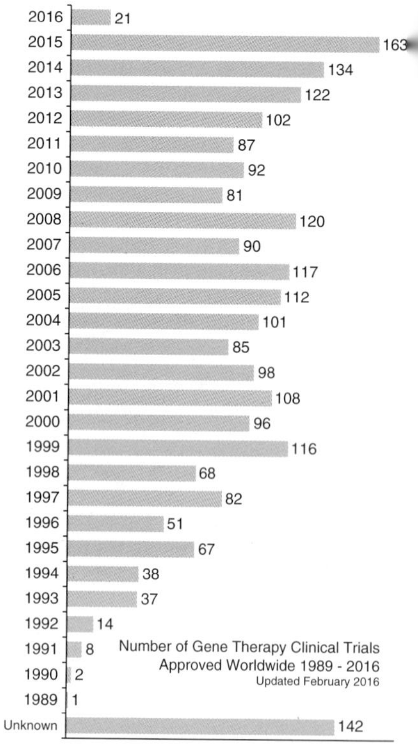

1 What problems did researchers have with early gene trials?

2 Describe the trend in numbers of gene therapy trials between 1989 and 2015 (Figure 6.105).

Figure 6.105 Numbers of approved gene therapy trials. Gene therapies against cancer and single gene disorders make up the largest trials

Gene therapies

Introducing genes from other organisms into humans would be unethical. But there is much potential in investigating **gene therapy** in humans to overcome inherited disorders.

Most gene therapy largely centre on inserting a normal version of an allele into cells that carry a defective version of that allele.

A deactivated virus is normally used as a vector to transfer the gene into the cell. But a major difficulty is how to deliver the replacement gene effectively. Gene therapy trials also assess the safety of the technique.

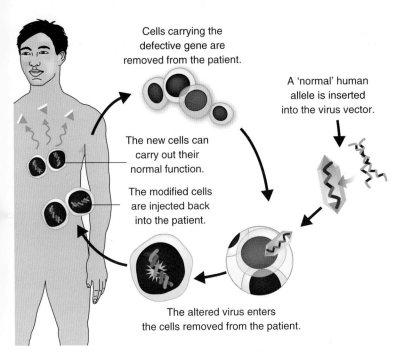

Cells carrying the defective gene are removed from the patient.

A 'normal' human allele is inserted into the virus vector.

The new cells can carry out their normal function.

The modified cells are injected back into the patient.

The altered virus enters the cells removed from the patient.

Figure 6.106 One type of gene therapy procedure

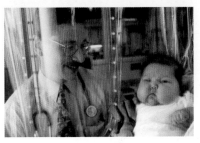

Figure 6.107 Many trials have been focused on correcting a severe immune system abnormality called SCID, or 'bubble-boy syndrome'

Currently there are thousands of gene therapy trials. And, as you have seen, another gene technology is showing great potential for improving human health. **Genome editing** involves replacing or removing sections of the DNA of the genome using 'molecular scissors'. Although not new, recent developments have improved the precision and efficiency of the DNA editing process.

Any successful gene therapy would not prevent the person from passing on an inherited condition to their children. It is the patient's body cells that are being modified. Any modification of reproductive cells, or germline gene therapy, would be both technically and ethically difficult. Germline gene therapy is currently not permitted by law.

3 Why were early attempts at gene therapy unsuccessful?

4 Explain one of the limitations of gene therapy.

5 What ethical argument could you give against developing gene therapy?

DID YOU KNOW?

One of the most publicised applications of gene therapy is for cystic fibrosis. The gene therapy formulation has been based on a plasmid rather than a virus, sprayed into the lungs of patients.

MATHS SKILLS

Sampling and scientific data

Learning objectives:

- understand why sampling is used in science
- be able to explain different sampling techniques
- be able to extract and interpret information from graphs.

KEY WORD

systematic
error
sampling

When undertaking clinical investigations, scientists are unable to test all people, so sampling is used.

Populations and samples

We cannot study every individual in a population, so we use a sample of the population.

Choosing the right size of sample is important. Carrying out studies is expensive so scientists don't want to use sample groups that are large, but the risk with small groups is that they aren't representative enough of the whole population. This is known as a 'sampling error' and it means that the results of the study don't indicate well what the population as a whole is like.

Scientists were investigating the effectiveness of a new antibiotic. For an antibiotic to be effective it should cure 95–100% of cases of an illness.

Imagine that the population taking the antibiotic is represented by a container of coloured balls. Each ball is a patient. Red balls represent patients who are not cured by the antibiotic. Blue balls represent the patients who are cured.

The scientists take a sample of 10 balls. The sample contains 1 red ball and 9 blue balls:

$$\frac{\text{patients not cured (red balls)}}{\text{all patients (red and blue balls)}} \times 100 = \text{\% chance of not being cured}$$

So

$$\frac{1}{10} \times 100 = 0.1 \times 100 = 10\% \text{ chance of not being cured.}$$

This suggests that the antibiotic is only effective for 90% of patients treated.

However, in another sample, this time of 100 balls, there are only two red balls:

$$\frac{2}{100} \times 100 = 0.02 \times 100 = 2\% \text{ chance of not being cured.}$$

The larger sample suggests that the antibiotic is 98% effective.

DID YOU KNOW?

Thalidomide relieved morning sickness in pregnant women. Pregnant women were not in the sample used to test thalidomide. Many babies born to mothers who took thalidomide had limb abnormalities.

REMEMBER!

A small error in a small sample can mean a large error.

When using a small sample size, a sampling error can easily be made, which makes the outcome unreliable. To avoid this sampling error, large-scale clinical trials that test new drugs in humans will likely involve thousands of patients.

1 Why do scientists use samples for investigations?

2 Figure 6.108 shows more samples in the antibiotic investigation.

    a Calculate the proportion of people who were cured in each sample.

    b How does sample size affect the results of the test?

Sampling techniques

Research aims to find consistent patterns in repeat samples which show relationships. Scientists select samples for clinical trials by:

- using random samples
- grouping individuals by characteristics, then randomly selecting people from each group
- focusing on a particular subset of a population.

The sampling technique used can affect the outcomes.

3 Why must care be taken when selecting the sampling method to be used?

4 Scientists studied 31 000 heart disease patients. They compared patients with high heart rates (more than 80 beats per minute) and low heart rates (less than 58 beats per minute). How could the sampling method be improved?

Looking at bias

Sample size needs to be considered as part of the research process. For a small population, 5–10% is a large enough sample size. For a larger population of size 'n', sample size = √n.

The symbol '√' means square root, so

√25 means the 'square root of 25'

The square root is the inverse of the square of a number.

For a population of 900, the sample size = √900 = 30.

There is a square root key on a scientific calculator.

Bias refers to **systematic** errors, which can give false outcomes. These must be eliminated wherever possible. In clinical trials, control groups are used (these are people with similar diet, weight etc.), along with an approach called blinding. Neither the patients nor the doctors can tell which are the test or the placebo drugs, so they don't know which patients get the test drug.

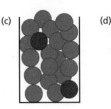
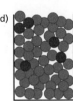

(a) (b) (c) (d)

Figure 6.108 How does sample size affect results?

5 Explain fully how bias in clinical trials can be minimised.

6 What sample size would you suggest for trials involving these total populations?

    a 36 patients
    b 169 patients
    c 729 patients
    d 136 161 patients

Check your progress

describe how to use some sampling techniques → describe how to use a transect line → explain how to perform accurate sampling

describe some uses of biotechnology → explain the advantages of some uses of biotechnology → evaluate some uses of biotechnology

describe the major causes of ill health → explain how diseases and lifestyle factors affect health → evaluate graphical data about lifestyle and health

recall a number of interacting factors which cause different diseases → explain how risk factors are linked to an increased rate of some non-communicable diseases → evaluate evidence linking risk factors and increased rates of disease

describe different types of tumours → describe lifestyle changes to reduce cancer risk → evaluate evidence linking smoking and cancer

describe the symptoms of some viral, bacterial, fungal and protist diseases → describe the transmission and control of different diseases → compare and contrast bacterial and viral diseases; evaluate control measures for malaria; explain the specificity of antibodies

describe how the body protects itself from pathogens → explain the role of the immune system → explain the impact of antibiotic-resistant bacteria

recall why vaccinations are used → explain how vaccinations trigger an immune response → evaluate the global use of vaccinations

describe the use of antibiotics and antivirals → explain how antibiotics and antiviral treat disease → explain the limitations of antibiotics

recall some plant diseases and plant defences → explain the identification and symptoms of some plant diseases; explain some plant defences → explain the use of monoclonal antibodies in identifying plant pathogens

Worked example

Viruses are pathogens that cause many diseases. Babies and children are vaccinated to protect them from many viruses.

1 **a Why are antibiotics not used to kill viruses in the body?**

They cannot kill them.

> The correct answer is that viruses live inside cells, where they are protected from the action of antibiotics.

b What is in a vaccine?

A weak form of the virus.

> Correct answer identified, although 'weak form' could be improved by replacing it with 'inactive or dead form'.

c What does the vaccine do in the child's body?

It makes antibodies.

> This is inaccurate. White blood cells/lymphocytes make antibodies.

d Why do pathogens make us feel ill?

They produce poisons.

> This is partially correct, but the answer should also include the fact that pathogens damage cells.

2 **a One type of tumour is known as benign. Name the other type of tumour and explain how it is different from a benign tumour.**

Cancer tumour spreads through the body.

> Incorrect tumour type identified. Correct answer is malignant tumour, but the difference is correct.

b Name a risk factor for lung cancer.

Smoking

> Correct answer identified.

3 **a Describe how malaria is spread by mosquitoes.**

Mosquitoes suck the blood of an infected person.

> Answer should also include how the mosquito then passes the protist pathogen/*Plasmodium* to an uninfected person.

b Explain how malaria is controlled by insecticide.

Insecticide kills eggs.

> Answer should mention mosquito eggs, and also include that mosquitoes lay their eggs in water.

End of chapter questions

Getting started

1. What are quadrats used for? `1 Mark`

2. Give one example of intensive farming. `1 Mark`

3. Write down the name of the technique that could be used to produce embryonic stem cells from a person's body cells. `1 Mark`

4. Choose a plant disease and describe how you would identify it. `2 Marks`

5. Name two risk factors for developing cardiovascular disease. `2 Marks`

6. What type of blood cells destroy bacterial pathogens? `1 Mark`

7. The graph shows the cases of polio from 1930 to 1969 in England and Wales. Polio vaccination was introduced in 1956.

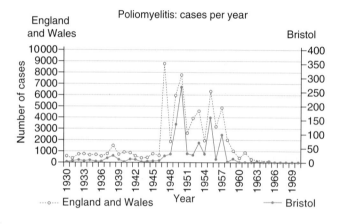

a In which year did the number of polio cases peak?

b How many years did it take for polio cases to fall to zero? `2 Marks`

Going further

8. Name a disease that is caused by a protist pathogen. `1 Mark`

9. What do vaccines contain? `1 Mark`

10. Explain how the spread of gonorrhoea can be controlled. `2 Marks`

11. Shireen has a sore throat caused by a bacterial pathogen, and a headache. What medicines should she take? Explain why. `4 Marks`

12 The graph shows the effect of two risk factors on mortality. Describe the patterns in the data.

2 Marks

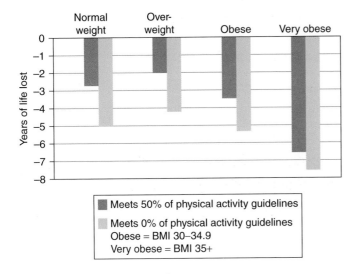

More challenging

13 A plant breeder is trying to produce a new variety of wheat that will withstand drought.

Describe how the plant breeder would do this.

4 Marks

14 Scientists have genetically engineered some crops to be resistant to herbicides.

Explain how herbicide resistance is beneficial to genetically modified (GM) crop production.

2 Marks

15 A group of scientists are investigating the effectiveness of a new antibiotic used to treat *Streptococcus pyogenes* bacteria. They test the antibiotic by spreading *Streptococcus pyogenes* bacteria on an agar jelly plate and place a small disc of filter paper containing the antibiotic in the centre of the dish. They then measured the radius of the 'zone of inhibition' shown in the diagram below.

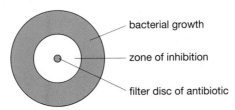

a The radius of the zone of inhibition was 12 mm. Calculate the area using the equation: Area = πr^2

when $\pi = 3.14$.

1 Mark

b For an antibiotic to be considered effective it should cure 95–100% of the cases of an illness. Out of a sample of 568 patients given the new antibiotic, 483 were cured.

Calculate the chance of not being cured.

1 Mark

16. The data shows the effects of cannabis use in 17–25 year olds in 2014. It is from the biggest study ever undertaken. Evaluate whether the data show a causal mechanism.

2 Marks

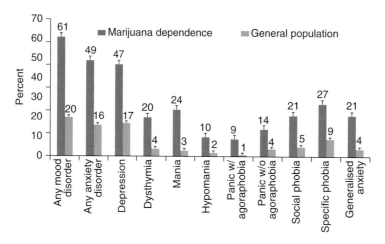

Most demanding

17. Explain how changing lifestyle factors can reduce the risk of developing a named non-communicable disease.

4 Marks

18. Jessica is carrying out an investigation into how many dandelions plants there are in her school playing field. The field is 20 metres by 30 metres. She selects 9 spots at random and samples each spot with a 1 m² quadrat. Jessica's results are shown below.

Sample number	Number of dandelion plants
1	5
2	4
3	2
4	4
5	3
6	1
7	3
8	2
9	4

Jessica calculates the mean number of dandelions to be 3.1.

a Calculate the median and mode values for the number of dandelions across the areas sampled.

1 Mark

b Use the data to estimate the number of daisy plants in the playing field.

1 Mark

19. After a baby is born, blood is left in the umbilical cord and placenta. The blood contains adult stem cells. Some scientists have reported that the stem cells found can repair other types of tissue. Others have not been able to repeat these results.

Some companies store cord blood until it might be needed by a patient.

Discuss the potential of stored umbilical cord blood in the treatment of medical conditions.

4 Marks

Total: 40 Marks

Glossary

A

abiotic factor physical or non-living conditions that affect the distribution of a population in an ecosystem, such as: light, temperature, soil and pH

accommodation ability of the eyes to change focus

acid rain rain water which is made more acidic by pollutant gases

active site the place on an enzyme where the substrate molecule binds

active transport where cells use energy to transport substances through cell membranes against a concentration gradient

ADH (antidiuretic hormone) a hormone released by the pituitary gland when blood plasma is too concentrated, it acts on the kidney to keep more water in the body

adrenaline a hormone released from the adrenal glands during a 'flight or fight' response

adult stem cells rare, undifferentiated cells found in some tissues in adults that can differentiate only into the cell type where they are found, e.g. cells in the bone marrow differentiate to become different types of blood cell

aerobic respiration respiration that involves oxygen

agar plate plastic dish, with a lid, containing a nutrient gel upon which bacteria are grown in a lab

agricultural inputs products, that need to be purchased, for use in farming, such as fertilisers and pesticides

allele a particular form of gene e.g. the blue eye colour allele of the eye colour gene

alveolus (plural: alveoli) air sacs; the site of gaseous exchange in the lungs

amino acids small molecules from which proteins are built

amylase a digestive enzyme (carbohydrase) that breaks down starch

anaerobic respiration respiration without using oxygen

antibacterial chemicals chemicals produced by plants as a defence mechanism which reduces the chance of bacterial infection; the amount produced will increase if the plant is under attack

antibiotic resistance markers a gene inserted into a cell, alongside the desired gene, which is resistant to an antibiotic; the marker allows the cells that have taken up the desired gene to survive when the culture of cells is treated with the antibiotic

antibody protein normally present in the body or produced in response to an antigen, which it neutralises, thus producing an immune response

antigen a specific marker found on most cells or toxins; for example, antigens can be detected in the lab to identify a plant disease. Antibodies detect specific antigens

antimicrobial resistance (AMR) an increasing problem in the twenty-first century whereby antibiotic resistant bacterial populations have increased due to overuse of antibiotics which kill the bacteria which are not resistant

antiseptic substance which is used on living tissues to prevent the growth of microorganisms

antitoxins chemicals produced by white blood cells (lymphocytes) that neutralise toxins

antivirals drugs used to treat viral infections; they are specific to the virus but can only slow down viral development

aorta artery that carries oxygenated blood from the left ventricle to tissues around the body

arteries blood vessels with thick elastic walls that carry oxygenated blood away from the heart under high pressure

artificial classification earlier ways of dividing organisms according to their habitat, for example, rather than common features and relationships with other organisms

artificial pacemaker a device fitted under the skin that sends out electrical impulses to control the heartbeat

aseptic technique measures taken to reduce contamination when preparing bacterial cultures, e.g. working with a flame

asexual reproduction reproduction involving only one parent

aspirin painkiller originally derived from willow bark, but which is now made industrially

ATP molecule used to provide energy for metabolic reactions

atrium (plural: atria) the anterior (nearer to the head) chambers of the heart that receive blood from the body or lungs

autoclave heated pressure vessel used to sterilize equipment and contaminated materials

B

bacterial growth curve an s-shaped growth curve with a steep decrease at the end, that shows how bacteria in culture increase in number exponentially until a build-up of toxins in the culture causes them to die off

barley powdery mildew a fungal disease that affects plants; it causes fluffy white growths on the surface of the leaf

barrier methods of contraception; where a condom or diaphragm is used to prevent sperm reaching an egg

basal metabolic rate the level at which chemical reactions take place in the body at rest

Benedict's test a test for sugar in which Benedict's reagent turns orange-red in the presence of sugar

benign tumour slow-growing, harmless mass of cells that does not spread to other parts of the body

binary fission the process by which a bacterium divides and doubles its numbers. E.coli can divide up to every 20 minutes

biodiversity range of all the different species living in an ecosystem, including plants, animals, fungi and protoctista

biological catalysts enzymes – molecules in the body that speed up chemical reactions

biological control a natural method of targeting a certain pest, with no risk of pollution or resistance developing in the pest

biomass the dry mass of organisms

biomass transfer efficiency the proportion of biomass that is passed on from one organism to its consumer, in a food chain

biotic factor factors caused by living organisms, such as: food availability and competition between species

Biruet reagent chemical indicator used to test for the presence of protein in a sample

blood sugar level the amount of glucose in the blood (controlled by the hormones, insulin and glucagon)

breed new form of animal created with particular characteristics, created through selective breeding

C

capillaries small blood vessels that are one cell thick and permeable for diffusion of gases; join arteries to veins

capillary network tree of capillaries surrounding alveoli that are adapted for efficient gaseous exchange

capture-recapture method of measuring the population size of animals in an area, which involves catching, marking, then re-catching the animals

carbohydrase enzyme that breaks down carbohydrates into simple sugars

carbohydrates one of the main groups of nutrients; e.g. glucose, starch

carbon cycle a natural cycle through which carbon moves by respiration, photosynthesis and combustion, in the form of carbon dioxide

carcinogen substance or virus that increases the risk of cancer, e.g. ionising radiation

cardiac muscle muscle that makes up the heart; it continuously contracts and relaxes

causal mechanism where a direct link has been made between a risk factor and a disease; e.g. smoking and lung cancer

cell cycle a series of three stages during which a cell divides

cell lines cells grown in a lab that are used to study a certain condition, cells used to make monoclonal antibodies are grown in the this way

cell membrane layer around a cell which helps to control substances entering and leaving the cell

cell wall outer barrier of plant cells, made of cellulose; form of plant defence as it prevents pathogens entering the cell

cellulose polymer of glucose; strengthening component of plant cell walls

central nervous system (CNS) collectively, the brain and spinal cord

cerebellum area at the base of the brain that coordinates muscular activity

cerebrum highly folded outer layer of the brain that controls consciousness, intelligence, memory and language

cervix the neck of the uterus

Charles Darwin scientist who proposed the theory of evolution by natural selection

chlorophyll pigment found in plants which is used in photosynthesis (gives green plants their colour)

chloroplast a cell structure found in green plants that contains chlorophyll

chromosomes thread-like structures of DNA in the cell nucleus

cilia tiny hair-like structures found throughout the respiratory system that beat together to move mucus out of the lungs

ciliary body part of the eye that secretes the fluid that supports the front part of the eye; it contains the ciliary muscle

clinical trial process during which a new drug is tested on patients and healthy individuals

clone in asexual reproduction, the offspring produced are identical to the parent (clones)

collision theory an explanation of enzyme action; enzymes cause more collisions between reactants thereby increasing the rate of reaction until reactants are used up

colony a spot containing millions of bacteria growing on an agar plate

colour blindness eye defect affecting the cones – receptor cells in the retina that allow us to perceive colour; sufferers cannot distinguish between certain colours

communicable disease infectious condition caused by a virus, protist, bacteria or fungi; e.g. HIV, tuberculosis

community all the plants and animals living in an ecosystem, e.g. a garden

competition when different species in an ecosystem compete for the same resources

complex diseases conditions that are caused by a combination of genetic and environmental factors

compost dead and decaying plant material

concentration gradient the difference between the amount of a substance on one side of a barrier (e.g. a membrane) and the other; particles diffuse down their concentration gradient

condom rubber sheath that covers the erect penis and prevents sperm reaching the egg; a barrier form of contraception

cones light-sensitive receptor cells in the retina that allow us to see in colour

conservation a way of protecting a species or environment

continuous variation characteristics that can take a range of different values on a continuous scale; e.g. height, weight

cooling the body loses heat through sweating

coordination centre region of the body that receives and processes information from receptors, e.g. brain, pancreas

cornea transparent region at the front of the eye through which light refracts when it enters the eye

coronary artery vessel that provides the heart muscle with oxygen and glucose for respiration

coronary heart disease a condition caused by build-up of fatty deposits in the coronary artery, leading to reduced blood flow and less oxygen and glucose reaching the heart tissue, which can cause a heart attack

correlation relationship between two sets of results

crown gall disease a bacterial disease in plants, caused by *Agrobacterium tumefaciens*. The bacteria cause plant tissues to grow in a disorganised way, to form swollen galls

culture the growing of cells in a lab

culture medium the liquid (nutrient broth) or gel (agar) in which bacteria are grown in a lab

cycle a relationship between two variables which rises and falls, predator-prey relationships follow a cyclical pattern

D

daughter cells cells produced during mitosis that are identical to the parent cell

deamination the removal of amino groups, as ammonia, from excess amino acids, in the liver

decomposer an organism that breaks down carbon in dead animals and plants

deforestation removal of large areas of trees to provide land for cattle or growing crops

dehydration result of the body losing too much water

denatured when an enzyme's shape changes so that the substrate cannot fit into the active site

diarrhoea a symptom of food poisoning; frequent passing of liquid stools

differentiation when cells gain certain features needed for their function; they become specialised

diffusion the net movement of particles from a high concentration to a lower concentration (along their concentration gradient)

diploid describes cells with two copies (or a pair) of each chromosome

directly proportional describes a relationship between two variables on a graph where the line of best fit goes through 0,0

discontinuous variation characteristics that can only take one of a set number of forms – there are no intermediates; e.g. blood group

distribution how living organisms are dispersed/spread out over an ecosystem

DNA (deoxyribonucleic acid) found as chromosomes in the nucleus – its sequence determines how our bodies are made, and gives each one of us a unique genetic code

dominant an allele that is always expressed, even if a different allele is present; represented by a capital letter

donor refers to the person or organism where donated cells or tissue come from

dormant describes seeds that have not germinated; they can be sprayed with the plant hormone gibberellins, which induces them to germinate

dose amount of a drug given to a patient

double-blind trial a drugs trial where neither doctors nor patients know whether the patient has received the test drug or the placebo

double circulation when blood flows in two separate circuits; e.g. in humans, blood flows from the heart to the lungs (1) and from the heart to the rest of the body (2)

double circulatory system where the blood is pumped to the lungs then returned to the heart before being pumped round the body

double helix the shape of DNA – two strands of nucleotides that wind around each other like a twisted ladder

E

ecosystem the interaction of a community of living organisms with the non-living parts of their surroundings

ecotourism measures aimed at reducing the impact of tourism on natural ecosystems, local plants, animals and communities

effector muscle or gland that brings about a response to a stimulus

efficacy how effective a drug is at preventing or curing the disease

egestion the process by which undigested plant material leaves the body of an organism in faeces

embryo screening the process whereby a few cells are taken from an embryo produced by IVF are checked for any defective genes

embryo transplants form of cloning where cells are taken from a developing embryo from a pregnant animal, separated and grown in culture then implanted into host mothers

embryonic stem cells unspecialised cells found in the early embryo that can differentiate into almost any cell type in the body

endocrine gland part of the body that releases chemical messengers, or hormones, directly into the bloodstream

endocrine system a control system in the body that communicates using chemical messengers, or hormones, to produce slow but long-lasting responses

endothermic reaction chemical reaction which takes in heat from the surroundings

environmental change a shift in the external conditions caused by human activity or a natural event

environmental variation differences between individuals that arise during development; e.g. scars

enzymes biological catalysts that increase the speed of a chemical reaction

epidemic an outbreak of a disease that spreads quickly to many people

epidermal tissues layers of cells that cover the top surface of a leaf; they let light penetrate

estimate a guess based on prior knowledge

ethanol product of anaerobic respiration in plant and yeast cells; used in the manufacture of alcoholic drinks

ethical whether a process is considered to be right or wrong, based on moral considerations

eukaryotic cells cells that contain a true nucleus in the cytoplasm e.g. plant and animal cells

evolution the gradual change in organisms over millions of years caused by random mutations and natural selection

evolutionary tree a diagram created by scientists that shows how animals are believed to have evolved from common ancestors

exchange surfaces specialised areas with large surface area to volume ratios for efficient diffusion

exothermic reaction chemical reaction in which heat is given out

extinction the elimination of all members of a species; there have been five mass extinctions over geological time

F

factory farming a form of intensive farming where animals are reared in sheds or cages under controlled conditions

fermentation anaerobic respiration in yeast cells; produces ethanol and carbon dioxide

fertiliser chemical containing minerals (nitrates, phosphates, potassium and magnesium) put on soil to improve plant growth

fertility drug combination of hormones given to a woman with low FSH levels to stimulate egg production

filtrate a solution which has passed through a filter, for example dissolved substances that cross into the kidney after the blood has been filtered

food security when all people have access to a consistent supply of food to meet their needs

fossil the remains of organisms that lived millions of years ago

fossil record an incomplete account of organisms that lived millions of years ago

fraction (in genetics) the number of people affected by a recessive condition expressed as a fraction could be 1/4

FSH (follicle stimulating hormone) a reproductive hormone that causes eggs to mature in the ovaries

fungicide chemical used to kill fungi

G

gametes the male and female sex cells (sperm and eggs)

gene section of DNA that contains the instructions for a particular characteristic

gene expression whether genes are switched on or off, which is regulated by non-coding DNA

gene mutation an error in the DNA sequence that codes for a gene, which can sometimes lead to a change in phenotype (e.g. peppered moths)

gene theory dogma developed in the twentieth century that brought together the work of many scientists on inheritance, DNA structure and the genetic code

gene therapy medical procedure where nucleic acid is used to treat a genetic disease

genetic code a sequence of three DNA bases that codes for a single amino acid

genetic cross a way of working out the probability of the genotype of the offspring produced from the parents' genotype for a particular characteristic, e.g. using a Punnett square

genetic engineering transfer of specific genes from one organism to another

genetic marker gene a gene inserted into a modified organism alongside the required gene; the marker gene is often resistant to an antibiotic, so that when cultures of cells are treated with that antibiotic, cells that do not contain the marker gene will be killed

genetic variation the product of meiosis, mutations and sexual reproduction, which all lead to changes in our genome

genome the entire genetic material of an organism

genome editing an experimental method of detecting and correcting defective genes in an individual

genomics the science of studying the human genome to increase our understanding of human DNA

genotype the alleles present for a particular gene make up the organism's genotype

germination the process by which a seed begins to develop and grow

global warming the increase in the Earth's temperature due to increases in carbon dioxide levels

glucagon hormone released by the pancreas that, along with insulin, controls blood glucose levels

GM crops varieties of crops that have had their genomes modified by the insertion of genes from a plant or other organism

goblet cells cells in the epithelium that produce mucus to trap dust particles

golden rice rice that has been genetically modified to contain β – carotene, which converts to vitamin A

gonorrhoea a sexually transmitted disease caused by bacteria, resulting in pain when urinating and a thick discharge from the vagina or penis

gradient the steepness or slope of a line plotted on a graph

graticule piece of glass or plastic onto which a scale has been drawn, which is used with a microscope

grouped bar chart bar chart where two or more sets of data are presented on the same graph

guard cells cells surrounding the stomata that open and close to control the exchange of gases and water loss

H

habitat the place where an organism lives in an ecosystem; e.g. the worm's habitat is the soil

haemoglobin chemical found in red blood cells which binds to oxygen to transport it around the body

haploid describes cells with a single chromosome from each pair (e.g. egg or sperm cells)

heterozygous a person who has two different alleles for a characteristic, e.g. someone with blond hair may also carry the allele for red hair

HIV (human immunodeficiency virus) virus transmitted through the exchange of body fluids that attacks the immune system

homeostasis the regulation of internal conditions, such as temperature, in the body

homozygous a person who has two alleles that are the same for a characteristic, e.g. a blue-eyed person will have two 'blue' alleles for eye colour

hormone chemical messenger that acts on target organs in the body

HPV a viral infection found in most women diagnosed with cervical cancer

hybrid infertile organism created through interbreeding organisms from two different species

hybridoma cells cells made from combining tumour cells with lymphocytes, to give cells that can produce antibodies and divide (for the production of monoclonal antibodies)

hydroponics growing plants in mineral solutions without the need for soil

hypothalamus control centre in the brain that produces hormones and links the nervous and endocrine systems

hypothesis a scientific question formed based on prior knowledge that can be tested in an experiment

I

immune system the organs and tissues of the body which help prevent and reduce pathogenic infection

immunity when the body is protected from a pathogen that it has already encountered enabling it to rapidly produce antibodies against it

inbreeding breeding closely related animals

incubation a period of time it takes a culture of bacteria to grow, either for cultures grown in a laboratory, or the time it takes a bacterial infection to make someone ill

indicator species organisms used to measure the level of pollution in water or the air

inoculating loop length of wire with a ring at the end used for transferring bacteria to an agar plate

insulin hormone made by the pancreas that controls the level of glucose in the blood

interbreeding organisms of the same species can interbreed to give fertile offspring

intercept the point where where two lines meet, often used in graphs to determine when a line crosses the y axis (y intercept)

interdependence where organisms depend on each other for survival e.g. plants need animals for carbon dioxide and seed dispersal; animals need plants for food and oxygen; i.e. they depend on each other for survival

interspecific competition competition between two different species of organism

intraspecific competition competition among organisms from the same species

inverse square law (in terms of light intensity and photosynthesis) the intensity of light is proportional to $1/d^2$ (where d = distance from the light source); for example, if the distance is doubled, the light intensity is quartered

in-vitro fertilisation (IVF) a fertility treatment, whereby an egg is fertilised with sperm outside the body, in a laboratory

iodine an orange solution used to test for starch (turns blue-black when starch is present)

iris part of the eye that has sets of muscles that control the size of the pupil and regulate the light reaching the retina

IUD (intrauterine device) a device containing hormones that is placed in the uterus to prevent a fertilised egg from implanting; a hormonal method of contraception

IVF cycle the process of IVF from stimulation of the ovaries to implantation of an embryo; if unsuccessful, another cycle can be attempted after about two months

K

keys reference charts used to identify the species of an unknown organisms

L

lactic acid product of anaerobic respiration in muscles

leaf cuticle tough waxy covering that prevents pathogens from entering the epidermis of plant leaves; a physical defence mechanism

lens part of the eye that focuses light rays on the retina

LH (luteinising hormone) a menstrual cycle hormone that stimulates an egg to be released from an ovary

lichen slow-growing plant that grows up trees

ligase enzyme used in genetic engineering that joins together the gene to be inserted into the host plasmid

limiting factor factors such as light, temperature and carbon dioxide, which affect the rate of photosynthesis

linear a straight line on a graph that indicates a strong relationship between the two plotted variables

lock and key hypothesis a model to explain how enzymes work; the substrate is the 'key' and the active site is the 'lock'

lumen the central part of a vessel

lymphocytes white blood cells that produce antibodies and antitoxins to destroy pathogens

lysis the bursting of a cell that occurs if it takes up too much water (e.g. if it was placed in water)

M

magnetic resonance imaging (MRI) scanning technique that uses strong magnetic fields to produce detailed images of the body; used to diagnose nervous system disorders

magnification the factor by which an image of an object is enlarged by a microscope; calculated as: size of image/size of real object

malignant tumour cancerous mass of cells that grows quickly and can spread to other parts of the body

mean average value calculated by adding up all the values in a data set then dividing by the number of values

medulla region at the base of the brain that controls unconscious activities, such as breathing

meiosis cell division that results in gametes being produced, with half the number of chromosomes as the parent cell

melanism darkening of appearance – a form of colour variation in animals, e.g. melanic moths

Mendelian inheritance name given to single-gene disorders, such as cystic fibrosis

menstrual cycle monthly cycle in females which is controlled by reproductive hormones

mental health a feeling of well-being, having a positive frame of mind

meristem regions at tips of roots and shoots where cell division and elongation take place

metabolic reactions processes whereby new substances are built; e.g. glucose is converted into glycogen

metabolism the sum of all reactions in a cell or the body

micrograph image captured using a microscope

microorganisms tiny organisms that can only be viewed with a microscope – also known as microbes

mimicry mechanical defence mechanism where a plant uses features to trick animals into not feeding or not laying eggs

mineral ions substances found in the soil that are essential for a plant's survival; e.g. plants need magnesium ions to make chlorophyll

mitosis cell division that results in genetically identical diploid cells

mixed population plants bred from two different varieties for their desirable traits

monoclonal antibodies antibodies made from cells that are cloned from one cell that are specific to one binding site on an antigen. They are used in medicine to treat cancer, and in research

monomers single units, such as sugar molecules, that join together in a long chain to form a larger molecule (polymer), e.g. cellulose

motor neurone nerve cell carrying information from the central nervous system to muscles

mutation where the DNA within cells has been altered

mutualism when two organisms live together and they both benefit from the relationship

N

natural classification the grouping of organisms according to their features and relationships with other organisms

natural selection process by which advantageous characteristics that can be passed on in genes become more common in a population over many generations

negative feedback a regulatory response to changes in the body which decreases levels that are too high, and increases levels that are too low

nervous system a control system in the body that uses electrical impulses to communicate rapidly and precisely

nets (in sampling organisms) nets are commonly used to collect airborne insects. This is a form of active collection

non-communicable disease conditions caused by environmental or genetic factors that are not spread among people; e.g. cancer, cardiovascular disease

non-invasive describes brain mapping techniques, such as MRI scans, that can be carried out without the need for surgery

nucleotide a molecule consisting of a sugar and phosphate group with a chemical base (A, T, C, G)

O

oestrogen the main female reproductive hormone produced by the ovaries

opiates a group of painkillers found in poppies

optic nerve nerve found at the back of the eye that carries impulses from the retina to the brain

optimum the conditions, in terms of temperature and pH, at which an enzyme works best

order of magnitude in microscopy, the difference between sizes of cells, calculated in factors of 10

organ group of tissues that carries out a specific function

organ system arrangement of organs in the body according to function; e.g. respiratory system

osmosis the diffusion of water molecules through a partially permeable membrane, from a dilute solution to a concentrated solution

ovulation release of an egg from the ovary

oxygen debt the amount of oxygen that the body needs to breakdown lactic acid after muscles undergo anaerobic respiration

oxyhaemoglobin bright red substance formed when oxygen binds to haemoglobin in red blood cells; this is how oxygen is transported to tissues

P

pandemic when an outbreak of a disease becomes global

parasitism a relationship between two organisms where one benefits and the other is harmed, e.g. tapeworms in humans

partially permeable membrane a membrane that allows some small molecules to pass through but not larger molecules

pathogen harmful microorganism that invades the body and causes infectious disease

peatlands areas of peat bog formed in marshlands; peat is partially decomposed leaf matter that is used as fuel and cheap compost

penicillin an antibiotic, isolated from Penicillum mould, which was discovered by Alexander Flemming

percentage a number or amount expressed per hundred

Petri dish plate, with a lid, used for growing bacteria in a lab

phagocyte a type of white blood cell that enters tissues and engulfs pathogens then ingests them

phagocytosis process by which a white blood cell (phagocyte) engulfs a pathogen

phenotype the characteristic that is shown or expressed

phloem specialised transporting cells which form tubules in plants to carry sugars from leaves to other parts of the plant

photosynthesis process carried out by green plants where sunlight, carbon dioxide and water are used to produce glucose and oxygen

phylogenetics the study of the relationships between species, and groups of organisms, and how they are related through their evolutionary history

pituitary gland known as the 'master gland' as it controls other endocrine glands, such as the thyroid gland

placebo a treatment that does not contain a drug

plasma straw-coloured liquid part of blood

plasmid small ring of DNA found in prokaryotic cells

plasmolysis/plasmolysed the shrinking of a plant cell due to loss of water, the cell membrane pulls away from the cell wall

platelets cell fragments which help in blood clotting

polymer a molecule, such as DNA, made up of repeating units

pooter a small resealable jar used for collecting insects

population the total number of one species in an ecosystem

potometer piece of equipment used to measure water uptake by plants

preclinical testing testing of a new drug in a lab using cells, tissues or live animals

predator animal (consumer) that kills and eats other animals

probability the likelihood of an event happening; e.g. the probability of a couple who are both heterozygous for cystic fibrosis having a child with cystic fibrosis is 0.25 i.e. there is a 1 in 4 chance

producers organisms in a food chain that make food using sunlight

progesterone reproductive hormone that causes the lining of the uterus to be maintained

progestogen-only pill (or mini pill or POP) contraceptive pill that only contains progesterone (not oestrogen), which may be more suitable (than the combined pill) for women who are older or have high blood pressure

proportion (in genetics) the number of people affected by a condition expressed in relation to the total population

proteases digestive enzymes that break down proteins into amino acids

protist a type of single-celled pathogen that causes malaria

pulmonary artery vessel that carries deoxygenated blood from the right ventricle to the lungs

pulmonary vein vessel that carries oxygenated blood from the lungs to the left atrium

Punnett square a grid used to determine possible outcomes of a genetic cross

pupil the hole in the center of the iris that allows light to pass through

pyramid of biomass table of dry weight of organisms at different trophic levels in an ecosystem, which forms a pyramid shape

Q

quadrat a square grid used to estimate the abundance of a species in a given area

qualitative reagents chemicals used to test for the presence of a substance in a sample

R

range a measure of spread; the difference between the biggest and smallest values in a set

rate the speed at which an event is occurring over time; can be calculated using the gradient on a graph

rate of photosynthesis is affected by temperature, light intensity, carbon dioxide concentration and amount of chlorophyll

ratio the relationship between two variables, expressed as 1:4, for example

reaction time the time it takes the body to respond to an event

receptors cells in the body that detect changes in the environment

recessive two copies of a recessive allele must be present for the characteristic to be expressed; represented by lowercase letters

red blood cells blood cells with a concave shape which are adapted to the transport of oxygen. As they move through the blood vessels they carry oxygen from the lungs to body cells

reflex action rapid automatic responses to a stimulus

reflex arc pathway taken by nerve impulses through the spinal cord during a reflex action

refraction the bending of light rays as they travel from one medium to another, e.g. as they enter the eye

regeneration restoration (of a habitat)

repeatability precision obtained when measurement results are produced in one laboratory, by a single operator, using the same equipment under same conditions, over a short timescale.

reproducibility a measure of the validity of a set of results; data that could be collected again by a different person

resolving power (resolution) the ability of a microscope to distinguish between two points; the resolving power of electron microscopes is higher than that of light microscopes

respiration the process used by all organisms to release the energy they need from food

restriction enzyme an enzyme used in genetic engineering that cuts both the gene to be inserted and the plasmid at a specific sequence

retina area at the back of the eye where light-sensitive receptor cells are found

ribosome structures in a cell where protein synthesis takes place

risk factor a lifestyle or genetic factor that increases the chance of developing a disease

rods light-sensitive receptor cells in the retina that allow us to see in dim light

root hair cells specialised cells in plant roots that are adapted for efficient uptake of water by osmosis and mineral ions by active transport

ruler-drop test an experiment used to measure reaction time whereby one person drops a ruler and the time it takes for another person to catch it is measured

S

Salmonella a type of bacteria that causes food poisoning

sampling techniques procedures used to test a hypothesis in an experiment

scale bar a line drawn on a micrograph used to measure the actual size of the object

scanning electron microscope (SEM) works by bouncing electrons off the surface of a specimen that has had an ultrathin coating of a heavy metal, usually gold, applied. Used to view surface shape of cells or small organisms

secondary consumer organism in a food chain that gets its energy from eating primary consumers

secondary tumour abnormal growth of cells that forms from a malignant tumour elsewhere in the body

seedbanks storage centres used to preserve (and safeguard) the biodiversity of crop and other plants

selective breeding process of breeding organisms with the desired characteristics (also known as artificial selection)

sensory neurone nerve cell carrying information from receptors to central nervous system

sex determination whether a fertilised egg develops into a male (XY) or female (XX) depends on the 23rd pair of chromosomes

sexual reproduction form of reproduction involving two parents, which introduces variation

sexually transmitted disease (STD) disease spread through sexual contact; e.g. HIV

specialised when cells or tissues become adapted to carry out their specific function

speciation formation of a new species over a long period of time, through separation of a population

species basic category of biological classification, composed of individuals that resemble one another, can breed among themselves, they can breed with members of other species – but they can at best form hybrids which are not fertile

sphere shape that has the smallest surface area compared with its volume

spores small seed-like structures released by a fungus to help it spread

stacked bar chart bar graph where two data sets are stacked on top of each other for each group/bar

standard form way of writing very large or small numbers using powers of ten; e.g. 1.0 × 10–3

starch a complex carbohydrate found in animals and plants

statins drugs that stop the liver producing so much cholesterol

stem cells unspecialised body cells (found in bone marrow) that can develop into other, specialised, cells that the body needs, e.g. blood cells

stents a treatment for heart disease; a catheter with a balloon attached is inserted to open up a narrowed coronary artery

sterilise the process of removing contaminated material (e.g. from an agar plate)

sticky ends these are overhanging lengths of DNA that are created during genetic engineering; the plasmid and the desired gene are cut by a restriction enzyme so that they both have sticky ends, which are then joined together by the enzyme ligase

stomata (singular stoma) small holes in the surface of leaves which allow gases in and out of leaves

substrate the protein or reactant in an enzyme-controlled reaction that fits exactly into the active site of a specific enzyme

surface area to volume ratio the relationship between the surface area of an organism or structure and its volume; SA:V ratios are large in single-celled organisms for efficient diffusion

suspensory ligaments ligaments in the eye that are attached to the ciliary muscle and hold the lens in place

sustainable long-lasting; something that can be maintained for future generations

sustainable fisheries measures to improve fish stocks, which were declining due to over-fishing, to include controls on net size and fishing quotas

synapse the gap between two neurones

T

target organ the site where a hormone has its effect

testosterone male sex hormone produced by the testes that stimulates sperm production

thyroxine hormone produced by the thyroid gland that increases the body's metabolism

tobacco mosaic virus (TMV) pathogen that causes mosaic pattern of discolouration on leaves and affects growth of plant

transcription the process by which genetic information is copied from DNA onto messenger RNA in the nucleus

transect line across an area to sample organisms

translation the process by which proteins are assembled using the mRNA template, on a ribosome

translocation the movement of sugars through a plant

transmission electron microscope (TEM) uses an electron beam to view thin sections of cells at high resolution

transpiration the movement of water up through a plant

transplant rejection when a patient's immune system reacts to and fights an implanted organ or stem cells from a donor because it treats them as 'foreign'

trend a pattern in a data set

trophic level feeding positions in a food chain

tropism the response of a plant by growing towards or away from a stimulus

tuberculosis a communicable disease caused by bacterial infection that usually affects the lungs

type 1 diabetes a condition where the pancreas cannot produce enough, or any, insulin

type 2 diabetes a condition where the body cells no longer respond to insulin produced by the pancreas

U

umbilical cord joins the foetus to the mother during pregnancy and is a source of stem cells

uncertainty a measure of the range about the mean, calculated by the range divided by two

V

vaccination injection of a small quantity of inactive pathogen to protect us from developing the disease caused by the pathogen

vaccine preparation of an inactive or dead form of a pathogen given by injection or nasal spray

valid refers to results that are accurate, representative and repeatable

valves flaps of tissue that prevent the backflow of blood in the heart and in veins

variant a new form of a gene that occurs through a change in the genetic code (mutation)

variation the differences between individuals brought about by both genetic and environmental influences

vascular bundle (veins) group of xylem and phloem cells that transport water and glucose around the plant

vasoconstriction in cold conditions, the diameter of small blood vessels near the surface of the body decreases, which reduces blood flow

vasodilation in warm conditions, the diameter of small blood vessels near the surface of the body increases, which increases blood flow

vector a carrier, usually a plasmid, used to transfer a gene into an organism to be genetically modified; also, mosquitoes are vectors – they spread malaria but don't cause it themselves

vena cava vein that carries deoxygenated blood from the body to the right atrium

ventilate the movement of air into and out of the lungs

ventricles the lower chambers of the heart that pump blood around the body (left) or back to the lungs (right)

W

Wallace (Alfred Russell) scientist that proposed the theory of evolution through natural selection, independently from Darwin

water potential a measure of the amount of water particles in a solution; pure water has the highest water potential

X

X-chromosomes sex chromosome present in males (XY) and females (XX)

xylem cells specialised for transporting water through a plant; xylem cells have thick walls, no cytoplasm and are dead, their end walls break down and they form a continuous tube

Y

Y-chromosomes sex chromosome found only in males

Z

zygote a fertilised egg cell

Index